Vygotsky and Sociology

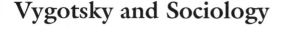
Building on earlier publications by Harry Daniels, *Vygotsky and Sociology* provides readers with an overview of the implications for research of the theoretical work which acknowledges a debt to the writings of L. S. Vygotsky and sociologists whose work echoes his sociogenetic commitments, particularly Basil Bernstein. It provides a variety of views on the ways in which these two, conceptually linked, bodies of work can be brought together in theoretical frameworks which give new possibilities for empirical work. The need for a creative fusion of the Vygotskian and sociological traditions has been traced through the publication of *Vygotsky and Pedagogy* and *Vygotsky and Research*. This book has two aims. First, to expand and enrich the Vygotskian theoretical framework; second, to illustrate the utility of such enhanced sociological imaginations and how they may be of value in researching learning in institutions and classrooms.

It includes contributions from long-established writers in education, psychology and sociology, as well as relatively recent contributors to the theoretical debates and the body of research to which it has given rise, presenting their own arguments and justifications for forging links between particular theoretical traditions and, in some cases, applying new insights to obdurate empirical questions.

Chapters include:

- Curriculum and pedagogy in the sociology of education; some lessons from comparing Durkheim and Vygotsky;
- Dialectics, politics and contemporary cultural-historical research, exemplified through Marx and Vygotsky;
- Sixth sense, second nature and other cultural ways of making sense of our surroundings: Vygotsky, Bernstein, and the languaged body;
- Negotiating pedagogic dilemmas in non-traditional educational contexts; and
- Boys, skills and class: educational failure or community survival? Insights from Vygotsky and Bernstein.

Vygotsky and Sociology is an essential text for students and academics in the social sciences (particularly sociology and psychology), student teachers, teacher educators and researchers as well as educational professionals.

Harry Daniels is Director of the Centre for Sociocultural and Activity Theory Research (Bath); Professor of Education: Culture and Pedagogy, Department of Education, University of Bath; Adjunct Professor, Centre for Learning Research, Griffith University, Brisbane, Australia; Research Professor, Centre for Human Activity Theory, Kansai University, Osaka, Japan; and Research Professor in Cultural Historical Psychology, Moscow State University of Psychology and Education.

Vygotsky and Sociology

Edited by Harry Daniels

Routledge
Taylor & Francis Group

LONDON AND NEW YORK

First published 2012
by Routledge
2 Park Square, Milton Park, Abingdon, Oxon OX14 4RN

Simultaneously published in the USA and Canada
by Routledge
711 Third Avenue, New York, NY 10017

Routledge is an imprint of the Taylor & Francis Group, an informa business

British Library Cataloguing in Publication Data
A catalogue record for this book is available from the British Library

Library of Congress Cataloging in Publication Data
Vygotsky and sociology / edited by Harry Daniels.
    p. cm.
  ISBN 978-0-415-67821-6 (hbk.) — ISBN 978-0-415-67822-3 (pbk.)
— ISBN 978-0-203-11299-1 (e-book) 1. Vygotskii, L. S. (Lev
Semenovich), 1896-1934. 2. Sociology. 3. Education. 4.
Psychology. I. Daniels, Harry.
  BF109.V95V95 2012
  300.92—dc23

                                                       2011052498

ISBN: 978-0-415-67821-6 (hbk)
ISBN: 978-0-415-67822-3 (pbk)
ISBN: 978-0-203-11299-1 (ebk)

Typeset in Galliard
by RefineCatch Limited, Bungay, Suffolk

MIX
Paper from
responsible sources
FSC
www.fsc.org   FSC® C004839   Printed and bound by CPI Group (UK) Ltd, Croydon, CR0 4YY

Contents

Figures and tables

Figures

Tables

Contributors

Raymond Brown, School of Education and Professional Studies, Griffith University, Nathan Campus, 170 Kessels Road, Nathan, Brisbane, Queensland 4111, Australia.

Seth Chaiklin, Centre for Sociocultural and Activity Theory Research, Department of Education, University of Bath, Bath BA2 7AY.

Harry Daniels, Centre for Sociocultural and Activity Theory Research, Department of Education, University of Bath, Bath BA2 7AY.

David H. Eddy Spicer, Centre for Sociocultural and Activity Theory Research, Department of Education, University of Bath, Bath BA2 7AY.

Arturo Escandón, Department of Spanish and Latin-American Studies, Faculty of Foreign Studies, Nanzan University, 18 Yamazato-cho, Showa-ku, Nagoya 466-8673, Japan.

Ruqaiya Hasan, Macquarie University, Australia.

Gabrielle Ivinson, Department of Social Sciences, Cardiff University.

Stephen Lerman, Department of Education, London South Bank University, 103 Borough Road, London SE1 0AA.

Andy Lock, School of Psychology, Massey University, Private Bag 11 222, Palmerston North, New Zealand.

Mariann Märtsin, School of Education and Professional Studies, Griffith University, Nathan Campus, 170 Kessels Road, Nathan, Brisbane, Queensland 4111, Australia.

Carolyn P. Panofsky, Rhode Island College, 600 Mount Pleasant Avenue, RI 02908, USA.

John Shotter, Department of Communication, University of New Hampshire, Durham, NH 03824-3586, USA.

Parlo Singh, Griffith University, Nathan Campus, 170 Kessels Road, Nathan, Brisbane, Queensland 4111, Australia.

Jennifer A. Vadeboncoeur, University of British Columbia, Faculty of Education, Educational and Counselling Psychology and Special Education, 2125 Main Mall, Vancouver BC V6T-1Z4, Canada.

Gordon Wells, Department of Education, Social Sciences 1, University of California, 1156 High Street, Santa Cruz, CA 95064, USA.

Michael Young, Faculty of Culture and Pedagogy, London Knowledge Lab, Institute of Education, University of London.

A brief introduction

Harry Daniels

In a discussion of the pitfalls created by the separation of sociology and psychology and long before the full extent of Vygotsky's writing had been revealed in the west, Adorno (1967) pointed to the challenges that are inherent in the production of a social science that makes a serious attempt to capture the totality of the social formation of mind. It is no surprise that Vygotsky himself drew on Marx and the French School of sociology in the guise of Durkheim and Janet (see Davydov (1995) and van der Veer and Valsiner (1988)). In the citation that follows he establishes a clear agenda:

> we must be profoundly historical and must always present man's behaviour in relation to the class situation at the given moment. This must be the fundamental psychological technique for every social psychologist. (Vygotsky, 1926/1997: 212)

In this book a group of academics who share an interest in progressing some aspects of the response to the challenge identified by Adorno that were partially addressed by Vygotsky, present their own arguments and justifications for forging links between particular theoretical traditions and, in some cases, applying new insights to obdurate empirical questions.

As I have argued in Daniels (2001, 2008) the application of Vygotsky's work by linguists, psychologists and educationalists has tended to focus on reasonably small-scale interactional contexts. The focus has often been on either how small groups create and negotiate social order or on meanings, their negotiation, the construction of identities and their careers as these emerge out of face-to-face encounters in well-defined contexts. There is little evidence of attention being directed to origins of specific forms of regulation of these contexts by factors which reside outside them. When this is attempted it is difficult to discern how relations internal to a context are themselves regulated by relations external to that context. In the case of institutions Marianne Hedegaard has remarked that institutions stand between persons and societal motives. Post-Vygotskian work has struggled to show how these societal motives are themselves reconstituted within institutions. Recent developments in the dialect of Activity Theory known as cultural-historical activity theory have drawn attention to the relations within and between activity systems in particular settings. However the calibration, description and analysis of the relations rely on a formulation of rules, community and division of labour which itself restricts the delicacy of the descriptions that can be derived.

This book has two aims. Firstly to expand and enrich the Vygotskian theoretical framework and secondly to illustrate the utility of such enhanced sociological imaginations that may be of value in researching learning in institutions and classrooms. It will come as no surprise to readers who have encountered my own writing in *Vygotsky and Pedagogy* (2001) and *Vygotsky and Research* (2008), that the writing of the British sociologist, Basil Bernstein, is a prominent feature in many of the chapters. Given the early influences on Vygotsky's own writing, it seemed appropriate to open with discussions concerning Durkheim and Marx.

In Chapter 1 Michael Young engages with issues concerning curriculum and pedagogy in the sociology of education and in so doing engages with the tensions and dilemmas that arise from a comparison of Durkheim and Vygotsky. His point of departure is the claim that they were both 'social epistemologists, interested in knowledge and the curriculum, and pedagogic theorists, interested in classroom practice' (p. 5). His chapter is an exploration of the ways in which that which counts as knowledge is deployed in both traditions. His roots are in sociology and he sees the benefits of utilising Vygotsky in the development of his chosen discipline

In Chapter 2 my colleague, Seth Chaiklin, examines the importance Marx and Vygotsky and their contribution to the development of what he terms the dialectical tradition. The central focus is on the development of this tradition and the contributions made by both writers rather than the contribution of one to the other.

He concludes that:

> The integrated objective of the dialectical tradition cuts across the traditional social scientific disciplines found at the beginning of the twenty-first century, and opens profound challenges for pursuing research that addresses the realisation of full human development. (p. 41)

Chapter 3 (my own chapter) draws attention directly to the work of Basil Bernstein, a sociologist who drew directly on Vygotsky (and Luria), Marx and Durkheim among others. I use the following quotation to set up, what I hope provides, an insight into the essence of his project which was to work on how:

> a given distribution of power and principles of control are translated into specialised principles of communication differentially, and often unequally, distributed to social groups/classes. And how such a differential/unequal distribution of forms of communication, initially (but not necessarily terminally) shapes the formation of consciousness of members of these groups/classes in such a way as to relay both opposition and change. (Bernstein, 1996: 93)

In this chapter I am particularly concerned with what is termed implicit or invisible mediation arguing that the, sometimes, exclusive focus on explicit visible mediational processes in and of itself truncates the account of social formation and disconnects the Vygotskian thesis from, what I consider to be, the necessary sociological imagination without which a theoretical opus develops not fit for the purpose which Vygotsky announced.

In Chapter 4 John Shotter and Andy Lock take an initial 'linguistic turn' in their examination of the relation between the two which is subsequently nuanced by what they term a 'corporeal turn'. The chapter's title 'Sixth Sense, Second Nature and Other Cultural Ways of Making Sense of Our Surroundings: Vygotsky, Bernstein, and the Languaged Body', points to a possible future for theoretical development rather than a retrospective account of what has been.

Chapter 5 by Ruqaiya Hasan returns to the focus on the concept of semiotic mediation, in which she also draws on Bernstein's sociology. In the way that Shotter and Lock announce the importance for young learners of the 'nature of the orientations, the ways of relating to their surroundings, the attitudes that they learn to adopt to events occurring around them – which they learn implicitly in the course of their everyday practical involvements with those around them' (p. 76), so Hasan adopts this orientation and yet infuses it with an analysis of Bernstein's discussion of knowledge structures. Taken together these opening chapters set the scene for discussions of empirical work which, to differing degrees, attend to notions of mediation, knowledge and dialectics.

In Chapter 6 Parlo Singh, Raymond Brown and Mariann Märtsin report studies of teachers working to negotiate pedagogic dilemmas in non-traditional educational contexts.

In Chapter 7 David Eddy Spicer develops an account of modalities of authority and the socialisation of the school in contemporary approaches to educational change. Both draw on Vygotsky and Bernstein.

In Chapter 8 Gordon Wells returns to the topic of semiotic mediation and in so doing draws on his early work conducted in Bristol and the development of an explanatory theory in empirical studies of the quality of parent–child interaction and home–school transitions. Here the relation between social structure is surfaced as it is in Chapter 9 by Gabrielle Ivinson as she discusses boys, skills and class and asks whether analysis should focus on educational failure or community survival.

In Chapters 10 and 11 Stephen Lerman and then Carolyn P. Panofsky and Jennifer A. Vadeboncoeur approach the same issue from different starting points. Lerman asks whether 'identity' is the most appropriate unit of analysis in researching and teaching mathematics, while Panofsky and Vadeboncoeur refigure the notion of the zone of proximal development in a discussion of schooling and social class. This is a topic which, at times, has struggled for survival in the context in which they work.

Lastly, in Chapter 12 Arturo Escandón, a Chilean working in Japan, examines the pedagogies of second-language acquisition and in so doing combines cultural-historical and sociological traditions again drawing on Bernstein and Vygotsky.

I am delighted to have been able to bring together this collection in which readers will find, as I have, a richness of innovative and creative social science deployed in attempts to realise some of the dreams of the early twentieth century.

References

Adorno, T. W. (1967) 'Sociology and Psychology', *New Left Review*, 67–80.

Bernstein, B. (1996) *Pedagogy, Symbolic Control and Identity: Theory, Research and Critique*, London: Taylor & Francis.

Daniels, H. (2001) *Vygotsky and Pedagogy*, London: Routledge.

—— (2008) *Vygotsky and Research*, London: Routledge.

Davydov, V. (1995) 'The Influence of L. S. Vygotsky on Education Theory, Research and Practice', *Educational Researcher*, 24: 12–21.

van der Veer, R. and Valsiner, J. (1988). 'Lev Vygotsky and Pierre Janet: On the Origin of the Concept of Sociogenesis', *Developmental Review* 8: 52–65.

Vygotsky, L. S. (1926/1997). *Educational Psychology*, trans. R. Silverman, Boca Raton, FL: St. Lucie Press.

1 Curriculum and pedagogy in the sociology of education

Some lessons from comparing Durkheim and Vygotsky

Michael Young

> the rules of classic art teach us by their arbitrary nature that the thoughts arising from our daily needs, sentiments and experiences are only a small part of the thoughts of which we are capable.
>
> (Paul Valéry, 1941)

Introduction

The distinction between curriculum and pedagogy in educational studies has a long history and has some parallels with the equally well-known distinction between 'structure' and 'agency' in social theory (Giddens, 1986). Both can be seen as a dividing line between the approaches to education adopted by Durkheim and Vygotsky, at least in how their ideas have been developed and used. My starting point takes a rather different and – I hope – more productive approach. It argues that, despite many 'mainstream' claims in their respective disciplines (sociology and psychology) Durkheim and Vygotsky were both, in the broad sense of the term, social epistemologists, interested in knowledge and the curriculum, *and* pedagogic theorists, interested in classroom practice. At the same time it would be misleading to claim that each did not emphasise the problems that were given priority by the other. Both were distinctive and in advance of their time in developing explicitly *social* theories of knowledge, although their respective approaches were very different. In this chapter, I shall concentrate on their social theories of knowledge, and the implications of the differences between them both for the sociology of education, and educational research generally. In relation to Vygotsky, the lack of attention to his theory of knowledge in the literature is noticeable. This no doubt reflects the fact that, despite the broad philosophical basis of his work, his ideas have been largely been taken up by psychologists. Thanks to the work of two philosophers, Derry (2003) and Bakhurst (2011), we now have a much fuller and more rounded view of the importance of epistemological issues in Vygotsky's work.

This chapter is a revised version of ch. 4 of *Bringing Knowledge Back in: From Social Constructivism to Social Realism in the Sociology of Education* (Abingdon: Routledge, 2008).

Durkheim, in contrast, has long been recognised as a sociologist of knowledge. However, the polemical style of some of his works[1] – he saw himself as an advocate of the reality of the 'social' *sui generis* as well as an analyst – and the fact that he did not explicitly refer to his theory of knowledge in his writings on education has meant that only recently has this been recognized as central to his educational theories Moore (2004), Young and Muller (2007).

Despite their different disciplinary origins, the two writers under discussion share two assumptions that were basic to their ideas about education. First is the idea that knowledge is not located 'in the mind' or in the material or experiential world. Both Durkheim and Vygotsky see knowledge as the outcome of men and women acting together on the world. In other words, both had an unambiguously *social* theory of knowledge. Secondly both recognized that the acquisition and transmission of knowledge is central to education. This does not of course mean, as some have supposed, that either relied on a mechanical or one-way metaphor of transmission. For Durkheim, as Paul Fauconnet says in his introduction to Durkheim's *Education and Sociology* 'the transmission [of knowledge] through the teacher to the pupil (or conversely) the assimilation by the child of a subject, seemed to him [Durkheim] to be the condition of real intellectual formation . . . Forms [of the mind] cannot be transmitted empty. Durkheim, like Comte, thinks that it is necessary to learn about things, to acquire knowledge' (1956:). Vygotsky expresses the crucial role of knowledge transmission slightly less directly in the way that he sees pedagogy as integral to a child engaging with 'theoretical' concepts and developing 'higher forms of thought'.

While neither Vygotsky or Durkheim offer a fully satisfactory social theory of knowledge, both raise the issue of knowledge as an educational issue in ways that most sociology of education and educational studies have ignored. More space in this chapter is given to Durkheim's work than that of Vygotsky. This is partly, because, as a sociologist, I am more familiar with Durkheim's work and partly because the issue of knowledge is at the centre of Durkheim's social theory and only indirectly addressed by Vygotsky.

By beginning with the similarities between Durkheim's and Vygotsky's approaches, my argument will be that while both can be understood as adopting a social realist approach to knowledge,[2] the ways that they conceptualized social reality were very different. One way of making a clear contrast between the two 'social realists' is that central to Durkheim's theory of knowledge is the idea of 'social structure', whereas Vygotsky's theory relies on the idea of 'social activity'.[3]

---

1 I am thinking of *The Rules of Sociological Method* (1938) and to some extent *Suicide* (1952).
2 The idea that knowledge is both 'socially' produced and acquired, but at the same time 'objective', and not reducible to the ideas of individuals.
3 Social Structure for Durkheim refers to the external constraints that are felt by members of a society and that give them a sense of who they are. In contrast, I interpret Vygotsky's reference to 'social activities' in its broader materialist sense, and close to Marx's use of the concepts 'human labour' and 'labour process'. However, unlike many Marxists, while including productive (or economic labour), in his concept of activity, Vygotsky

I will return to the concepts 'social structure' and 'social activity' later in the chapter.

Section 2 outlines Durkheim's theory of knowledge and the problems that arise from his concept of 'social structure' and its neglect of the dimension of social activity. It draws on both his early anthropological work (Durkheim, 1912/1965; Durkheim and Mauss, 1970), and his later lectures on the pragmatism of William James (Durkheim, 1984).

Section 3 describes Vygotsky's social activity-based theory of knowledge and how it emphasizes just those issues that Durkheim neglects. It notes that Vygotsky's emphasis on 'social activity' appears to preclude him from treating knowledge as something that can be conceptualized as separate from its uses. The importance of being able to separate knowledge from its uses is of course Durkheim's key point in his critique of pragmatism (Durkheim, 1984), and has profound implications for his approach to the curriculum. Section 4 explores the contrasts between Durkheim and Vygotsky's theories in more detail and develops more fully the analytical distinction between 'structure' and 'activity'. Section 5 turns to some issues raised by the leading English Durkheimian, Basil Bernstein. Although I focus largely on Bernstein's last book (Bernstein, 2000), his ideas about educational knowledge can be traced back to his earliest papers on the curriculum (Bernstein, 1971). I show how both the strengths and some of the problems with Durkheim's approach re-emerge in Bernstein's more developed theory of educational knowledge. Section 6 traces some of the ways in which Vygotsky's ideas have been developed, especially by the Finnish socio-cultural theorist, Yrjö Engeström, and how Engeström's approach highlights the problems that an activity-based theory of knowledge can lead to. I conclude by suggesting some of the educational implications of the distinction between structure-based and activity-based approaches to knowledge and the lessons contemporary researchers can learn from the Vygotsky–Durkheim comparison.

Despite being located within the different disciplinary traditions of sociology and psychology, and living and working in contexts as different as pre-First World War France and post-revolutionary Russia, Durkheim and Vygotsky had much in common as social theorists and educational thinkers. Both had social theories of knowledge that were closely related to their ideas about education. This point about Vygotsky having a social theory of knowledge is especially significant as it has been largely neglected in the psychologically oriented tradition of activity theory that has built on his work. Both shared a fundamentally evolutionary approach to knowledge and human development that was common to most progressive intellectuals in the early decades of the twentieth century. Both held *differentiated*

---

does not reduce the concept of activity to its economic dimensions. Here I use it in a way that I hope is consistent with Vygotsky to refer to the ways people in history have engaged in collective activities (these included, in early societies, as both Vygotsky and Durkheim recognized, the economic activities of hunting and gathering) to appropriate the natural world for their survival needs, and later for the creation of wealth, knowledge and institutions.

theories of knowledge; they recognized that knowledge is not a seamless web – that theoretical or context-independent knowledge and everyday or context-bound knowledges have different structures and different purposes. Both saw formal education as the main source of, and condition for, people to acquire the capacity for generalization, and both recognized that the acquisition of context-independent or theoretical knowledge was the main, albeit not the only, goal of formal education.

On the other hand, Durkheim and Vygotsky differed both on the aspects of human development that they saw as fundamental, and how they conceptualized the 'social' in their theories of mind and knowledge. It is also relevant that Durkheim had a far greater concern with education's integrative role in a society. This is not surprising when, as in the France of his time, the old religious bonds were weakening and when new, for Durkheim 'amoral' forms of economic activity that threatened the integrity of society, were expanding. In contrast, Vygotsky was living in a society in which a new concept of man – socialist man – was being created. It is hardly surprising, therefore, that they had different ideas about the social character of knowledge. Both recognized that human beings are social in ways that have no equivalent among animals. Both interpreted man's social relations as fundamentally *pedagogic*. In other words, both saw that it is through the ability of human beings not just to adapt to their environment like animals but to develop in response to pedagogy, especially but not only when they are young, that they become members of societies and create knowledge beyond anything previous generations could conceive of. It was for these reasons, that unlike later sociology and psychology of education, both saw education and integral to the social (and in Vygotsky's case, development) theories and vice versa. They differed, however, in how they interpreted the origins of this fundamental human sociality. Although both were creatures of the Enlightenment and believed in the progressive possibilities of science, Durkheim tended to look backwards for the foundations of knowledge and equate them with sources of social stability, whereas Vygotsky's more activist approach looked forward to men and women's capacities for developing higher forms of thought and creating a socialist society. Before exploring the implications of these differences, the next two sections focus separately and in more detail on Durkheim and Vygotsky's ideas.

Durkheim's theory of knowledge

For Durkheim, the fundamental *sociality* of human beings is the basis of his social theory of knowledge; everything that is human is social for Durkheim. Human society, he argued, originated in the collective relations found in the most primitive societies (the clan system in those he studied). For Durkheim, the sociality of early human beings was expressed in their membership of clans and the social identity this gave them. It was through their ability to distinguish clans (and learn that one was a member of one and not the others) that Durkheim and Mauss (1970) located the origins of logic (the grouping of things into discrete categories). Durkheim argued that totems associated with primitive religions (usually an animal, a bird or a fish) were collective representations which defined what clan someone was in (and therefore who they were). He built his social theory of the foundations of knowledge on his account of totemic religion and it was from this starting point that he developed his distinction between 'the sacred' and 'the profane'. In laying the social foundations of logic without which no other knowledge is possible, Durkheim described these primitive forms of totemic religion as a kind of proto-science.

He set out to show that, despite being experienced by members of primitive societies (and described by anthropologists) as *religious* beliefs and practices, the collective representations which emerged from and constituted the clan structures are, in form at least, remarkably like the ideas of modern logic. He is, it can be argued, inverting the dominant rationalism of his time which assumed that logical ideas are innate or 'in the mind'. As he and Mauss put it:

> (it is not) that the social relations of men are based on the logical relations between things, in reality, it is the former which have provided the prototype for the latter . . . men classified things because they were divided into clans. (Durkheim and Mauss, 1970: 82)

Social scientists keep returning to Durkheim's ideas a century later, not because subsequent ethnographical evidence supports them (often it does not) but because, almost uniquely, he offers a convincing *sociological* account of the most basic categories of human thought (or, as he put it, of the foundations of knowledge). The power, objectivity and generality of knowledge are, for Durkheim, located in the generality of society for its members. Furthermore, in making a distinction between the totemic classifications which hold primitive societies together, and what he and Mauss refer to as the 'technological classifications that [merely] reflect usage', Durkheim is suggesting how we might develop a social theory of the origins of our most fundamental categories that we largely take for granted such as 'analytical' and 'descriptive', 'theoretical' and 'everyday', and 'cause' and 'effect'. In other words he is offering us the basis for a social theory of the differentiation of knowledge. His social theory of knowledge is therefore also the basis for a theory of the curriculum; it implies a set of principles for the selection of curriculum knowledge. This is a point that I will return to.

In a footnote to their book *Primitive Classifications*, Durkheim and Mauss make a clear distinction between their idea of social classifications and the ways that members of primitive societies classify what Durkheim and Mauss refer to as:

> the things on which they lived according to the means they used to get them. (1970: 81)

They saw the latter type of classification as 'mere divisions . . . *and not schemes of classification*' (*ibid.*; my italics).

Why did Durkheim make such a sharp distinction between religious or totemic classifications and what he referred to as technological (or practical/useful) classifications? My view is that this distinction is fundamental to his theory of knowledge and his theory of society, which are in a sense the same. This point needs some elaboration. Furthermore, his tendency to elide the sociological meanings that he gives to religion, knowledge and society, points also to some problems with his approach. Firstly, it is arguable that his whole theory of knowledge collapses if the reason for making the distinction between 'social' and 'technological' classifications is not accepted. The case that he makes for the social basis of knowledge assumes that the clans of which primitive men and women were members and the collective rituals that sustained them had an epistemological priority over any other forms of social grouping or relations that they may have been involved in – almost a kind of anti-materialist doctrine. Secondly, despite his criticisms of Kant, Durkheim was at heart a rationalist, who accepted the idea that reason (and its specification as logic) was the unique quality that made people human (and different from other animals); the activities they engaged in to survive did not distinguish them from animals; they also had to survive! Reason was also, for Durkheim, the basis of our objectively true knowledge of the world, and hence it was the foundation of science. On the other hand, Durkheim was deeply dissatisfied with the accounts of the origins of human reason that were prevalent in his time. These, and the problems with them that he identified, can be summarized briefly in the following very schematic terms:

1   *Rationalism* – this refers to the argument by Kant and his followers that reason is innate in the human mind. For Durkheim this was an unproveable assertion and therefore like faith, an unreliable basis for knowledge or truth. Furthermore, it was also unable to account for the great diversity of beliefs in different societies.

2   *Empiricism* – this is the claim, by those such as John Locke, that reason is grounded in experience (or the sensations that our mind receives) that is disciplined by scientific method. For Durkheim, sensations are an unreliable and inadequate basis for explaining the universality and compelling force of logic in human affairs.

3   *Hegelian dialectics* – Hegel grounded reason in history and ontology – in our being as humans. This was a view of reason and logic that Durkheim did not explicitly engage with. As an admirer of Comte's positivist sociology, he would presumably have seen Hegel's approach as unscientific.

4   *Dialectical materialism* – this views the grounds for knowledge and truth in human labour, and the contradictions that arise as people struggle through their labour to appropriate the material world. Durkheim dismisses this (Marxist) view with the argument that 'the world of representations is superimposed upon its material substratum, far from arising from it' (Durkheim, 1912/1965: 461). Although recognizing that the material world always 'left its mark' on human affairs, Durkheim asserts the '*sui generis*' reality of social or collective representations.

Durkheim's social (or more specifically, societal) theory of knowledge and reason was his attempt to overcome the weaknesses he saw in these four approaches.

Thirdly, Durkheim separated the two kinds of classification because he thought that logical classification must be prior to any classification related to usage. In other words men lived in clans and developed a sense of themselves as clan members before they developed classifications. As he and Mauss put it in explaining why they were not paying attention to technological classifications:

> we have tried above all to throw some light on the [social] origins of the logical procedure which is the basis of scientific classifications. (Durkheim and Mauss 1970: 82)

An understanding of 'the word' precedes an understanding of 'the world' was the way he was to express this later in his account of the curriculum and the development of knowledge in medieval French universities (Durkheim, 1938/1977).

Fourthly, Durkheim was seeking an answer to why we find logic so compelling; in other words, where, he asked, did its undoubted power over our thinking come from? For Durkheim this power could never arise out of its usefulness in terms of satisfying specific needs. Consequences, he argued, are inevitably unreliable criteria for truth; things might always be different. The power of logic has to refer to factors that are a priori and external to any specific human activity. In other words, to restate a key Durkheimian point, the compelling power of logic, and hence knowledge, has to come from society as a reality *sui generis*.

His explicit dismissal of the importance of what he and Mauss refer to as 'technological' classifications arises from (a) his focus on *the foundations* of knowledge or logic and (b) his concept of society *as a whole* as the grounds for truth and objectivity and the basis for the humanity of all men and women and their sense of identity. As Worsley (1956) argues, it is the morphology of the societies that he studied – in particular their clan structure – that Durkheim took as his model for the social origins of the basic categories of logic, and hence of the foundations of knowledge. In linking the classes of clan, sub-clan and tribe to the rules of logic, he claims to have the basis for extrapolating a social theory based on primitive societies to the collective representations of any society, however complex.

Undoubtedly Durkheim does focus on societies as wholes, which is not surprising given the lack of differentiation in these primitive societies; they were *the* exemplar of what he referred to as 'mechanical solidarity'. Furthermore, he gives little attention to the activities that take place within them or their internal structures; the question is: does this matter for his theory of knowledge? The problem can be illustrated in relation to hunting and gathering that were the means of subsistence in the societies that he studied. These activities themselves play no part in his account. He refers to society and social relationships in largely abstract terms, with no reference to their content or to the specific activities and interests or members. Another example of his separation of structure and content is to be found in his descriptions of how the totems that represent deities are associated with different plants and animals and become symbolic repositories of spiritual forces. Durkheim noted that plants and animals were arbitrarily assigned to clans as totems; it was their function that was important to him.

Worsley (1956) argues that this neglect of the survival or subsistence activities of members of the aboriginal societies which he studied leads to weakness in Durkheim's theory of knowledge as a general theory. The members of these societies did not cultivate the land, they had no flocks or herds of animals and had few techniques of food preservation. As a result, procuring food through hunting and gathering was a very high priority. This meant that the ways in which particular areas of land were classified and the different seasons were distinguished were vital for a clan's survival. For Worsley, these subsistence classifications warrant the same epistemological importance as the clan relations that Durkheim focused on. However, it is only clan relationships that Durkheim was concerned with. It was as if man's relationship to the material world was of secondary importance. Durkheim did not appear to take account of the fact that religious beliefs such as totemism and clan relations developed in specific environments and that clan-based societies also develop forms of systematic and relatively objective 'technical' classifications that arise from needing to identify and use animals and plants for food and clothing. In other words, it could be that there is not just a clan (and therefore a societal) basis for classifications, but a material basis as well.

The general point is that for Durkheim, the universality of the categories of thought that he is concerned with arises from the generality of the collective representations that he identified, and not from the specific social experiences of survival in particular environments. He separates the collective clan activity of primitive societies from the activities of clan members as they wrestle their livelihood from nature, without seeing that this may introduce problems for his theory of classifications. In his critique of Durkheim, Worsley (1956) wants to relativize the fundamental categories of thought to the specific circumstances of particular societies. From Durkheim's point of view, this would remove both their fundamental objectivity and their societal basis.

Durkheim makes a powerful case for the social basis of the foundations of knowledge or logic. As Cuvillier (1955) puts it, truth for Durkheim is a *social* reality, but it cannot be explained in terms of the practical needs that lead societies to develop particular kinds of 'technological' classifications. Durkheim contrasts thought which is speculative (with its roots in the 'sacred') with action, which he expresses as a form of 'sudden release', or immediate response to need – in other words, as 'profane'. As a result, his theory offers a sociology of the foundations of knowledge and truth, and a theory of the basic differentiation of knowledge. On the other hand, it does not take us very far as a theory of the specialization of knowledge, which has been the dominant feature of industrialisation. We have a starting point for a social theory of knowledge, but a number of problems are left unresolved. One is how science, with foundations modelled on what is general to any society, is used to transform the very specific worlds of everyday life. A second problem is whether Durkheim's categories of 'sacred' and 'profane' can be the basis for a social theory of the curriculum – a problem taken up most creatively from Durkheim in the work of Basil Bernstein.

The next section turns to Vygotsky's theory of knowledge. It is distinguished from Durkheim's in three ways. Firstly, as indicated earlier, it is a far less developed aspect of his thinking. Secondly, it does not separate the foundations of knowledge from 'technological classifications', or specific knowledges such as science and technology. Thirdly, it locates the origins of knowledge not, like Durkheim, in social structures that are general to all societies, but in the human activities that have historically been involved in transforming the natural world.

Vygotsky's theory of knowledge

Whereas Durkheim quite explicitly developed a theory of knowledge in his books *Primitive Classifications* (with Marcel Mauss, 1970) and *Elementary Forms of Religious Life* (1912/1965), Vygotsky's primary focus was on human development, or the development of mind, not knowledge. He wanted to show that:

> Human nature [*and specifically, human minds*] have changed in the course of history. (Luria and Vygotsky, 1992: 41; my addition in italics)

Again in contrast to Durkheim, who set out to counter arguments of those like Comte and Saint Simon who associated specialization and the division of labour with societal fragmentation, Vygotsky began by criticizing the individualism that dominated the psychology of his time. His interest was in conceptualizing a social and cultural theory of mind that countered prevailing individualist and a-historical tendencies in psychology. So it was with somewhat different purposes that Vygotsky turned to anthropological studies of primitive peoples. Like Durkheim, he did not himself undertake any ethnography; unlike him, he seems to have relied largely on the secondary analyses of Lévy-Bruhl, rather than on original ethnographies.

Vygotsky drew an important and fundamental lesson from Lévy-Bruhl that brought him close to Durkheim – that thought and mind are social. However, whereas for Durkheim it was the formal similarities between the minds of primitive and modern man that were important, Vygotsky took over Lévy-Bruhl's view that it was the differences between the two that mattered. As he put it:

> the higher psychological functions of primitive man are profoundly different from those same functions in civilised man . . . the very type of thinking . . . [is] . . . a historical variable. (Luria and Vygotsky, 1992: 44)

Also in contrast to Durkheim (and Lévy-Bruhl), Vygotsky stressed the crucial epistemological importance of the practical subsistence activities of members of primitive societies. Vygotsky's view was that even primitive man was capable of:

> objective logical thinking whenever the purpose of his actions is direct adaptation to nature. (Luria and Vygotsky, 1992: 45)

Unlike Durkheim (and like Lévy-Bruhl), Vygotsky saw no positive role for religion. Whereas for Durkheim, religion was the structural precursor of science, Vygotsky saw the germ of modern science and technology in the:

> tools, hunting, animal husbandry, agriculture and fighting all [of which] demand from man real and not just apparent logical thought. (*Ibid.*)

These were just those activities that Durkheim dismissed as contingent and 'merely technological' forms of classification.

In contrast to Lévy-Bruhl, who did not differentiate between science and modern thought (both for him constituted the largely undifferentiated and superior common sense of modern societies), Vygotsky made a clear distinction between science and everyday or common-sense concepts that had significant similarities with Durkheim's distinction between the 'sacred' and the 'profane'.

We can conclude this brief account of Vygotsky's ideas about knowledge by suggesting that he located his social theory of knowledge in just what Durkheim disregarded – people's struggle to appropriate nature for their survival. Thus, in a broad sense, he was a materialist, and at first sight, Vygotsky's historical approach to knowledge appears more grounded in the realities of social existence than Durkheim's. However, it has a number of problems. Firstly, he seems to take for granted the progressive transformation of mankind's pre-scientific struggles for survival into modern scientific forms of thought. There is no space in his theory for identifying the conditions for this transformation on the lines developed by Max Weber and powerfully argued for in contemporary terms by Ernest Gellner (1992). Secondly, the relationship between Vygotsky's evolutionary theory of the development of knowledge and the emergence of higher forms of thought and his theory of the development of the human mind in children is unclear. The developmental link which he wants to make between 'the real logical thought demanded by primitive man in animal husbandry and agriculture' (Luria and Vygotsky, 1992) and the higher forms of 'scientific' thinking that can be acquired through the pedagogy of formal education is more implicit than explicit. The development of Vygotsky's distinction between scientific (theoretical) and everyday concepts appears to have arisen more from his early critique of Piaget than from any explicit relationship to his genetic and materialist account of human development. Finally, Vygotsky appears to take for granted the issues which were of primary concern to Durkheim – namely the objectivity and compelling power of logic and the necessarily social foundations of knowledge.

Further aspects of the differences between Durkheim and Vygotsky

It can be argued that there are significant formal similarities between Vygotsky's idea of theoretical concepts and Durkheim's idea of the 'sacred' in terms of the criteria that they specify for each. Both are expressed as involving systematic relationships between concepts and being independent of specific contexts. Both provide the potential for speculation, connection and generalization. Both are separate from everyday practices (although the emphasis placed by the two writers on this separation is different) although derived from them. Vygotsky distinguishes between reality reflected in consciousness (theoretical concepts) and in immediate sensation (everyday concepts) as qualitatively different ways of thinking. He refers to their relationship as a 'dialectical leap', but we are left in considerable doubt as to what he means by this. Vygotsky's approach to his two types of concept can be seen as dialectical in the simple sense that he sees them as embedded in and related to each other in an ongoing process. This appears to be in stark contrast to Durkheim's view that:

> in all the history of human thought there exists no example of two categories (the sacred and the profane) so profoundly differentiated or so radically opposed. (Durkheim, 1961: 53)

For Durkheim, society (as a structure that is independent of the social activities that has generated it) shapes and constitutes the forms of social classification independently (almost) of the activities of any specific society. Vygotsky, on the other hand, saw just these activities – the working on and transforming of nature – as the fundamental basis of human development (and therefore of knowledge) in history. The question that remains is what is the relation between this view of social activity and how it develops, and Vygotsky's distinction between theoretical and everyday concepts. It has been argued by Wertsch (1985) and others that Vygotsky had an overly teleological view of history, and endorsed an overly abstract view of rationality that was a legacy of an uncritical view of the Enlightenment. This critique that is countered, effectively in my view, by Bakhurst (2011). However, regardless of whether this is a correct view of Vygotsky's ideas about rationality, human society would seem to be impossible without some notion of future and purpose which are the aspects of the Enlightenment most sharply criticized by anti-humanists (Gray 2003) .

One way of focusing on the contrasts between Durkheim and Vygotsky that has direct relevance to the sociology of education is by exploring further the structure–activity distinction that I began with. Durkheim and Mauss argue that what they referred to as primitive classifications:

> are not singular or exceptional . . . on the contrary [they] seem connected . . . to the first scientific classifications . . . [having] all their essential characteristics. They are systems of hierarchized notions . . . standing in fixed relationships to one each other and together form a single whole . . . like science, they have a purely speculative purpose. Their object is not to facilitate action, but to advance understanding, to make intelligible the relations which exist between things . . . [they] are intended, above all, to connect ideas, to unify knowledge. (1970: 81)

Durkheim is thus able to develop his social theory of the foundations of knowledge by arguing that the structure of society is homologous with the structures of logic, and therefore with the foundations of all knowledge. The strengths of such a theory are that:

- it treats society as the foundation of knowledge and as separate from and not reducible either to other social relations or institutions, to individual members, or to the ways knowledge is used (as in the case of technology and tools);
- it highlights classifications or rules of exclusion and inclusion within a hierarchical system as necessary features of societies and of any knowledge that claims objectivity (X is either X or not X);
- it makes explicit the link by relating identity and knowledge between the clan (or society) that I am a member of to my knowledge of myself and the world; and
- it offers a justification for a social a-priorist theory of knowledge unlike pragmatism that relies on uses or consequences as criteria of truth. Unlike Hegel and Marx, it does not rely on a providential view of workings of reason or of the inevitability of positive outcome of the clash of social classes in history.

However, in avoiding 'technological' types of classifications that arise from the exigencies of survival and need, and by assuming that the principles that he identified about the social basis of knowledge in the most primitive societies hold for every society, Durkheim treats the foundations of knowledge as almost outside of both society and history. He is assuming in effect that though social, the foundations of knowledge have no history – they are almost universal. The problem with this conclusion is that it can rob the idea of 'the social' or 'society' of any content. In other words, it appears to rob it of any culture that is specific to particular societies. It is also at odds with debates within philosophy which have led to changes in ideas about logic (Collins, 2000). Also, being only concerned with foundations, Durkheim's theory robs knowledge of its content. The challenge to Durkheim posed by Worsley and other social anthropologists is that even in those primitive societies, the clan structure was not the only basis for the development of social classifications. A social theory of even the foundations of knowledge may be more complex than Durkheim hoped. His rejection of the epistemological significance of technological classifications remains difficult to justify.

Despite the similarities between Durkheim and Vygotsky summarized earlier in this chapter, I suggested that the latter could be seen as beginning with just the problems that the former avoided – the activities of men and women as they struggle to appropriate the natural world. Unlike Durkheim, Vygotsky takes man's productive relationships with the natural world, not his social relationships, as his starting point. At the same time, his concept of human development involves the emergence of higher forms of thinking, which do not automatically arise from man's relationship with the natural world but depend on the pedagogy of formal education, and the specific development of science as a social institution. Unlike Durkheim, Vygotsky sees science as replacing religion; the latter is not a kind of proto-science. He sees no need for a model and an explanation of the emergence of theoretical knowledge with autonomy from practical concerns. For Vygotsky the interplay between theoretical and everyday concepts is the source of knowledge and new ideas. How, then, for Vygotsky, are these systems of theoretical concepts developed from practical subsistence activities, and how do they gain their objectivity? Knowledge ('scientific concepts' is probably the nearest Vygotsky gets to referring to knowledge) is not a separate social category for Vygotsky; it is a result of the evolution of man's relationship with his environment. For Vygotsky, knowledge, we can assume, develops in the process of mediation between consciousness and the world, as theoretical and practical concepts shape and develop each other. For Vygotsky the relationship between science and technology is, implicitly, seamless; he thus has difficulty in accounting for the growth of knowledge except in broad evolutionary terms. In parallel, his explicit blurring of science and technology is at odds with his stress on the importance of the distinct roles and forms of theoretical and everyday concepts and their interaction in the pedagogy of formal education.

We have, therefore, two social theories of knowledge. One is structure based: despite its social origins, it sets the foundations of knowledge apart from the lived world; it is this separation that for Durkheim is the condition for freeing the intellect and for innovation and new knowledge to be developed. At the same time, as a social theory it has its origins in that lived world; human beings need to make sense of it, and it provides us with the categories for speculating about the world beyond ourselves. However, once we move out of Durkheim's primitive societies with their clans, it is far from clear how the concept of society and its generality, or the nature of the knowledge that is being referred to, are to be specified.

The second theory of knowledge is social activity based; it arises from our collective activity in trying to shape the world to our purposes; it remains embedded in the world, and the objectivity of the explanations it provides arises from the success or failure of our efforts at transforming it. This 'dialectical' or pragmatic model of the relations between theory and practice that is expressed in the interdependence of scientific and everyday concepts is not adequate on its own in accounting for new knowledge. It requires some notion of purpose, some teleology – Lenin's 'socialist man', for example, however provisional, and a more explicit notion of the separateness as well as the embeddedness of theoretical concepts from the everyday. Without these additional elements, one is left with a 'logical utilitarianism' (to use Durkheim's term for criticizing pragmatism) that does not account for the 'hard' objective character of truth as something external to us, or for the remarkable growth of science and technology, and their impact on society, in the last two centuries. There are thus two problems with Vygotsky's theory of knowledge. The first is that his idea of scientific or theoretical concepts is too general, and too lacking in specificity in the generalizations that it offers. His criteria for theoretical concepts do not provide us with any way of differentiating concepts in the various fields of specialist knowledge that might be the basis of curricula. The second problem is that whereas Durkheim offers no way of conceptualizing how science transforms the everyday world, Vygotsky focuses only on the process of transformation between scientific and everyday concepts, and does not distinguish between science and technology. We are left with only formal criteria (their interrelatedness) for distinguishing theoretical concepts from any other. I shall return to these problems in a brief discussion of post-Durkheimian and post-Vygotskian developments.

Post-Durkheimian approaches to knowledge

Almost the only post-Durkheimian developments in the sociology of knowledge are those associated with the work of Basil Bernstein and those who have drawn on his ideas. This is not the place to describe the complex body of Bernstein's ideas. I will, however, pick up a number of issues that I have raised in relation to Durkheim and which reappear in Bernstein's work. I shall consider his concept of classification, his idea of the social, and his model of science. Bernstein first drew on Durkheim's idea of the relationship between classifications and social order in his justly acclaimed paper, 'On the Classification and Framing of Educational Knowledge' (Bernstein, 1971). In that paper, he distinguished between curricula based on strong classification between different fields of knowledge and strong framing between school and everyday knowledge, and those characterized by weak classification and weak framing. Like Durkheim, his focus was on relations between knowledge contents, not the contents themselves. This can lead to a rather static and a-historical view of knowledge and curriculum categories that allows strong disciplinary boundaries to be treated as themselves almost beyond history and as the only condition for knowledge production and acquisition. It does not provide a framework that deals adequately with new forms of knowledge classification that may not be disciplinary in the traditional sense or with the historicity of disciplinarity itself. Bernstein returned to the issue of knowledge in a chapter in his last book (Bernstein, 2000), in which he distinguished between vertical and horizontal knowledge structures. His model for vertical knowledge structures has some parallels with Durkheim's clan model of primitive society. Also like Durkheim, Bernstein relies on a somewhat idealized notion of science (in his case physics) in terms of which less vertical forms of knowledge are compared, inevitably unfavourably. On the other hand, following Durkheim, Bernstein's great strengths are that he offers us (a) a sociology of *knowledge* as something *sui generis*, not just as a sociology of knowers and their interests and standpoints (Moore, 2004). Educational knowledge – or its selection and pacing in the curriculum – becomes, from his perspective, something to be studied sociologically as a phenomenon in its own right, with its own distributional consequences, not just as another social institution or as he once put it 'as a relay of other institutions and structures'. Bernstein also takes up a point that was referred to but not developed by Durkheim when he argues that knowledge classifications are both identity relations and hierarchical relations as well as knowledge relations – they include and exclude. This opens up a whole new set of research questions about pedagogy and changes in the teaching profession.

Post-Vygotskian developments

Given that Vygotsky's ideas about science and knowledge were implicit rather than explicit in his theory of human development, it is not surprising that they have been vulnerable both to being used in oversimplified ways and to being the subject of simplistic criticisms. Post-Vygotskians have tried to go beyond his formulation of the theoretical–everyday distinction, and what they take to be his rather narrow concentration on formal schooling. However, such developments rely on two highly problematic assumptions that are prevalent in much contemporary educational research. These concern (a) the very idea of science, or indeed any knowledge, being able to make claims to truth that are more reliable than common sense and (b) that schooling may not provide the only or even the unique conditions for the acquisition of theoretical concepts. The influence of Vygotsky's ideas or at least interpretations of them in the expansion of research into work-based and experiential learning is a case in point. I have discussed elsewhere some of the problems that arise if Vygotsky's key pedagogic distinction between theoretical and everyday concepts is dispensed with (Young, 2008).

The Finnish researcher Yrjo Engeström is an exception to most other post-Vygotskians. Here I will mention his attempt to go beyond Vygotsky's theoretical–everyday distinction (Tuomi-Grohn and Engeström, 2003). Engeström argues that in any classroom, workplace or community it is possible to develop what he refers to as 'theoretically grounded concepts' which go beyond the distinction between theoretical and everyday concepts, and provide the tools for actors to understand and change the world. I will restrict myself to making two observations on this move. Firstly, in disconnecting the acquisition of theoretical concepts from its institutional location in specialized educational institutions such as schools, colleges and universities, where it was located by Vygotsky, Engeström seems to be denying that there may be institutional specificities associated with the acquisition of particular types of knowledge. This conclusion could have serious policy implications, especially in developing countries, and could provide a justification for not expanding schooling (the opposite of Vygotsky's intention). Second, although Vygotsky stressed the interrelationship of theoretical and everyday concepts in the process of learning, he also stressed their distinctiveness, and did not argue that their differences could be blurred in the interests of solving particular problems; it follows that Engeström's formulation of 'theoretically grounded concepts' represents a break with, rather than a development of, Vygotsky's ideas. It may be that by his focus on the embeddedness as well as the distinctiveness of theoretical and everyday concepts, Vygotsky did not, like

Durkheim, see it as necessary to try to articulate more precisely the nature of their distinctiveness.

Vygotsky emphasized the distinctiveness of theoretical and everyday concepts as the basis for a pedagogy that would enable learners in schools to acquire theoretical concepts and then use them to reinterpret the world of the 'everyday'. This distinctiveness also implicitly provided the grounds for his theory of knowledge. However, neither Vygotsky nor Engeström, as far as I am aware, discuss the possibility of different types of theoretical concept (as in the case of concepts associated with different disciplines and school subjects), or the possible relationships between them. As a result, the Vygotskyian tradition has, with few exceptions, focused on the relationship between theoretical and everyday concepts as a developmental process and scaffolding structure and played down how the two types of concepts are distinguished in content and structure. In relativizing the idea of scientific or theoretical concepts, post-Vygotskian revisionists such as Wertsch seem to be in danger of losing what was distinctive about his pedagogic theory and its links with his theory of knowledge.

The one post-Vygotskian who took what might be described as a more Durkheimian approach to knowledge was the Russian V. V. Davydov. Davydov started with Vygotsky's critique of crude 'transmission' models of pedagogy and his observation that:

> direct instruction in concepts is impossible . . . [The teacher] who attempts to use this approach achieves nothing but a mindless learning of words . . .
> (quoted in Engeström, 1991: no page numbers)

He pointed out that much teaching in schools is like this, and is likely to continue in that way. This, he explains, is partly due to inadequacies that he sees in Vygotsky's definition of scientific concepts. However, his criticisms are of a completely different kind to those referred to earlier. Whereas postmodernist critics seek to weaken Vygotsky's emphasis on science and schooling, Davydov sets out to strengthen Vygotsky's scientific concepts by making them more explicit. He argues that a failure to specify the content of scientific concepts means that it is hard to distinguish them from empirical or everyday concepts. It is worth elaborating on his ideas a little, as he remains, in my view, an important example of someone who tried to build on Vygotsky's largely implicit theory of the curriculum.

On the assumption that everyday knowledge gives us only 'abstractions' – in the sense that it never provides 'the whole picture', Davydov followed Marx in 'arguing that teaching theoretical knowledge must involve ascending from the abstract to the concrete'. It followed for him that teachers need a theory of the development of knowledge to enable them to identify topics which embody the core or 'kernel' concepts of any particular field. The problem with Davydov's formulation is that there is no general theory of the development of knowledge as is assumed by dialectical method; we only have accounts of the development of different fields such as physics and history. His approach thus lays itself open to a theory of knowledge defined bureaucratically, and to knowledge selection becoming a state function – one way of looking at some forms of National Curriculum. One fruitful line of enquiry might be to treat Davydov's approach as a form of genericism (Bernstein, 2000) and to compare it with contemporary approaches to genericism such as critical thinking, meta-cognition and thinking skills, which play down content and stress processes.

Conclusions

When I first encountered Vygotsky's work almost ten years ago, I was struck by the extraordinary and largely neglected similarity of his and Durkheim's core distinctions – Durkheim's 'sacred' and 'profane' sources of meaning and Vygotsky's 'scientific' and 'everyday' concepts. However, as I tried to locate the two sets of distinctions in the whole body of the thought of each writer and in their approaches to knowledge, I became increasingly aware of the differences between them and their different purposes in each theory. As I have set out to show, they offer, in effect, two very different approaches to developing a social theory of knowledge with very different practical implications – Durkheim (via Bernstein) primarily for the curriculum and Vygotsky primarily for pedagogy.

Daniels (2001) describes the aims of pedagogy as:

> helping children make links between their everyday understanding and . . . schooled knowledge (or scientific concepts).

With the somewhat different emphasis referred to earlier, the purpose of the curriculum for Davydov is to 'teach theoretical understanding'. Both of these formulations derive from Vygotsky, and in my view, it is hard to see Durkheim disagreeing with them. However, as researchers or curriculum developers, we are still left with the big questions. What concepts? What theories? What selection of knowledge? And on what basis do we decide?

Vygotsky addresses the pedagogic questions in his discussion of the interrelationships between theoretical and everyday concepts. He does not, at least for me, deal adequately with the foundational or content questions. What are the non-arbitrary grounds for curriculum choices?

Durkheim does address at least the first of these types of question about foundations, in terms of the externality and objectivity of knowledge that needs to be the basis of the curriculum. Durkheim's model for the social basis of knowledge is, however, limited by depending on the idea of 'society as a whole'; he therefore addresses only the foundations of knowledge. His concept of the sacred (as the basis for speculative thought and the development of science) and his criticism of the seamlessness of pragmatism and other social constructivisms is more helpful to curriculum developers and has been taken further by Bernstein with his typology of knowledge structures and how they can embody weak or strong classification and framing, or, as he later expressed it, the principle of verticality. However, as I argued earlier, Bernstein's concept of vertical knowledge is over-reliant on an idealized notion of science, and the debatable assumption that it provides a model for knowledge in general.

Contrasting the theories of Durkheim and Vygotsky has emphasized their differing weaknesses and strengths rather than leading to a new theory. They remind us of two things that are important for the sociology of education. First, like any educational theory, it must have a theory of 'what is worthwhile knowledge'. Durkheim's concept of the sacred as it was developed by Bernstein offer powerful resources for such a theory, as well as the basis for a critique of the trends to vocationalism, curriculum relevance and modularization which increasingly dominate government policies across the world. Vygotsky in emphasizing the relational character of his theoretical–everyday concept distinction offers a powerful way of conceptualizing teaching and learning. He points to theory of pedagogy that directs our attention to the activities of teachers and students that are the necessary conditions for students to acquire powerful theoretical concepts – and in the broadest sense, to be educated. Thus in their differences and similarities, Durkheim and Vygotsky provide a strong basis for the future of the sociology of education.

References

Bakhurst, D. (2011) *The Formation of Reason*, Chichester, UK: Wiley-Blackwell.

Bernstein, B. (1971) *Class Codes and Control*, vol. 1, London: Routledge.

—— (2000) *Pedagogy, Symbolic Control and Identity*, Oxford: Rowan and Littlefield.

Collins (2000) *The Sociology of Philosophies*, Cambridge, MA: Harvard University Press.

Cuvillier, F. (1955) 'Introduction', to Durkheim, E., *Pragmatism and Sociology* (1984).

Daniels, H. (2001) *Vygotsky and Pedagogy*, London: RoutledgeFalmer.

Derry, J. (2008) 'Abstract Rationality in Education: From Vygotsky to Brandom', *Studies in Philosophy of Education*, 27(1): 49–62.

Durkheim, E. (1912/1965) *The Elementary Forms of Religious Life*, trans. K. Fields, New York: Free Press.

—— (1938/1977) *The Evolution of Educational Thought: Lectures on the Formation and Development of Secondary Education in France*, trans. P. Collins, London: Routledge and Kegan Paul.

—— (1956) *Education and Sociology*, New York: Free Press.

—— (1984). *Pragmatism and Sociology*, trans. J. C. Whitehouse and J. B. Alcock, with intro. by F. Cuvillier, Cambridge: Cambridge University Press.

Durkheim. E and Mauss, M. (1970) *Primitive Classifications*, Chicago: University of Chicago Press, 81–2.

Engeström, Y. (1991) *Learning by Expanding*. Available online at: http: //lchc.ucsd.edu/ MCA/Paper/Engeström/expanding/toc.htm (last accessed 28 February 2007).

Engeström, Y. and Gronin, T. (eds.), *Transfer and Boundary Crossing*, London: Pergamon.

Gellner, E. (1992) *Reason and Culture*, Oxford: Blackwell.

Giddens, A. (1986) *Sociology: A Brief But Critical Introduction*, Cambridge: Polity.

Luria, A. R. and Vygotsky, L. S. (1992) *Ape, Primitive Man and Child*, Hemel Hempstead: Harvester Wheatsheaf.

Moore, R. (2004) *Education and Society*, Cambridge: Polity.

Tuomi-Grohn, T. and Engeström, Y. (2003) *Between School and Work: New Perspectives on Transfer and Boundary Crossing*, Oxford: Pergamon.

Valéry, P. (1941) *Selected Writings of Paul Valery*, New York: New Directions.

Wertsch, J.V. (1990) 'The Voice of Rationality in a Socio-Cultural Approach to the Mind', in Moll, L. (ed.) *Vygotsky and Education*, Cambridge: Cambridge University Press.

Worsley, P. (1956) 'Emile Durkheim's Theory of Knowledge', *Sociological Review*, 4(1): 47–62.

Young, M. and Muller, J. (2007) 'Truth and Truthfulness in the Sociology of Educational Knowledge', *Theory and Research in Education*, 5(2): 173–201.

Young, M. (2008) *Bringing Knowledge Back in: From Social Constructivism to Social Realism in the Sociology of Education*, London: Routledge.

2 Dialectics, politics and contemporary cultural-historical research, exemplified through Marx and Vygotsky

Seth Chaiklin

Marx and Vygotsky. These two researchers are often named together in accounts about cultural-historical research. How might one understand the relationship between their scientific projects? Given that many different relationships between Marx and Vygotsky might potentially be explored, a principled strategy is needed to focus the discussion on the thematic interest of the present volume – namely to expand and enrich contemporary research grounded in or motivated by 'Vygotskian theory'. Given that Marx's ideas are already viewed as having some relation to Vygotsky's, the interest in enrichment or expansion circles back on itself to the initial question of how to understand their relationship.

The strategy followed in this chapter is grounded in the contention that it is productive (and necessary) to consider Marx and Vygotsky as important moments in the historical development of a tradition of thought, which in this chapter is termed *dialectical tradition*.[1] The approach is to identify and illuminate key issues in these historical streams of thought that they drew upon and responded to in their scientific work, and which are still salient for contemporary scientific work.

This strategy breaks with the typical way that Vygotsky and Marx are addressed in contemporary discussions, where Vygotsky's ideas are supplemented or elaborated with ideas from Marx. In this way, the initial question about the relationship between Marx and Vygotsky becomes transformed to a question about the meaning of dialectical tradition, and the ways in which their work embodies, extends and falls short of the ideals of this tradition.

A complex of distinct ideas have served as sources of theoretical inspiration and orientation within the cultural-historical tradition. These ideas include a monistic

---

1 As best I can tell, there is no standard meaning or widespread use of the expression *dialectical tradition*. Forster (1993) used the expression to refer to the long tradition of philosophers (starting from the fifth century BC) identified by Hegel (and including himself) as seeking 'to show that thought was in fundamental ways self-contradictory' (p. 149). The present chapter extends this referential scope beyond this epistemological focus to include ontological, political and methodological concerns found within the cultural-historical tradition, as well as Hegel and Marx. This broader usage, which is more indexical than denotational, may lead to confusion in some quarters (because many of these ideas are not strictly related to the tradition discussed by Forster), but this term will be used for now, until a better descriptive term can be established.

approach to psychology, inspired partly from Spinoza (seventeenth century); a (modern) materialist view expressed by French philosophers in the eighteenth century, and focused on conditions for human development (a problem which Hegel, Feuerbach and Marx developed further); the formation of concepts developed by Hegel, and its further development and application by Marx; and historical materialism from Marx and Engels.

As far as I know, this complex of ideas does not have a standard designation among twenty-first-century philosophers as a philosophical school or tradition (Jan Derry; Uffe Juul Jensen, personal communications, 08/02/2011 and 12/10/2011, respectively). The metaphoric idea of 'the dialectical river' is used to refer to several different interrelated lines of thought that flow together (i.e., currents and counter-currents), originating from different sources (e.g., dialectic, historical materialism), from which one might draw a particular configuration of ideas, such as just named. The metaphor is meant to underscore that there is no fixed, doctrinal monolith that is 'the' dialectical tradition; rather, one might speak of the cultural-historical tradition embodying 'a' dialectical tradition, such as discussed in this chapter.

If there is no standard designation, then why trust the designation sketched here? A satisfying answer would require a detailed historical analysis to show that main figures in the dialectical river (e.g., Marx, Hegel, Vygotsky, Ilyenov) engage with and refer to many common sources and ideas. The proposal sketched here is drawn from the kinds of issues that appear in their texts, along with the issues highlighted in secondary literature (from across different disciplines). Many secondary sources, often independently, come to highlight similar streams of these ideas in their accounts and analysis, which inclines one to believe that there is a coherent tradition of thought, even if it has not achieved the usual organisational forms that mark an institutionalised discipline or category.[2]

In pointing to this river of ideas, I am also – consistent with a dialectical perspective – forming the contents of the river, and its implications for cultural-historical research. The purpose is to be an active participant in this river of thought, seeking to articulate these ideas and their practical consequences, and engage with the substantive issues that arise from those issues that are unquestionably part of this flow.

This chapter introduces an idea of dialectical tradition as a comprehensive perspective for scientific work, including analytic perspectives about goals and purposes for research, conceptions about the objects of analytic focus (i.e., ontological dimensions), and conceptions about the kinds of scientific analyses that one seeks to make (i.e., epistemological dimensions). This tradition includes a complex of ideas about the nature and development of human life (both individually and collectively), embodied in an interrelated network of concepts

---

2 As an illustration of this point, a similar broad interpretation of dialectical tradition can be found among dialectical anthropologists (e.g., Diamond, Scholte, and Wolf, 1975), where, consistent with the metaphor, they emphasise many of the same historical sources and relations mentioned here, while also drawing on others not included here.

and issues, along with implications and consequences that arise from these interrelations.

To work in this tradition (as it has developed historically) is to have an overarching view of the scientific project in which one is engaged, going beyond a mere collection of conceptual or analytical techniques that can supplement an existing research approach.

A main goal of this chapter is to point to the idea and possibilities of conceptualising a dialectical tradition (rather than a Vygotskian tradition per se) as a frame for contemporary cultural-historical research, and to expand attention to themes of the tradition described here. Another goal is to suggest that contemporary research has barely begun to recognise (or engage) the deep issues that have motivated this tradition of thought, where some issues are already embodied in Vygotsky's research (e.g., concepts of freedom and full human development), but which have not been taken up in contemporary practice.

To contribute to this engagement, this chapter does the following things. First, there is a review of how other researchers have engaged analytically with conceptual relations between Vygotsky and Marx, as a way of highlighting the current state of the intellectual commitments and accomplishments of the contemporary cultural-historical research community. Main conclusions from this review are that (a) there has not been much discussion of their conceptual relations in the existing research literature, and (b) many of these discussions have focused on what ideas from Marx have been taken up by Vygotsky. Then there is a brief discussion of the idea of dialectical tradition in relation to the cultural-historical tradition (including Vygotsky and Marx), followed by discussions that highlight some key ideas from this dialectical tradition.

Three distinctive implications of these ideas are elaborated: a focus on full human development; the idea of dialectical tradition as a comprehensive research perspective, and some methodological consequences for understanding the relation between research and practice and for formulating research questions. The present exposition remains an interpretative proposal or sketch. More systematic introduction, explanation and justification of this tradition must be addressed elsewhere.

Current research on Marx–Vygotsky relations

In general, there is not much literature that discusses specific aspects of Marx's thought in relation to Vygotsky's work (e.g., Elhammoumi, 2002: 90–1, identifies several well-known introductory texts that do not discuss Marxian aspects in Vygotsky). Veresov (2005: 31–2) notes that a contradictory image arises in the existing literature that discusses Vygotsky's conceptual relations to Marxism (in part because the meaning of Marxism is difficult to establish in a coherent way). Packer (2008) suggests that 'exploring the Marxist framework to Vygotsky's conception and practice of psychology would appear an important yet neglected task' (p. 9). He also lists previous commentators who have mentioned the lack of engagement with this aspect of Vygotsky's thought. The specific conclusions of these individual reviewers are consistent with the following crude search using Google Scholar to get an impression of the extent of contemporary discussions about the relation between Vygotsky and Marx. Piaget, an important development psychologist who is often discussed in relation to Vygotsky, is also included in the search to provide a comparative perspective for interpreting the observed numbers.

Figure 2.1 shows the search terms used and the number of hits identified for these terms, and percentages for selected pairs. (Searches were also conducted with the research databases ERIC, PsycINFO and Web of Science, which gave even more limited results than those reported here.) The main patterns are interpreted to show that (a) Piaget is discussed in relation to Marx nearly as frequently as Vygotsky (b) Vygotsky, Piaget, and Marx are discussed together almost as frequently as discussing Marx and Vygotsky alone, and (c) there is little indication that Marx is particularly important to discuss in relation to Vygotsky. A speculative explanation for point (b) is that many of the found texts are general introductory discussions that mention (but do not elaborate) intellectual connections. The global or rough impression from point (c) is consistent with the just-mentioned observations from those who have looked directly at the extent to which existing literature discusses the relation between Marx and Vygotsky.

The specific and particular historical relationships between Vygotsky and Marx are interesting and useful to examine. To date, among the few researchers who have tried to address the inadequate analysis of the relation between Vygotsky and Marx, the tendency has been to identify ideas within Vygotsky's work (e.g., focus on development of consciousness, the idea of labour as mediating action) that have been accepted in contemporary research practice, and that can be traced either directly or conceptually to ideas in Marx's work (e.g.,

Search term	Number of hits (rounded to nearest hundred)	
Vygotsky Marx	9,500	10%
Vygotsky	99,600	
Piaget Marx	19,700	7%
Piaget	300,000	
Vygotsky Piaget	36,500	37%
Vygotsky	99,600	
Vygotsky Piaget Marx	4,200	45%
Vygotsky Marx	9,500	
Marx	1,160,000	

Figure 2.1 Number of hits from Google Scholar (June 2011)

Elhammoumi, 2002; Lee, 1985; Langemeyer and Roth, 2006: 24–6; Packer, 2008: 9–11; Veresov, 2005).

There is nothing wrong with this kind of intellectual or historical contextualisation. Considerably more elaboration about this relation is no doubt needed, especially given that most contemporary reception of the relations between Vygotsky and Marx have either been ignored, or simply noted without entering into any substantive detail. Such comparative studies can be instructive for locating Vygotskian ideas (e.g., the need to study mediating instruments, or the importance of social interaction) in a broader tradition of thought, but they are unlikely to enrich our conceptual understanding of these ideas, unless new conceptual relations can be elaborated. This kind of comparative study is not pursued here because it raises additional discussions that are tangential to the present focus[3] of characterising their work within broader intellectual concerns.

Beyond a specific focus on the relations between Marx and Vygotsky, there are also a few texts in the research literature that bring conceptual resources from this broader tradition into contact with cultural-historical research. One small subgenre identifies important ideas in Marx's texts that have not been addressed or taken up adequately in contemporary cultural-historical research. For example, Jones (2009) suggests that current developments in cultural-historical theory have moved away specifically from Marx's analysis of capitalist production, citing several recent papers that have come to a similar view (p. 46), where these papers have focused more specifically on a model of activity put forward by Engeström. A related (and even smaller) subgenre has articulated some of the methodological consequences of a dialectical perspective in relation to the cultural-historical tradition (as well as discussed how these ideas can be misapplied) (Langemeyer and Roth, 2006). Elhammoumi's (2006) criticism of a science that focuses on individuals (p. 33), can be viewed as trying to move in this direction of drawing analytic consequences for further development of cultural-historical research from a general understanding of dialectics.

Otherwise it has not been possible to identify any existing research literature on Vygotsky that focuses, in a comprehensive way, on the significance of the dialectical tradition for understanding the substance and direction of his research programme. This state of the literature is not particularly surprising, especially if one considers that most social scientific researchers in the twenty-first century do not have an educational history or a scientific community that provides working conditions for developing such discussions, but it is intellectually problematic, if one is committed to following the implications of dialectical ideas, including interpreting ideas from Vygotsky and Marx within a dialectical perspective.[4]

---

3 For example, to clarify that one can engage with Marx and the dialectical tradition without a need to engage with dialectical materialism and Marxism-Leninism, or that there is no need to frame Vygotsky as attempting to create a 'marxist' psychology.

4 Beyond a strict focus on Vygotsky, one can find some works within the cultural-historical tradition (e.g., Duarte, 2006; Jantzen, 2004) that reflect the dialectical tradition described here (even if they are sometimes framed as marxist tradition).

The dialectical tradition and cultural-historical research

There are several reasons for wanting to look at the broader intellectual ideas and currents – stemming from the seventeenth, eighteenth and nineteenth centuries – from which Vygotsky and Marx drew inspiration. There is a traditional value within academic research to try to understand a researcher's approach in relation to their own intentions and in relation to the whole of their work. As Davydov and Radzikhovskii (1985) note in relation to Vygotsky, this can be done in part by considering the 'logic of the development for the specific scientific tradition to which he was objectively related and to which he subjectively attached himself' (p. 39). Similar points can be made for other key researchers in the initial generations of the cultural-historical tradition (e.g., Leontiev, El'konin, Davydov), where this point is generalised to refer to the dialectical tradition. Even if these researchers do not necessarily refer to or use all the same ideas in this river, it is usually possible to provide textual sources to at least indicate their awareness of these ideas.

A second academic value is the need to build on existing ideas. The dialectic tradition remains a viable and rich intellectual tradition, provided that contemporary cultural-historical researchers are able to recognise and engage with this tradition.

Third, it can be productive to consider the historical complex of issues being addressed within a research tradition, rather than using a single person to define the research programme. In this perspectival shift, the specific relations between Vygotsky and Marx recede somewhat into the background. While it can be useful and productive to make direct comparisons of their substantive relations it is important not to reduce or limit the dialectical conception to that which is found within Marx and Vygotsky alone. The significance of such comparisons is enriched by understanding the broader history of ideas within which Marx and Vygotsky were engaged. By recognising the broader range of issues embedded in their work, it becomes possible to draw on and engage with the streams of thought and analysis in this range of ideas, and not simply to be a Marxist or a Vygotskian.

The critical claim here is that Marx and Vygotsky's work can be seen as grounded in, oriented to, and animated by common themes, some of which will be elaborated in a moment. There is no reason to believe that Vygotsky had access to or encountered all the ideas presented in this chapter (or conversely that this chapter has addressed all the ideas found in Vygotsky). There may also be ideas and arguments found in Vygotsky's texts that are weak or contradictory to this dialectical tradition (e.g., Davydov notes that Vygotsky did not have the benefit of Ilyenkov's analysis of dialectics). Furthermore, Marx and Vygotsky, each pursuing their own substantive research area, drew on many other intellectual sources that were relevant to the problems they were investigating (hence there is no problem that Marx engages with and draws on classical political economists, or that Vygotsky draws on Janet, Köhler, Lévy-Bruhl, Thurnwald and other psychologists and anthropologists). To view Marx and Vygotsky's work as stemming from a common tradition of ideas is not to limit or distort their projects to fit a Procrustean bed; rather it is to recognise the comprehensive perspective from which they were working. These relations are highlighted in order to engage with and further develop the general problems in this tradition of thought, and not simply to note some historical characteristics about Vygotsky and Marx.

Implications of this view

The preceding arguments have put forward some reasons for wanting to look at the broader intellectual perspective within which Vygotsky was working. In this strategic focus, Vygotsky's work is portrayed as a moment in the historical development of this dialectical theoretical framework, rather than the 'germ' or 'origin' from which a conceptual framework has grown. From this point of view, one may be post-Vygotsky in a chronological sense but, as will be developed here, there are many dimensions in this dialectical tradition that were also explicit in Vygotsky's work, which deserve to be continued, and which have not been taken up in any obvious ways in contemporary research.

This interest to interpret Vygotsky as embodying a dialectical research tradition may be construed (by some) as a negation of scientific approaches where re-searchers want to draw on selected aspects from Vygotsky's work. The analyses presented here are not meant to deny that some researchers may want to retain (a selective version of some) Vygotskian ideas as the 'sun' around which their theoretical system revolves, or as one ingredient in a contemporary stew – where ideas from Marx or this dialectical tradition may or may not be included. Nor does it deny that one can try to select aspects from Vygotsky's thought that are consistent with other intellectual traditions (e.g., Bakhurst's, 2009, framing of Vygotsky as being in a philosophical rationalist tradition). This pluralistic perspective accepts that there is no 'true' Vygotsky to be revealed. But the argument that viewing Vygotsky's theoretical perspective as grounded in a dialectical tradition is also meant as a challenge for those who want to work with a 'restricted' or 'transformed' version of his ideas. At the very least, it highlights that different research communities may be working with some of the same explicit ideas from Vygotsky, but with different underlying intentions.

Key ideas in the dialectical tradition

A distinctive feature of the dialectical tradition is its multifaceted engagement with the historical conditions of human life – both as a motivation for and objective of research. Five key ideas within the dialectical tradition are selected and highlighted in an integrated way to elaborate the meaning of *multifaceted engagement*.[5] The first three ideas are ontological; while the other two are epistemological, to underscore the comprehensive, integral nature of the dialectical tradition.

A key ontological idea in the dialectical tradition is that persons transform their conditions, aiming to produce and reproduce conditions for their life. As an

---

5 As characterised here, there is no single key defining idea or starting assumption for the dialectical tradition. The idea of 'multifaceted engagement' is meant to highlight, in an organised way, implications of interrelated currents of thought in the dialectical tradition.

ontological idea, it becomes a starting point for analysis and understanding, rather than a conclusion. This characteristic is a permanent feature of all human life, appearing in its origins thousands of years ago, and remaining constantly in the present forms. Processes of transformation can range from dramatic industrial processes (e.g., steel production, energy production based on nuclear fission) to common everyday processes such as using writing technologies for organising action (e.g., making to-do lists, sending messages), or preparing food to eat, and using dishes, cutlery and napkins in the eating process. In other words, it is difficult (probably impossible) to find any sphere or aspect of human life that does not involve processes of transformation of material.

Ways of acting are developed historically. This second key ontological idea, which draws on the first, notes that possibilities for human action are formed through experiences of transforming nature, encountering problems, new demands, and so forth. This conception applies generally, both in relation to the activity of individual persons (i.e., an ontogenetic process), and to practices, whether organised locally, nationally, or transnationally. This assumption does not imply that action is always determined, only that action is oriented to historical traditions in relation to specific practices.

A third ontological idea is that individuals develop as a consequence of these interactions. An important implication is the dissolution of the idea of 'natural' as a significant and independent dimension of human action.

Drawing on these three ideas, a fourth key idea, now epistemological, is that research should aim at analytic understanding of the origins and development of these processes. In this sense, the historical conditions of human life becomes an objective for research.

A fifth key idea, also epistemological, is that research should focus on the possibilities for the development of human life. This idea is rooted in the three ontological ideas: the forms and practices of human life are not necessarily static, or marked with fixed or eternal characteristics, and it is possible for humans (including researchers) to engage in the creation, development and transformation of conditions. The aim is not simply to document the historical forms that have developed, but to understand how existing conditions may distort possibilities for full human development and/or to find ways of creating conditions to support such development.

Taken together, these five key ideas highlight a central orienting focus in the dialectical tradition on the consequences of transformative human action and the qualities and development of societal conditions for individual development. These ideas are closely related to each other, providing analytic constraints and elaborations when they are deployed together in specific investigations.

The dialectical tradition cannot be reduced to these five key ideas and implications of their interrelations; they were presented as a way to give a quick orientation to main perspectives in this tradition. Many other aspects must be elaborated. Figure 2.2 presents some of them in schematic form, drawing in part on the key ideas. These aspects are presented in list form for purposes of exposition. Ideally this presentation should be developed as a historical analysis, showing the

---

1 Committed to a scientific approach (i.e., analytic, empirical).

2 Start with as few assumptions as possible.

    a Objects[a] are never 'given' or 'received'

    b No fixed/stable human essence

    c No (given a priori) separation of individual and society[b]

3 Pay attention to the whole (i.e., relationships and interactions needed in production).

4 Trace the consequences of the ontological fact that humans produce and reproduce their conditions of life as way of establishing conclusions.

    a Consider material aspects[c] as primary

    b Use a historical approach in this trace (immanent analysis, unfolding of internal relations)

    c Need to understand the interactions that form objects

    d Focus on understanding the origins of phenomena rather than merely describing them

5 Oriented toward concept of freedom and problem of full human development.

a Includes persons, organisations and institutions
b Of course there are individuals, but not in the sense as proposed by Hobbes or Rousseau, where persons exist independently of society
c Including actions and demands motivated by laws, policies and traditions

---

Figure 2.2 Some conceptual aspects of the dialectical tradition

unfolding of these ideas as consequences that arise from the ontological idea about humans producing conditions for their life. In other words, conclusions about human nature and human ways of acting are achieved as analytic results, rather than a priori assumptions. In this sense the list in Figure 2.2 is not a list of a priori assumptions (which would appear to violate the second point on the list), but reflect the historical understanding that has developed among Hegel, Marx, Vygotsky and others who have worked in the dialectical tradition. For now, they must remain as assertions or predictions that this kind of analysis (and its possible revision) reflect the spirit (i.e., central, essential aspects) of the dialectical tradition. This list focuses primarily on central methodological abstractions of the dialectical perspective. To work productively with these interconnected ideas, it becomes necessary to gain control over many important technical concepts (e.g., the idea of abstractions, appearances and reality, rising from abstract to concrete, germ cells or primary relations, societal need).

Implications and elaborations

The remainder of this chapter takes up the following three points.

1   To give an impression of the dialectical river, the last point in Figure 2.2 is discussed in more detail, which will highlight that a notion such as freedom

can be studied as a scientific concept, arising from analysis and not from a priori or normative assertion about preferred conditions. At the same time, the focus on freedom and full human development appears to be the main place within the dialectical tradition where a normative position appears. This normative position has necessary consequences for choices of research topics.

2   The dialectical tradition as a comprehensive research perspective.

3   As presented here, the key ideas and Figure 2.2 may give the (wrong) impression that dialectical researchers should remain at a global (or sociological) plane of analysis, standing outside or beyond the daily actions by which persons produce and reproduce their life conditions. The points described here articulate starting points for analysis and action, providing useful conceptions for constituting the focus of concrete research objectives about specific human practices, and ways to approach those objectives. A simple example about school-based research on subject-matter learning is discussed to illustrate ways to use these ideas.

Freedom and full human development

The concept of *freedom* is central in the dialectical tradition. It provides an orienting point for social scientific research, and gives substantive content to the idea of full human development. A main aim of research in the dialectical tradition is understanding how to create conditions for full human development. Because it is not common to encounter these issues within contemporary cultural-historical research, several different sources of ideas in the history of thought are reviewed briefly to indicate more concretely how concepts of freedom and full human development are used in the dialectical tradition.

While these expressions may seem comprehensible without further explanation, there are different ways that these general ideas have been concretised historically, with different underlying ontological assumptions, and their meaning can be quite different from popular understandings. These expressions do not refer to a single idea or special view, that can be located easily and originally with any single thinker; rather there are a series of related different ideas, which can be assembled into possible meanings, as implied by the 'river' analogy.

Given the commitment to develop theoretical conceptions about societal and human issues through scientific analysis, concepts such as freedom and full human development are, in the first instance, ontological assumptions (or empirical discoveries), without any particular normative value. That is, freedom and full human development describe particular existential states, without requiring that researchers must give them preferred or special status. However, it is common in this stream of ideas to give normative preference to understanding how to realise the conditions described by these concepts (see Gould, 1978: 103, who also notes and discusses this point extensively in relation to Marx's *Grundrisse*).

The following discussion starts with the notion of human development, and then shows one relation to the dialectical concept of freedom. Concern about human development was especially prominent during the period in the eighteen century known as the Enlightenment, where it was common to find optimistic perspectives about the possibilities for human development and (moral) perfection. In this connection, there was much reflection and discussion about the role and necessity of education for individual development.

Consequences of societal conditions. There was concern during this period (e.g., Rousseau, 1762/1974) that because of societal conditions (i.e., division of labour), an individual may only develop special talents for their profession, therefore education should supply individuals with the abilities and experiences that allow full development of personality, which in turn would allow persons to play their full part in society. (The same theme can be found among the ancient Greeks, Plato and Aristotle, in their discussions of education for citizenship and moral virtue.) A similar focus on education and concern for the consequences of societal conditions for human development was also found at the same time among eighteenth-century French materialists (e.g., Helvétius, Holbach), who were inspired by ideas from Locke, Condillac and to some extent Leibniz. These materialists focused on the idea of the perfectibility of a changeable human nature, that persons were born neither good nor bad (in contrast to Rousseau who views persons as naturally good), where the development of human nature depends on the interests, circumstances and institutions in society, including education. This complex of assumptions, along with additional assumptions about the ideal of human life, leads to a conclusion that the form of education, in the sense of the totality of the individual's life conditions, was critical for the possibilities of full human development. The assumptions of the French materialists are more consistent with a collectivist assumption found in socialist political philosophy, that the full development of individuals depends on the conditions under which one lives, and that efforts to abolish the contradiction between particular interests and those of the common good will create conditions for the full development of individuals. The ontological assumption about human nature found in Rousseau (as well as Adam Smith and Adam Ferguson) (and which is often used to justify a politically liberal philosophy) is that humans are born with a fixed and stable essence, which can come to full expression, provided that artificial restrictions from societal institutions are not placed in the way. Here is an example of the consequences of the third ontological assumption discussed previously.

Societal conditions and freedom. The consequences of societal conditions for human development was a theme that was adopted and investigated further by both Hegel (e.g., *Elements of the Philosophy of Right*) and Marx (e.g., *German Ideology*, ch. 1; *Capital*, vol. 3, such as ch. 47, or p. 959). For both Hegel and Marx, there was a concern about the idea of freedom as an expression of full human development. In their view, freedom is the power to act self-consciously in accordance with reason, trying to shape conditions for reproducing life and realising potentialities. Note that 'power to act' is meant to refer to actuality and not potential. If there are not conditions to act according to reason, then a person is not free. (See Westphal, 1993 for a helpful overview of the *Philosophy of Right*, and Wood, 1993: 216–19. Both emphasise Hegel's primary focus on realisation of human freedom.)

Similarly, *reason* refers to a theoretical understanding of the essence of the situation (i.e., the conceptual relations from which observable appearances are generated). In other words, much in the same spirit of Spinoza (discussed in a moment), the development of freedom requires the development of an understanding of the situation in which one finds oneself.

Full human development and freedom. The idea of full development, as developed by Marx, is grounded in part in Aristotelian thought, which views the realisation of a thing's essence as a fulfilment of its potentiality, which is its end or good. Thus, freedom does not mean being free from external hindrances, but free to develop according to one's essence. A second way to conceptualise human nature is to draw on an ontological assumption that the nature or essence of persons are in their societal relations (cf. Marx's sixth thesis on Feuerbach).[6] This statement presents a conception of the essence of humans as reflecting the societal relations into which they enter, hence the concern about the implications of societal conditions for human life, and rejection of a fixed or static meaning of essence. This idea can be understood as related to the views of the French materialists, where human beings are both the result and the subject of the dynamic of historical forms in social life. While this formulation may appear trivially obvious, it is important to note that it stands in sharp contrast and opposition to another obvious idea, such as just seen from Rousseau, that humans are born with particular natural characteristics, or that societal life is the result of expression of individual human mental characteristics. Therefore, full human development is connected to mastering one's ability to act freely in relation to existing historical conditions.

Marx understands freedom in a historical way, where there are stages of social development (for discussion and explanation, see Brien, 2006: chs. 3 and 4; Gould, 1978: ch. 4). In other words, freedom is not an a priori philosophical definition, but a consequence of the conditions of human life, and the development of human capabilities in relation to those conditions. This point highlights that the study of freedom is not a normative question, but a matter of studying the possibilities of human development.

A third way to consider human nature is found in the substance monism of the seventeenth-century philosopher Spinoza. It is difficult to explain this idea adequately in a brief form (cf. Bennett, 1984), but an important consequence for the present discussion is that by not separating mental and physical phenomena, Spinoza rejects the idea of 'free will' as the source of free human action – which would imply a separate 'mental' substance that was the source of action. Spinoza considered all human actions and states of mind to be determined, where the task (both personally and scientifically) is to understand the causes of these actions and

---

6 In the sixth thesis, Marx writes: 'Aber das menschliche Wesen ist kein dem einzelnen Individuum innewohnendes Abstraktum. In seiner Wirklichkeit ist es das Ensemble der gesellschaftlichen Verhältnisse' (1845/1961: 6).

(But human essence is not something abstract, residing in the specific individual. In its reality, it is the ensemble of societal relations. [author's translation])

states. Freedom in Spinoza's view is self-determination. That is, as one becomes more knowledgeable, one can become free of external influences by making one's own states and activities a result of one's own causal activity. These ideas about freedom are very similar to the arguments found from Hegel and Marx. This perspective also fits well with the materialist perspective.

These ways of thinking about freedom are not normative. Rather they present analytic implications about how to understand the meaning of the concept, growing from assumptions of human nature (e.g., the ontological ideas discussed previously). As elaborated in a moment, these ideas about freedom also illustrate the idea of the dialectical river, where related ideas can be drawn into analysis.

Implications of full human development. The point about full human development is raised here because of its implications for contemporary research practice; it is not simply a practical anachronism. This focus arises from a concern to understand human life in a fundamental or comprehensive way. Implicit in this concern is a belief that the more we (as researchers and humans) can understand about humans – as individuals and as collectives (in the form of groups, organisations, states, etc.) – the better we will be able to create conditions that support the development of the conditions under which we live, in relation to our understanding of human life (what some might call 'the good life'). Is such a belief naïve, platitudinous or trivial? These are not rhetorical questions, because they raise fundamental issues about the objective of social science, and the possibilities to work towards that objective.

Concern about the good life has been found repeatedly in human philosophical and religious investigation (e.g., Cottingham, 1998). Aristotle is known for his analyses of *eudaimonia*, which is translated as *happiness* or maybe more appropriately *human flourishing*, while it is well documented that Hegel and Marx were familiar with and oriented to responding to these ideas (e.g., Leopold, 2007: 238–41, for one illustration).

Dialectical tradition as comprehensive perspective

The dialectical tradition was described earlier as a comprehensive perspective for research. It is now possible to return to this idea, elaborating it further in light of the material just presented. The dialectical tradition is comprehensive in that it functions as what Vygotsky (1926/1997) calls a general science, which elaborates 'the foundations and problems of a whole area of being' and provides 'the philosophy of the special disciplines' (p. 247). This perspective cuts across the disciplinary boundaries (which originated in the nineteenth century) that differentiate the social sciences in the twenty-first century. For example, psychology is usually understood as the study of individuals; sociology the study of groups in society. In contrast, it may be appropriate and productive to view the dialectical tradition as its own science, and not simply a theoretical perspective that fits within or combines existing special disciplines (e.g., psychology, sociology). The following discussion elaborates these ideas, where the main point is to highlight several distinctive features that serve to unify the dialectical tradition as an integral research perspective.

As already noted, one foundational focus for the dialectical tradition is conditions for realisation of full human development, which involves the realisation of freedom. This focus makes it possible for Hegel (within philosophy), Marx (within sociology), and Vygotsky (within psychology) to be oriented centrally to this issue, in relation to their specific studies. The following small collection of quotes are offered to indicate the plausibility that they are drawing on a common river of thought in relation to the idea of freedom. For example, 'Hegel . . . based his political philosophy on the analysis and fulfillment of individual human freedom' (Westphal, 1993: 234). '[Hegel] conceives the human self as free in the radical sense that its identity, and therefore the content of its self-realization, is the result of its own activity' (Wood, 1993: 217). 'Marx sees freedom . . . as . . . activity or labor itself, conceived as activity of self-realization' (Gould, 1978: 102). 'It should be noted that the problem of human freedom and self-determination was of great importance for Vygotsky, though the explicit discussion of this problem is not common in his writings' (Aidman and Leontiev, 1991: 148).[7]

Second, the idea of dialectic, as an analytic conception, and the material grounding in human transformation of conditions are central in how they have pursued their investigations (see Haug, 2005, for a historical overview). The following quotation from Vygotsky (1926/1997) shows the idea of dialectic (as applied in psychology) as a study of consequences of material transformations, focusing on the whole of human practice ('dialectic of man').

> what we may now call the general psychology . . . is the science of the most general forms of movement (in the form of behavior and knowledge of this movement), i.e., the dialectic of psychology is at the same time the dialectic of man as the object of psychology, just as the dialectic of the natural sciences is at the same time the dialectic of nature. (p. 256)

Note that Vygotsky describes a general psychology in its most general form as a dialectic, where the dialectic of man (i.e., the historical development of transformations of materials and conditions) is the object of psychology. Marx and Hegel are focused on the same dialectic, but elaborated in relation to their 'special disciplines'. For a brief illustrative elaboration of this idea in relation to psychology, see Kravtsov (2010: 53–4). Also note that Vygotsky, drawing from Engels, makes

---

7 They give no evidence for their assertion, but here are two small indicators. First, it striking that the word *freedom* barely appears in Vygotsky's (1926/1997) 100-page manuscript on the crisis in psychology, but he chooses to draw on a quotation from Engels about a 'leap into the kingdom of freedom' as a way to conclude his manuscript, noting that this leap 'inevitably puts the question of the mastery of our own being, of its subjection to the self, on the agenda' (p. 342). Second, in a 1932 notebook, Vygotsky wrote: 'The cent[ral] problem of all psychology is freedom' (quoted in Zavershneva, 2010: 66).

an analogy to the natural sciences. Regardless of whether one accepts Engels' proposal about a dialectic of nature, the critical point is that this dialectical tradition is aimed at a scientific (i.e., empirically grounded) approach to investigating human life.

In another passage, Vygotsky explains his idea of dialectics as a general science, providing some support for the idea that Vygotsky viewed his work as following in the dialectical tradition (even if there is not extensive discussion of these philosophical ideas in his published works).

> The key to general psychology as a part of dialectics lies in these words: this correspondence between thinking and being in science is at the same time object, highest criterion, and even method, i.e., general principle of the general psychology. (p. 256)

Third, the idea of the dialectical tradition as a general science is not meant to suggest that it is only a philosophical or metatheoretical perspective, defined a priori. As Vygotsky (1926/1997) notes, there is an interactive quality between a general science and its special disciplines:

> The general science's fundamentally guiding and supreme role, so to speak, does not follow from the fact that it stands above the sciences, it does not come from above, from logic, i.e., from the ultimate foundations of scientific knowledge, but from below, from the sciences themselves which delegate the authorization of truth to the general science. The general science, consequently, develops from the special position it occupies with regard to the special ones: it integrates their sovereign ties, forms their representative. (p. 256)

Vygotsky was speaking primarily about psychology in the preceding quote, but the point can be generalised to the dialectical tradition, as already noted in relation to Hegel, Marx and Vygotsky. In this sense, the general science gives specific ideas for how to approach concrete research problems.

A fourth distinctive feature of the dialectical tradition is what it seeks to achieve (i.e., its purpose as a scientific discipline). It is not so common to see a description of the purpose of psychology or sociology (beyond the previously named general descriptions). Perhaps it is taken for granted in these disciplines that the aim is to 'describe the nature of reality', where the description is to provide an account of observed states of being. Within the dialectical tradition, this kind of objective would be rejected, primarily because of the conception that 'being' and 'reality' in the human world are historically formed, where the task is to explain the genesis of these appearances rather than describe the existing conditions,[8] with an eye on transformations of conditions that improve possibilities for human development.

8 Further explanation would require more detailed discussion of the idea of appearance and essence (e.g., Sayers, 1985: ch.3), to highlight the idea of theoretical concepts in relation to appearance.

In other words, it is not sufficient to justify a study in terms of 'because it is there'; at the very least one must try to understand how these forms appeared and their meaning in relation to full human development.

A fifth (though not unique) aspect of the dialectical tradition is its reflexive understanding of the purposes of research. Researchers are part of the historical practice they are studying. Research should be conceptualised in a way so that it becomes a part of the further development of the human practice(s) being studied, rather than remaining outside of these practices. Whether research is used in practice or not is a different question, but the products of research can be conceptualised in relation to the practices being studied. For example, are researchers working for private interests? Or do they seek to engage universally with the societal relations in which they are studying? Historically, the dialectical tradition has been oriented to the societal relations.[9] The Marx quotation was oriented towards all persons in society, which of course would apply to researchers as well. This concern provides a significant challenge for how researchers want to conceptualise the relation of their work to the practices they study. The issue is whether a research approach has a way to explicitly conceptualise the meaning of 'improvement of conditions' in a way that becomes embodied in the research approach. This kind of conceptualisation is fundamentally different from simply having a desire for improvement. It involves a direct engagement with understanding what kinds of analyses will engage with conditions of human development. It is not sufficient to appeal to a division of scientific labour, or seek an accumulation of empirical or theoretical results, without understanding how they are related to this issue.

Implications of a dialectical perspective for research

The focus on human freedom has consequences for conceptualising the relation between research and practice, where the aim of research is to understand how to create conditions for human development that promote freedom. This aim has consequences for the kinds of analyses undertaken.

As a simple example, children's learning in school can be viewed as development of action in relation to production of life conditions, and the meaning of those

---

9 Erst wenn der wirkliche individuelle Mensch den abstrakten Staatsbürger in sich zurücknimmt und als individueller Mensch in seinem empirischen Leben, in seiner individuellen Arbeit, in seinen individuellen Verhältnissen, *Gattungswesen* geworden ist, erst wenn der Mensch seine »forces propres« als *gesellschaftliche* Kräfte erkannt und organisiert hat und daher die gesellschaftliche Kraft nicht mehr in der Gestalt der *politischen* Kraft von sich trennt, erst dann ist die menschliche Emanzipation vollbracht (Marx, 1843/1976: 370).

(Not until the actual individual person takes back into himself the abstract citizen, and as a distinct person in his existential life, in his particular work and in his particular situation, becomes a *species-being*, not until a person recognises and organises their own powers as *societal* powers, not as *political* powers that are separated from themselves, only then will human emancipation be brought to completion. [author's translation])

actions for development – as a person within those life conditions. School teaching creates possibilities for the development of this action. Forms of school teaching reflect school as an institution, which is historically constituted in a particular society. Actions within an individual school or individual classroom are likely to be formed in relation to those larger historical processes, while still having some of its own local historical developments. A singular focus on symbolic thinking processes (including emotional processes) and subject-matter content would not make sense, because it loses the meaning of these processes and content in relation to a person who is developing in relation to production of life conditions. These formulations reflect consequences of the third and fourth points in Figure 2.2. (See Duarte, 2006, for more elaborated discussion.)

Because these conditions are understood as historically formed, then one might be oriented to see beyond the current classroom-teaching conditions, and how they can be formed. If the conditions of human development depend on pedagogical practices, then what is the point of merely documenting our in-adequate practices? These kinds of framing conceptions open many different kinds of questions that might potentially be asked.

Each research project does not necessarily have to reconstruct the historical development of the institutions being studied, but there is a recognition that nothing is fundamental or necessary about present institutional forms, and a recognition that humans are creating these practices with particular intentions and purposes. Even a presumably simple and neutral question such as 'what is going on?' (in a school classroom) becomes unclear once one recognises, beyond description of observed actions, there is also a need to understand the intentions that are organising the observed appearance. Do these appearances reveal the achievement of or failure to realise intentions? These kinds of questions do not usually get raised in academic discussions, but they cut to the heart of some of the contemporary demands for 'relevance' or 'impact' from publicly supported academic research.

The issue of freedom and full human development brings additional con-siderations about what kinds of studies to conduct. Attention may shift from documenting what is going on to focusing on analysing practices in relation to creating conditions (in forms and content of teaching, in organisational structures, in institutional policies) to support children's development. In this sense, the results of the research are oriented to developing the practice, and in that sense can become part of the practice.

Closing reflections

This chapter has put forward the proposal that Vygotsky's research should be conceptualised as rooted in a dialectic tradition, where Vygotsky (Marx and Hegel) are important figures in the historical development of this tradition. In relation to this tradition, much contemporary research practice is still 'pre'-Vygotskian (if 'Vygotskyian' is used to indicate this tradition). The present chapter was motivated by the belief that these perspectives are inadequately known by cultural-historical researchers, which hinders more active and self-conscious engagement with issues found within this tradition. A few important characteristics were sketched here, and it was suggested that the tradition should be understood as an integral research perspective in its own right, rather than a subset or combination of existing disciplines.

It is understandable that contemporary researchers have not always had adequate preparation or support to work in this way, but if there is intellectual substance in this tradition, then it seems worth trying to reconceptualise the goals of cultural-historical research, even if the initial attempts are feeble relative to where we should be getting. As a first step, it should be possible to focus more attention on conceptualising the idea of human development and the consequences for its realisation within specific practices. In this connection, it is important to underscore that concepts such as freedom and full human development are not offered here as an invitation for free speculation about their possible meaning. As noted, these concepts grow out of a conceptual analysis, with meanings that often run counter to common views. These different meanings, in and of themselves do not give them more value, but one must engage with the ideas already developed, given that they arise in the conceptual system of ideas.

In considering the future development of the dialectical tradition within twenty-first century university environments, one might consider implications of the hypothesis from the dialectical tradition that 'intellectual production is determined by the form of material production' (Vygotsky, 1930/1994: 177). Contemporary conditions for research have been organised largely by a technical division of labour that leaves one part of human life to psychologists, another to sociologists, a third to anthropologists, a fourth to economists, and so forth. From that point of view, it is not so surprising that many persons who work with the cultural-historical tradition are found in interdisciplinary organisations (including departments or schools of education). The integrated objective of the dialectical tradition cuts across the traditional social scientific disciplines found at the beginning of the twenty-first century, and opens profound challenges for pursuing research that addresses the realisation of full human development.

Acknowledgements

Thanks to Mariane Hedegaard and Harris Chaiklin for editorial responses and to Ken Westphal for important contrarian responses, all of which helped to clarify the exposition.

References

Aidman, E. V. and Leontiev, D. A. (1991) 'From Being Motivated to Motivating Oneself: A Vygotskian Perspective', *Studies in Soviet Thought*, 41: 137–51.
Bakhurst, D. (2009) 'Vygotsky's Demons', in H. Daniels, M. Cole and J. V. Wertsch (eds.), *The Cambridge Companion to Vygotsky*, Cambridge: Cambridge University Press, 50–76.
Bennett, J. F. (1984) *A Study of Spinoza's Ethics*, Cambridge: Cambridge University Press.

Brien, K. M. (2006) *Marx, Reason, and the Art of Freedom*, 2nd edn, Amherst, NY: Humanity Books.

Cottingham, J. (1998) *Philosophy and the Good Life*, Cambridge: Cambridge University Press.

Davydov, V. V. and Radzikhovskii, L. A. (1985) 'Vygotsky's Theory and the Activity-Oriented Approach in Psychology', in J. V. Wertsch (Ed.), *Culture, Cognition, and Communication: Vygotskian Perspectives*, Cambridge: Cambridge University Press, 35–65.

Diamond, S., Scholte, B., and Wolf, E. (1975) 'Anti-Kaplan: Defining the Marxist Tradition', *American Anthropologist*, 77: 870–6.

Duarte, N. (2006) 'Education as Mediation between the Individual's Everyday Life and the Historical Construction of Society and Culture by Humankind', in P. H. Sawchuk, N. Duarte and M. Elhammoumi (eds.), *Critical Perspectives on Activity*, Cambridge: Cambridge University Press, 211–37.

Elhammoumi, M. (2002) 'To Create Psychology's Own Capital', *Journal for the Theory of Social Behaviour*, 32: 89–104.

—— (2006) 'Is There a Marxist Psychology?', in P. H. Sawchuk, N. Duarte and M. Elhammoumi (eds.), *Critical Perspectives on Activity*, Cambridge: Cambridge University Press, 23–34.

Forster, M. (1993) 'Hegel's Dialectical Method', in F. C. Beiser (ed.), *The Cambridge Companion to Hegel*, Cambridge: Cambridge University Press, 130–70.

Gould, C. C. (1978) *Marx's Social Ontology: Individuality and Community in Marx's Theory of Social Reality*, Cambridge, MA: MIT Press.

Haug, W. F. (2005) 'Dialectic', *Historical Materialism*, 13: 241–65.

Hegel, G. W. F. (1991) *Elements of the Philosophy of Right*, ed. A. H. Woods; trans. H. B. Nisbet, Cambridge: Cambridge University Press (original work published 1821).

Jantzen, W. (2004) *Materialistische Anthropologie und postmoderne Ethik*, Bonn: Pahl-Rugenstein.

Jones, P. (2009) 'Breaking away from *Capital?* Theorising Activity in the Shadow of Marx', *Outlines*, 11(1): 45–58.

Kravtsov, G. G. (2010) 'On the Methodological Strategies of Classical and Nonclassical Psychology', *Journal of Russian and East European Psychology*, 48(4): 53–60.

Langemeyer, I. and Roth, W.-M. (2006) 'Is Cultural-Historical Activity Theory Threatened to Fall Short of Its Own Principles and Possibilities as a Dialectical Social Science?', *Outlines*, 8(2): 20–42.

Lee, B. (1985) 'Intellectual Origins of Vygotsky's Semiotic Analysis', in J. V. Wertsch (ed.), *Culture, Communication and Cognition*, Cambridge: Cambridge University Press, 66–93.

Leopold, D. (2007) *The Young Marx*, Cambridge: Cambridge University Press.

Marx, K. (1961) Thesen über Feuerbach [Theses on Feuerbach], in *Karl Marx/Friedrich Engels – Werke* (Band 3, 5–7). Berlin: Dietz Verlag (original work written 1845).

Marx, K. (1970) 'Feuerbach. Opposition of the Materialist and Idealist Outlook', ed. C. J. Arthur; trans. W. Lough, C. Dutt and C. P. Magill, in K. Marx and F. Engels, *The German Ideology*, New York: International.

—— (1976) 'Zur Judenfrage' [On the Jewish question]. in *Karl Marx/Friedrich Engels – Werke* (Band 1, 347–77). Berlin: Dietz Verlag (original work published 1843).

—— (1991) *Capital*, vol. 3. *The Process of Capitalist Production as a Whole*, trans. D. Fernbach, London: Penguin.

Packer, M. (2008) 'Is Vygotsky Relevant? Vygotsky's Marxist Psychology', *Mind, Culture and Activity*, 15: 8–31.

Rousseau, J. J. (1974) *Émile*, trans. B. Foxley, London: Dent (original work published 1762).

Sayers, S. (1985) *Reality and Reason: Dialectic and the Theory of Knowledge*, Oxford: Blackwell.

Spinoza, B. (1996) *Ethics*, ed. and trans. E. Curley, London: Penguin (original work published 1676).

Veresov, N. (2005) 'Marxist and non-Marxist Aspects of the Cultural-Historical Psychology of L. S. Vygotsky', *Outlines*, 7(1): 31–49.

Vygotsky, L. S. (1994) 'Socialist Alteration of Man', trans. T. Prout, in R. van der Veer and J. Valsiner (eds.), *Vygotsky Reader*, Oxford: Blackwell (original work published 1930), 175–84.

—— (1997) 'The Historical Meaning of the Crisis in Psychology: A Methodological Investigation', trans. R. van der Veer, in R. W. Reiber and J. Wollock (eds.), *The Collected Works of L. S. Vygotsky*, vol. 3, *Problems of the Theory and History of Psychology*, New York: Plenum Press (original work written 1926), 233–343.

Westphal, K. R. (1993) 'The Basic Context and Structure of Hegel's *Philosophy of Right*', in F. C. Beiser (ed.), *The Cambridge Companion to Hegel*, Cambridge: Cambridge University Press, 234–69.

Wood, A. W. (1993) 'Hegel's Ethics', in F. C. Beiser (ed.), *The Cambridge Companion to Hegel*, Cambridge: Cambridge University Press, 211–33.

Zavershneva, E. I. (2010) 'The Way to Freedom', *Journal of Russian and East European Psychology*, 48(1): 61–90.

3 Vygotsky and Bernstein

Harry Daniels

The point of departure of this chapter is the understanding that the way in which the social relations of institutions are regulated has cognitive and affective consequences for those who live and work inside them. The current state of the art in the social sciences struggles to provide a theoretical connection between specific forms, or modalities, of institutional regulation and consciousness. Attempts which have been made to do so tend not to be capable of generating analyses and descriptions of institutional formations which are predictive of consequences for individuals. At the same time, social policy tends not to engage with the personal consequences of different forms of institutional regulation. This chapter will discuss an approach to making the connection between the principles of regulation in institutions, discursive practices and the shaping of consciousness. This approach is based on the work of the British sociologist Basil Bernstein and the Russian social theorist Lev Vygotsky.

From the sociological point of view Bernstein outlined the challenge as follows:

> The substantive issue of . . . [this] theory is to explicate the process whereby a given distribution of power and principles of control are translated into specialised principles of communication differentially, and often unequally, distributed to social groups/classes. And how such a differential/unequal distribution of forms of communication, initially (but not necessarily terminally) shapes the formation of consciousness of members of these groups/classes in such a way as to relay both opposition and change. (1996: 93)

The following assertion from Vygotsky recasts the issue in a more psychological vein but with the same underlying intent and commitment:

> Any function in the child's cultural [i.e. higher] development appears twice, or on two planes. First it appears on the social plane, and then on the psychological plane. First it appears between people as an inter-psychological category, and then within the child as an intra-psychological category. This is equally true with regard to voluntary attention, logical memory, the formation of concepts, and the development of volition . . . it goes without

saying that internalization transforms the process itself and changes its structure and functions. Social relations or relations among people genetically underlie all higher functions and their relationships. (1981: 163)

Taken together, the Vygotskian and Bernsteinian social theory have the potential to make a significant contribution to the development of a theory of the social formation of mind in specific pedagogic modalities. Following Bernstein, pedagogy may be thought of a sustained process whereby somebody acquires new forms or develops existing forms of conduct, knowledge, practice and criteria, from somebody or something deemed to be an appropriate provider and evaluator (Bernstein, 2000). Defined in this way, the general practitioner, the policy maker, the therapist, the broadcaster and the journalist are all involved in a form of pedagogic practice.

A sociological focus on the rules which shape the social formation of dis-cursive practice may be brought to bear on those aspects of psychology which argue that cultural artefacts, such as pedagogic discourse, both explicitly and implicitly, mediate human thought and action. Socio-cultural theorists argue that individual agency has been significantly under-acknowledged in Bernstein's sociology of pedagogy (e.g. Werstch, 1998a). Vygotsky's work provides a compatible account which places emphasis on individual agency through its attention to the notion of mediation. Sociologists complain that post-Vygotskian psychology is particularly weak in addressing relations between local, interactional contexts of 'activity' and 'mediation', where meaning is produced and wider structures of the division of labour and institutional organisation act to specify social positions and their differentiated orientation to 'activities and 'cultural artefacts' (e.g. Fitz, 2007).

Many sociologists have sought to theorise relationships between forms of social relation in institutional settings and forms of talk. Socio-cultural psychologists, working in the post-Vygotskian tradition, have done much to understand the relationship between thinking and speech in a range of social settings with relatively little analysis and description of the institutional arrangements that are in place in those settings.

> We can never 'speak from nowhere', given that we can speak (or more broadly, act) only by invoking mediational means that are available in the 'cultural tool kit' provided by the Socio-cultural setting in which we operate . . . this does not mean that we are mechanistically determined by, or are mere puppets of, the mediational means we employ, but it does mean that constraints of some kind always exist. (Wertsch *et al.*, 1995: 25)

Vygotsky provided a rich and tantalising set of suggestions that have been taken up and transformed by social theorists as they attempt to construct accounts of the formation of mind which to varying degrees acknowledge social, cultural and historical influences. There is also no doubt that Vygotsky straddled a number of disciplinary boundaries. Davydov (1995: 15) went as far as to suggest that he was involved in a creative reworking of the theory of behaviorism, gestalt psychology, functional and descriptive psychology, genetic psychology, the French school of sociology, and Freudianism.

Recent developments in post-Vygotskian theory have witnessed considerable advances in the understanding of the ways in which human action shapes and is shaped by the contexts in which it takes place. They have given rise to a significant amount of empirical research within and across a wide range of fields in which social science methodologies and methods are applied in the development of research-based knowledge in policy making and practice in academic, commercial and industrial settings. His is not a legacy of determinism and denial of agency; rather, he provides a theoretical framework which rests on the concept of mediation. These developments have explored different aspects of Vygotsky's legacy at different moments. As Puzyrei notes, his work constitutes a dynamic resource for modern-day researchers who will explore different facets of the texts we have available in line with their own interests and to some extent the prevailing Zeitgeist. These wider social influences are seen to have mediated the development and uptake of the theory itself.

> Vygotsky's cultural-historical theory (like any great theory) resembles a city. A city with broad new avenues and ancient, narrow backstreets known only to longtime residents, with noisy, crowded plazas and quiet, deserted squares, with large, modern edifices and decrepit little buildings. The individual areas of that city may not be situated on a single level: while some rise above the ground, others are submerged below it and cannot be seen at all. In essence, it is as though there were a second city that has intimate and complex associations with the ground-level city but completely invisible to many. And the sun rises above it all and the stars come out over it at night. Sometimes dust storms and hurricanes rage, or the rain beats down long and hard and 'the sky is overcast'. Life is a constant feeling of effervescence. Holidays and the humdrum follow one another. The city changes, grows, and is rebuilt. Whole neighborhoods are demolished. The center is sometimes over here, sometimes over there. And so it goes. (2007: 85–6)

Smardon takes this line of argument somewhat further in suggesting that the Vygotskian way of seeing the world has been and continues to be marginalised in some academic settings:

> The Vygotskian project has been largely overlooked outside of the field of educational psychology, where Stetsenko argues it is still marginalized in comparison to other, more dominant theoretical models. Furthermore, Marxist psychology has never been a part of American sociology, a discipline that has instead focused on macrosociological Marxist models. Thus, the Vygotskian project exists at the marginal nexus of both psychology and sociology. (2010: 70)

The reasons for formation of this marginal position may be that in attempting to resolve the disconnection between disciplinary imaginations it manages to offend both. Whatever the reasons, it is clear that many disciplines contributed to the formation of Vygotsky's ideas. For example, van der Veer (1996) argued that Humboldt with reference to linguistic mediation and Marx with reference to tool-use and social and cultural progress influenced Vygotsky's concept of culture. He suggested that the limitations in this aspect of Vygotsky's work are with respect to non-linguistically mediated aspects of culture and the difficulty in explaining innovation by individuals. Vygotsky's writing on the way in which psychological tools and signs act in the mediation of social factors does not engage with a theoretical account of the appropriation and/or production of psychological tools within specific forms of activity within or across institutions. Just as the development of Vygotsky's work fails to provide an adequate account of social praxis, so much sociological theory is unable to provide descriptions of micro-level processes, except by projecting macro-level concepts onto the micro level unmediated by intervening concepts, through which the micro can be both uniquely described and related to the macro level.

Among sociologists of cultural transmission, Bernstein (2000) provides a sociology of this social experience which is compatible with, but absent from, Vygotskian psychology. His theoretical contribution was directed towards the question as to how institutional relations of power and control translate into principles of communication and how these differentially regulate forms of consciousness. It was through Luria's attempts to disseminate his former colleague's work that Bernstein first became acquainted with Vygotsky's writing.

> I first came across Vygotsky in the late 1950s through a translation by Luria of a section of Thought and Speech published in *Psychiatry* 2 1939. It is difficult to convey the sense of excitement, of thrill, of revelation this paper aroused: literally a new universe opened. (1993: xxiii)

This paper along with a seminal series of lectures given by Luria at the Tavistock Institute in London sparked an intense interest in the Russian cultural-historical historical tradition and went on to exert a profound influence on post-war developments in English in education, the introduction of education for young people with severe and profound learning difficulties and theories and practices designed to facilitate development and learning in socially disadvantaged groups in the UK. In November 1964 Bernstein wrote a letter to Vygotsky's widow outlining her late husband's influence on his developing thesis:

> As you may know, many of us working in the area of speech (from the perspective of psychology as well as from the perspective of sociology) think that we owe a debt to the Russian school, especially to works based on Vygotsky's tradition. I should say that in many respects, many of us are still trying to comprehend what he said. (1964b: 1)

It was Vygotsky's (1978) non-dualist cultural-historical conception of mind claims that 'intermental' (social) experience shapes 'intramental' (psychological) development that continued to influence his thinking. This was understood as a mediated process in which culturally produced artefacts (such as forms of talk, representations in the form of ideas and beliefs, signs and symbols) shape and are shaped by human engagement with the world (e.g. Vygotsky, 1987; Daniels, 2008).

> Language here is a system of meanings, a relay for the social, a primary condition for the formation of consciousness and the levels and variety of its function. Relation to (the social) precedes relations within (the individual). This insight was of course, Mead's, much earlier than Vygotsky but his insight produced a very different model. The I/Me dualism of the Meadian self is a dualism endemic to European thought, perhaps even to christianity, with its distinction between inner/outer, individual/society. The relaying, mediating role of language is shared with Durkheim. (Bernstein, 1993: xiv)

However, as Atkinson notes, despite his acquaintance with the various philo-sophical and anthropological authors on language and symbolism including Cassirer and Whorf and Vygotsky and Luria, Bernstein's approach epitomises an essentially macro-sociological point of view.

> It is undoubtedly true that in Bernstein's general approach there is little or no concern for the perspectives, strategy and actions of individual social actors in actual social settings. (1985: 32)

Durkheim influenced both Vygotsky and Bernstein. On the one hand Durkheim's notion of collective representation allowed for the social interpretation of human cognition, on the other it failed to resolve the issue as to how the collective representation is interpreted by the individual. This is the domain so appropriately filled by the later writings of Vygotsky. The fact that Bernstein has utilised Mead and Vygotsky in the formulation of his model allows for the exploration of interpersonal relations at the face-to-face level in the classroom. Many of the symbolic interactionist and Vygotskian insights can be subsumed into his model which affords the wider social dimension a central place in a general thesis.

Although Vygotsky discussed the general importance of language and schooling for psychological functioning, he failed to provide an analytical framework to analyse and describe the real social systems in which these activities occur and reflect. Vygotsky never indicated the social basis for this new use of words. The social analysis is thus reduced to a semiotic analysis which overlooks the real world of social praxis (Ratner, 1997).

> The feature that can be viewed as the proximal cause of the maturation of concepts, *is a specific way of using the word*, specifically the functional application of the sign as a means of forming concepts.(Vygotsky, 1987: 131)

While it is quite possible to interpret 'a specific way of using the word' to be an exhortation to analyse the activities in which the word is used and meaning negotiated, this was not elaborated by Vygotsky himself. The analysis of the structure and function of semiotic psychological tools in specific activity contexts is not explored. The challenge is to address the demands created by this absence. Bernstein recognised the need for such an endeavour in his early writing.

> Different social structures may generate different speech systems or linguistic codes. The latter entail for the individual specific principles of choice which regulate the selections he makes from the totality of options represented by a given language. The principles of choice originally elicit, progressively strengthen, and finally stabilize the planning procedures an individual uses in the preparation of his speech and guide his orientation to the speech of others. (1964a: 56)

Bernstein outlined a model for understanding the construction of pedagogic discourse. In this context pedagogic discourse is a source of psychological tools or cultural artefacts.

> The basic idea was to view this (pedagogic) discourse as arising out of the action of a group of specialised agents operating in specialised setting in terms of the interests, often competing interests of this setting. (1996: 116)

In Engeström's (1996) work within activity theory, which to some considerable extent has a Vygotskian root, the production of the outcome of activity is discussed but not the production and structure of cultural artefacts such as discourse. The production of discourse is not analysed in terms of the context of its production that is the rules, community and division of labour which regulate the activity in which subjects are positioned. It is therefore important that the discourse is seen within the culture and structures of schooling where differences in pedagogic practices, in the structuring of interactions and relationships and the generation of different criteria of competence will shape the ways in which children are perceived and actions are argued and justified.

The application of Vygotsky by many social scientists (e.g. linguists, psychologists and sociologists) has been limited to relatively small-scale inter-actional contexts often within schooling or some other form of educational setting. The descriptions and the form of analysis are in some sense specific to these contexts. Sociologists have drawn on ethnomethodology or symbolic interactionism (see Makitalo and Saljo, 2002, for a discussion). Here the focus is on the creation and negotiation of social order by participants in clearly defined and categorised settings. Data collection tends to focus on what is said. As Bernstein notes, extra-contextual structures of power and their discursive regulation are necessarily excluded from the analysis.

He also notes the limitations of symbolic interactionism which, from his point of view:

> focuses upon meanings, their negotiation, the construction of identities and their careers as these emerge out of face to face encounters in well bounded contexts. Here there is opportunity for showing relations to external constraints and possibilities in which interactions are embedded but not necessarily determined. Yet there still remains the crucial conceptual issue of explicating this interrelation. This is not solved by a set of boxes which only index the very processes to be described. Symbolic interaction provides sensitive and insightful descriptions of interactions within the pedagogic format. The description it gives necessarily stems from its own selective focus. It tends to take for granted, that it does not include in its description, how the discourse itself is constituted and recontextualized. The theory focuses upon interactional formats rather than the way the *specialisation of knowledge is constructed*. From the point of view of Vygotsky the '*tool*' is not subject to analysis, although the articulation of the zone of proximal development may well be. This absence of focus is common to both linguistics and psychology. (1993: xix)

In his work on schooling, Bernstein (2000) argues that pedagogic discourse is constructed by a recontextualizing principle which selectively appropriates, relocates, refocuses and relates other discourses to constitute its own order. He argues that in order to understand pedagogic discourse as a social and historical construction attention must be directed to the regulation of its structure, the social relations of its production and the various modes of its recontextualising as a practice. For him symbolic 'tools' are never neutral; intrinsic to their construction are social classifications, stratifications, distributions and modes of recontextualising.

The language that Bernstein (2000) has developed allows researchers to take measures of institutional modality. That is to describe and position the discursive, organizational and interactional practice of the institution. His model is one that is designed to relate macro-institutional forms to micro-interactional levels and the underlying rules of communicative competence. He focuses upon two levels: a structural level and an interactional level. The structural level is analysed in terms of the social division of labour it creates (e.g. the degree of specialisation, and thus strength of boundary between professional groupings) and the inter-actional with the form of social relation it creates (e.g. the degree of control that a manager may exert over a team member's work plan). The social division is analysed in terms of strength of the boundary of its divisions; that is, with respect to the degree of specialisation (e.g. how strong is the boundary between professions such as teaching and social work or one school curriculum subject and another). Thus the key concept at the structural level is the concept of boundary, and structures are distinguished in terms of their relations between categories. The interactional level emerges as the regulation of the transmission–acquisition relation between teacher and taught (or the manager and the managed); that is, the interactional level comes to refer to the pedagogic context and the social relations of the workplace or classroom or its equivalent. Power is spoken of in terms of classification, which is manifested in category relations that themselves generate recognition rules. Possession of this allows the acquirer to recognise a difference that is marked by a category, as would be the case of the rules that allow a professional to be recognised as belonging to a particular professional group. This is not simply a matter of finding out which service someone belongs to; it also refers to the ways that forms of talk and other actions may be seen to be belonging to a particular professional category or grouping. When there is strong insulation between categories (i.e. subject, teachers), with each category sharply distinguished, explicitly bounded and having its own distinctive specialisation, then classification is said to be strong. When there is weak insulation, then the categories are less specialised and their distinctiveness is reduced, and classification is said to be weak. Bernstein (1996) refined the discussion of his distinction between instructional and regulative discourse. The former refers to the transmission of skills and their relation to each other, and the latter refers to the principles of social order, relation and identity. Whereas the principles and distinctive features of instructional discourse and its practice are relatively clear (the what and how of the specific skills/competences to be acquired and their relation to each other), the principles and distinctive features of the transmission of the regulative are less clear, as this discourse is transmitted through various media and may indeed be characterised as a diffuse transmission. Regulative discourse communicates the school's (or any institution's) public moral practice, values beliefs and attitudes, principles of conduct, character and manner. It also transmits features of the school's local history, local tradition and community relations. Pedagogic discourse is modelled as one discourse created by the embedding of instructional and regulative discourse. This model of pedagogic discourse provides a response to one of the many theoretical demands which have remained unfulfilled in the post-Vygotskian framework. The rejection of the cognitive–affective dualism which Vygotsky announced was not followed by a model within which a unitary conception of thinking and feeling could be discussed and implemented within empirical research.

Different institutional modalities may be described in terms of the relationship between the relations of power and control, which gives rise to distinctive discursive artefacts. For example, with respect to schooling, where the theory of instruction gives rise to a strong classification and strong framing of the pedagogic practice, it is expected that there will be a separation of discourses (school subjects), an emphasis upon acquisition of specialised skills; the teacher will be dominant in the formulation of intended learning and the pupils are constrained by the teacher's practice. The relatively strong control on the pupils' learning, itself, acts as a means of maintaining order in the context in which the learning takes place. This form of the instructional discourse contains regulative functions. With strong classification and framing, the social relations between teachers and pupils will be more asymmetrical; that is, more clearly hierarchical. In this instance the regulative discourse and its practice are more explicit and distinguishable from the instructional discourse. Where the theory of instruction gives rise to a weak classification and weak framing of the practice, then children will be encouraged to be active in the classroom, to undertake enquiries and perhaps to work in groups at their own pace. Here the relations between teacher and pupils will have the appearance of being more symmetrical. In these circumstances it is difficult to separate instructional discourse from regulative discourse, as these are mutually embedded. The formulation of pedagogic discourse as an embedded discourse comprising instructional and regulative components allows for the analysis of the production of such embedded discourses in activities structured through specifiable relations of power and control within institutions. Bernstein provides an account of cultural transmission which is avowedly sociological in its conception. In turn the psychological account that has developed in the wake of Vygotsky's writing offers a model of aspects of the social formation of mind which is underdeveloped in Bernstein's work. The Socio-cultural account of the social, cultural and historical context is insufficient for the task that Vygotsky set himself in his attempt to formulate a general social theory of the formation of mind. Bernstein's account of social positioning within the discursive practice that arises in institutional settings taken together with his analysis of the ways in which principles of power and control translate into principles of communication allows us to investigate how principles of communication differentially regulate forms of consciousness.

Bernstein's work provides the basis for a language of description which may be applied at the level of principles of power and control which may then be translated into principles of communication. Different social structures give rise to different modalities of language which have specialised mediational properties. They have arisen, have been shaped by, the social, cultural and historical circumstances in which interpersonal exchanges arise and they in turn shape the thoughts and feelings, the identities and aspirations for action of those engaged in interpersonal exchange in those contexts. Hence the relations of power and control, which regulate social interchange, give rise to specialised principles of communication. These mediate social relations. I intend to develop an account of the production of psychological tools or artefacts, such as discourse, that will allow for exploration of the formative effects of the institutional context of production at the psychological level. This will also involve a consideration of the possibilities afforded to different social actors as they take up positions and are positioned in social products such as discourse. This discussion of production thus opens up the possibility of analysing the possible positions that an individual may take up in a field of social practice.

> To understand his views on what underlies the social subject's participation in discourse is to understand the true meaning of speaking each act of speaking is a social event, behind which lies the history of the individual and so the history of the community of which the individual is a member.
> (Hasan, 2001: 6)

Discourse may mediate human action in different ways. There is visible (Bernstein, 2000) or explicit (Wertsch, 2007) mediation in which the deliberate incorporation of signs into human action is seen as a means of reorganising that action. This contrasts with invisible or implicit mediation that involves signs, especially natural language, whose primary function is *in* communications which are part of a pre-existing, independent stream of communicative action that becomes integrated with other forms of goal-directed behaviour (Wertsch, 2007). Invisible semiotic mediation occurs in discourse embedded in everyday ordinary activities of a social subject's life.

As Hasan argues, Bernstein further nuances this claim:

> what Bernstein referred to as the 'invisible' component of communication (see Bernstein 1990: 17, figure 3.1 and discussion). The code theory relates this component to the subject's social positioning. If we grant that 'ideology is constituted through and in such positioning' (Bernstein 1990: 13), then we grant that subjects' stance to their universe is being invoked: different orders of relevance inhere in different experiences of positioning and being positioned. This is where the nature of what one wants to say, not its absolute specifics, may be traced. Of course, linguists are right that speakers can say what they want to say, but an important question is: what is the range of meanings they freely and voluntarily mean, and why do they prioritize those meanings when the possibilities of making meanings from the point of view of the system of language are infinite? Why do they want to say what they do say? The regularities in discourse have roots that run much deeper than linguistics has cared to fathom. (2001: 8)

This argument is all the stronger through its reference to a theoretical account which provides greater descriptive and analytical purchase on the principles of regulation of the social figured world, the possibilities for social position and the voice of participants.

These challenges of studying implicit or invisible mediation have been approached from a variety of theoretical perspectives. Holland *et al.* (1998) have studied the development of identities and agency specific to historically situated, socially enacted, culturally constructed worlds in a way which may contribute to the development of an understanding of the way in which the development of social capital is situated. This approach to a theory of identity in practice is grounded in the notion of a figured world in which positions are taken up constructed and resisted. The Bakhtinian concept of the 'space of authoring' is deployed to capture an understanding of the mutual shaping of figured worlds and identities in social practice. They refer to Bourdieu (1977) in their attempt to show how social position becomes disposition. They argue for the development of social position into a positional identity into disposition and the formation of what Bourdieu refers to as 'habitus'. Bernstein is critical of habitus, arguing that the internal structure of a particular habitus, the mode of its specific acquisition, which gives it its specificity, is not described. For him, habitus is known by its output not its input (Bernstein, 2000).

Wertsch (1998a) turned to Bakhtin's theory of speech genres rather than habitus. A similar conceptual problem emerges with this body of work. While Bakhtin's views concerning speech genres are 'rhetorically attractive and impressive, the approach lacks . . . both a developed conceptual syntax and an adequate language of description. Terms and units at both these levels in Bakhtin's writings require clarification; further, the principles that underlie the calibration of the elements of context with the generic shape of the text are underdeveloped, as is the general schema for the description of contexts for interaction' (Hasan, 2005). Bernstein acknowledges the importance of Foucault's analysis of power, knowledge and discourse as he attempts to theorise the discursive positioning of the subject. He complains that it lacks a theory of transmission, its agencies and its social base.

Hasan brings Bernstein's concept of social positioning to the fore in her discussion of social identity. Bernstein (1990: 13) used this concept to refer to the establishing of a specific relation to other subjects and to the creating of specific relationships within subjects. As Hasan (2005) notes, social positioning through meanings are inseparable from power relations. Bernstein provided an elaboration of his early general argument:

> More specifically, class-regulated codes position subjects with respect to dominant and dominated forms of communication and to the relationships between them. Ideology is constituted through and in such positioning. From this perspective, ideology inheres in and regulates modes of relation. Ideology is not so much a content as a mode of relation for the realizing of content. Social, cultural, political and economic relations are intrinsic to pedagogic discourse. (1990: 13–14)

Here the linkage is forged between social positioning and psychological attributes. This is the process through which Bernstein talks of the shaping of the possibilities for consciousness. The dialectical relation between discourse and subject makes it possible to think of pedagogic discourse as a semiotic means that regulates or traces the generation of subjects' positions in discourse. We can understand the potency of pedagogic discourse in selectively producing subjects and their identities in a temporal and spatial dimension (Diaz, 2001: 106–8). As Hasan (2005) argues, within the Bernsteinian thesis there exists an 'ineluctable relation between one's social positioning, one's mental dispositions and one's relation to the distribution of labour in society. Here the emphasis on discourse is theorised not only in terms of the shaping of cognitive functions but also, as it were invisibly, in its influence on dispositions, identities and practices' (Bernstein, 1990: 33).

Within Engeström's approach to cultural-historical activity theory (CHAT) the subject is often discussed in terms of individuals, groups or perspectives/views. I would argue that the way in which subjects are positioned with respect to one another within an activity carries with it implications for engagement with tools and objects. It may also carry implications for the ways in which rules, community and the division of labour regulate the actions of individuals and groups.

Holland *et al.* have studied the development of identities and agency specific to historically situated, socially enacted, culturally constructed worlds. They draw on Bakhtin (1978, 1986) and Vygotsky to develop a theory of identity as constantly forming, and person as a composite of many often contradictory, self-understandings and identities which are distributed across the material and social environment and rarely durable (1998: 8). They draw on Leont'ev in the development of the concept of socially organised and reproduced *figured worlds* which shape and are shaped by participants and in which social position establishes possibilities for engagement. They also argue that figured worlds:

> [D]istribute 'us' not only by relating actors to landscapes of action (as personae) and spreading our senses of self across many different fields of activity, but also by giving the landscape human voice and tone. Cultural worlds are populated by familiar social types and even identifiable persons, not simply differentiated by some abstract division of labour. The identities we gain within figured worlds are thus specifically historical developments, grown through *continued participation in the positions defined by the social organization of those worlds' activity.* (Holland *et al.*, 1998: 41; my emphasis)

This approach to a theory of identity in practice is grounded in the notion of a figured world in which positions are taken up, constructed and resisted. The Bakhtinian concept of the 'space of authoring' is deployed to capture an understanding of the mutual shaping of figured worlds *and* identities in social practice. Holland *et al.* (1998) refer to Bourdieu (1977) in their attempt to show how social position becomes disposition. They argue for the development of social position into a positional identity into disposition and the formation of what Bourdieu refers to as 'habitus'. It is here that I feel that this argument could be strengthened through reference to a theoretical account which provides greater descriptive and analytical purchase on the principles of regulation of the social figured world, the possibilities for social position and the voice of participants.

Engeström (1999), who has tended to concentrate on the structural aspects of CHAT, offers the suggestion that the division of labour in an activity creates different positions for the participants and that the participants carry their own diverse histories with them into the activity. This echoes the earlier assertion from Leont'ev:

> Activity is the minimal meaningful context for understanding individual actions . . . In all its varied forms, the activity of the human individual is a system set within a system of social relations . . . The activity of individual people thus *depends on their social position*, the conditions that fall to their lot, and an accumulation of idiosyncratic, individual factors. Human activity is not a relation between a person and a society that confronts him . . . in a society a person does not simply find external conditions to which he must adapt his activity, but, rather, these very social conditions bear within

themselves the motives and goals of his activity, its means and modes. (1978: 10; my emphasis)

In activity, the possibilities for the use of artefacts depends on the social position occupied by an individual. Sociologists and sociolinguists have produced empirical verification of this suggestion (e.g., Bernstein, 2000; Hasan, 2001; Hasan and Cloran, 1990). My suggestion is that the notion of 'subject' within activity theory requires expansion and clarification. In many studies the term 'subject perspective' is used, which arguably infers subject position but does little to illuminate the formative processes that gave rise to this perspective.

Holland *et al.* also argue that multiple identities are developed within figured worlds and that these are 'historical developments, grown through continued participation in the positions defined by the social organization of those worlds' activity' (1998: 41). This body of work represents a significant development in our understanding of the concept of the 'subject' in activity theory. As Roth notes:

> Goals and actions are free-floating, generally intelligible, cultural-historically contingent possibilities. Because concrete embodied actions articulate between society and the self, a person's identity does not constitute a singularity but is itself inherently intelligible within the cultural unit. It is because of what they see each other doing that two (or more) persons come to 'recognize themselves as mutually recognizing one another'. Publicly visible actions serve as the ground of recognizing in the other another self that recognizes in me its corresponding other. It is this linkage between self and other through patterned embodied actions that have led some to theorize identity in terms of agency and culture in which a person participates. (2007: 144)

For my point of view there remains a need to develop the notion of 'figured world' in such a way that we can theorise, analyse and describe the processes by which that world is 'figured'. Bernstein's (1990: 13) concept of social positioning seems to me to concur with the analysis outlined by Holland *et al.* (1998). He relates social positioning to the formation of mental dispositions in terms of the identity's relation to the distribution of labour in society. It is through the deployment of his concepts of voice and message that Bernstein forges the link between division of labour, social position and discourse, and opens up the possibilities for a language of description that will serve empirical as well as analytical purposes. The distinction between what can be recognised as belonging to a voice and a particular message is formulated in terms of distinction between relations of power and relations of control. Bernstein (1990) adapted the concept of voice from his reading of *The Material Word* by Silverman and Torode (1980).

> From this perspective classificatory (boundary) relations establish 'voice'. 'Voice' is regarded somewhat like a cultural larynx which sets the limits on

what can be legitimately put together (communicated). Framing (control) relations regulate the acquisition of this voice and create the message (what is made manifest, what can be realized)'. (Bernstein, 1990: 260)

In his last book he continues:

> Voice refers to the limits on what could be realized if the identity was to be recognized as legitimate. The classificatory (boundary) relation established the voice. In this way power relations, through the classificatory relation, regulated voice. However voice, although a necessary condition for establishing what could and could not be said and its context, could not determine what was said and the form of its contextual realization; the message. The message was a function of framing (control). The stronger the framing the smaller the space accorded for potential variation in the message. (2000: 204)

Thus social categories constitute voices and control over practices constitutes message. Identity becomes the outcome of the voice–message relation. Production and reproduction have their social basis in categories and practices; that categories are constituted by the social division of labour and that practices are constituted by social relations within production/reproduction; that categories constitute 'voices' and that practices constitute their 'messages'; message is dependent upon 'voice', and the subject is a dialectical relation between 'voice' and message (Bernstein, 1990: 27).

Hasan (2001: 8) suggests that Bernstein's analysis of how subjects are positioned and how they position themselves in relation to the social context of their discourse offers an explanation of discursive practice, in terms of the relations of power and control which regulate speaking subjects. However, the theoretical move which Bernstein makes in relating positioning to the distribution of power and principles of control opens up the possibility of grounding the analysis of social positioning and mental dispositions in relation to the distribution of labour in an activity. Through the notions of 'voice' and 'message' he brings the division of labour and principles of control (rules) into relation with social position in practice. This theoretical stance suggests that activity theory could also develop a language of description which allows for the parameters of power and control to be considered at structural and interactional levels of analysis. A systematic approach to the analysis and description of the formation of categories through the maintenance and shifting of boundaries and principles of control as exercised within categories would bring a powerful tool to the undoubted strengths of activity theory. This would then allow the analysis to move from one level to another in the same terms, rather than treat division of labour and discourse as analytically independent items. Bernstein argues that positioning is in a systematic relation to the distribution of power and principles of control. I suggest that this approach to understanding the notion of social positioning as the underlying, invisible component which 'figures' (as in Holland *et al.*, 1998) practices of communication, and gives rise to the shaping of identity provides an important potential development from the current status of third-generation activity theory.

Such a development requires a theoretical account of social relations and positioning. The theoretical move which Bernstein makes in relating positioning to the distribution of power and principles of control opens up the possibility of grounding the analysis of social positioning and mental dispositions in relation to the distribution of labour in an activity. Through the notions of 'voice' and 'message' he brings the division of labour and principles of control (rules) into relation with social position in practice. The implication is that 'subject' in an activity-theory-driven depiction should be represented by a space of possibility (voice) in which a particular position (message) is taken up. Thus subject would be represented by a socially structured zone of possibility rather than a singular point. This representation would signify a move to attempt to theorise the subject as emerging in a world that was 'figured' by relations of power and control.

The language that Bernstein has developed allows researchers to take measures of school modality. That is, to describe and position the discursive, organisational and interactional practice of the institution. He also noted the need for the extension of this work in his discussion of the importance of Vygotsky's work for research in education.

His theoretical perspective also makes demands for a new methodology, for the development of languages of description which will facilitate a *multilevel* understanding of pedagogic discourse, the varieties of its practice and contexts of its realization and production (1993: xxiii).

This approach to modelling the structural relations of power and control in institutional settings taken together with a theory of cultural–historical artefacts that invisibly or implicitly mediate the relations of participants in practices forms a powerful alliance. It carries with it the possibility of rethinking notions of agency and reconceptualising subject position in terms of the relations between possibilities afforded within the division of labour and the rules that constrain possibility and direct and deflect the attention of participants.

It accounts for the ways in which the practices of a community, such as school and the family, are structured by their institutional context and that social structures impact on the interactions between the participants and the cultural tools.

Thus, it is not just a matter of the structuring of interactions between the participants and other cultural tools; rather it is that the institutional structures themselves are cultural products that serve as mediators in their own right. In this sense, they are the 'message', that is, a fundamental factor of education. As Hasan (2001) argues, when we talk, we enter the flow of communication in a stream of both history and the future. When we talk in institutions, history enters the flow of communication through the invisible or implicit mediation of the institutional structures. There is therefore a need to analyse and codify the mediational structures as they deflect and direct attention of participants and as they are shaped through interactions which they also shape. In this sense, combining the intellectual legacies of Bernstein and Vygotsky permits the development of cultural-historical analysis of the invisible or implicit mediational properties of institutional structures which themselves are transformed through the actions of those whose interactions are influenced by them. This move would serve to both expand the gaze of post-Vygotskian theory and at the same time bring sociologies of cultural transmission into a framework in which institutional structures are analysed as historical products which themselves are subject to dynamic transformation and change as people act within and on them.

References

Atkinson, P. (1985) *Structure and Reproduction: An Introduction to the Sociology of Basil Bernstein*, London: Methuen.

Bakhtin, M. M. (1978) 'The Problem of the Text', *Soviet Studies in Literature*, 14(1): 3–33.

——— (1986) *Speech Genres and Other Late Essays*, ed. Caryl Emerson and Michael Holquist, trans. Vern W. McGee, Austin, TX: University of Texas Press Slavic Series 8.

Bernstein, B. (1964a). 'Elaborated and Restricted Codes: Their Social Origins and Some Consequences', *American Anthropologist*, 66(6): 55–69.

——— (1964b) letter to Vygotsky's widow (mimeo).

——— (1990) *The Structuring of Pedagogic Discourse*, vol. 4, *Class, Codes and Control*, London: Routledge.

——— (1993) Foreword, in H. Daniels (ed.), *Charting the Agenda: Educational Activity after Vygotsky*, London: Routledge.

——— (1996) *Pedagogy Symbolic Control and Identity: Theory, Research, Criticism*, London: Taylor & Francis.

——— (2000), 'Pedagogy, Symbolic Control and Identity: Theory, Research, Critique', rev. edn, Lanham, MD: Rowman & Littlefield.

Bourdieu, P. (1977) *Outline of a Theory of Practice*, Cambridge: Cambridge University Press.

Daniels, H. (2008) *Vygotsky and Research* (London: Routledge).

Davydov, V. V. (1995) 'The Influence of L. S. Vygotsky on Education Theory, Research, and Practice', *Educational Researcher*, 24(3): 12–21.

Diaz, M. (2001) 'The Importance of Basil Bernstein', in S. Power, P. Aggleton, J. Brannen, A. Brown, L. Chisholm and J. Mace (eds.), *A Tribute to Basil Bernstein 1924–2000*, London: Institute of Education, University of London, 106–8.

Engeström, Y. (1996) 'Development as Breaking away and Opening up: A Challenge to Vygotsky and Piaget', *Swiss Journal of Psychology*, 55: 126–32.

——— (1999a). 'Activity Theory and Individual and Social Transformation', in Y. Engeström, R. Miettinen and R.-L. Punamäki (eds.), *Perspectives on Activity Theory*, Cambridge: Cambridge University Press, 19–38.

——— (1999b). 'Innovative Learning in Work Teams: Analyzing the Cycles of Knowledge Creation in Practice', in Y. Engeström, R. Miettinen and R.-L. Punamäki (eds.), *Perspectives on Activity Theory*, Cambridge: Cambridge University Press, 377–404.

Fitz, J. (2007) 'Knowledge, Power and Educational Reform: Applying the Sociology of Basil Bernstein' (review essay), *British Journal of Sociology of Education*, 28(2): 273–9.

Hasan, R. (2001) 'Understanding Talk: Directions from Bernstein's Sociology', *International Journal of Social Research Methodology*, 4(1): 5–9.

—— (2005) 'Semiotic Mediation, Language and Society: Three Exotripic Theories: Vygotsky, Halliday and Bernstein', in J. J. Webster (ed.), *Language, Society and Consciousness: Ruqaiya Hasan*, London: Equinox.

Hasan, R. and Cloran, C. (1990) 'A Sociolinguistic Study of Everyday Talk between Mothers and Children', in M. A. K. Halliday, J. Gibbons and H. Nicholas (eds.), *Learning, Keeping and Using Language*, vol. 1, Amsterdam: John Benjamins.

Holland, D., Lachiotte, L., Skinner, D. and Cain, C. (1998) *Identity and Agency in Cultural Worlds*, Cambridge, MA: Harvard University Press.

Leont'ev, A. N. (1978) *Activity, Consciousness and Personality*, Englewood Cliffs, NJ: Prentice Hall.

Makitalo, A. and Saljo, R. (2002) 'Talk in Institutional Context and Institutional Context in Talk: Categories as Situated Practices', *Text*, 22 (1): 57–82.

Mead, G. H. (1934) *Mind, Self and Society*, ed. Charles W.Morris, Chicago: University of Chicago Press.

Puzyrei, A. A. (2007) 'Contemporary Psychology and Vygotsky's Cultural-Historical Theory', *Journal of Russian and East European Psychology*, 45(1): 8–93.

Ratner, C. (1997) *Cultural Psychology and Qualitative Methodology: Theoretical and Empirical Considerations*, London: Plenum.

Roth, W. M. (2007) 'Heeding the Unit of Analysis', *Mind, Culture and* Activity, 14(3): 143–9.

Silverman, D. and Torode, B. (1980) *The Material Word: Some Theories of Language and Its Limits*, London: Routledge.

Smardon, R. (2010) 'A Sociological Response to Stetsenko Restructuring Science Education', *Cultural Studies of Science Education*, 2(1): 69–88 (DOI: 10.1007/ 978-90-481-3996-5_6).

van der Veer, R. (1996) 'The Concept of Culture in Vygotsky's Thinking', *Culture and Philosophy*, 2(3): 247–63.

Vygotsky, L. S. (1978) *Mind in Society: The Development of Higher Psychological Processes*, ed. and trans. M. Cole, V. John-Steiner, S. Scribner and E. Souberman, Cambridge, MA: Harvard University Press.

—— (1981) 'The Genesis of Higher Mental Functions', in James Wertsch (ed.), *The Concept of Activity in Soviet Psychology*, Armonk, NY: M. E. Sharp.

—— (1987) *The Collected Works of L. S. Vygotsky*, vol. 1, *Problems of General Psychology*, including vol. *Thinking and Speech*, ed. R. W. Rieber and A. S. Carton, trans. N. Minick, New York: Plenum.

Wertsch, J. V. (1998a) 'Review of Basil Bernstein, Pedagogy, Symbolic Control and Identity: Theory, Research, Critique', *Language in Society*, 27(2): 257–9.

—— (1998b). *Mind as Action*, New York: Oxford University Press.

—— (2007) 'Mediation', in H. Daniels, M. Cole and J. V. Wertsch (eds.), *The Cambridge Companion to Vygotsky*, New York: Cambridge University Press.

Wertsch, J., del Rio, P. and Alvarez, A. (1995) 'Socio-cultural Studies: History, Action and Mediation', in J. Wertsch, P. del Rio and A. Alvarez (eds.), *Socio-cultural Studies of Mind*, Cambridge: Cambridge University Press.

4 Sixth sense, second nature, and other cultural ways of making sense of our surroundings

Vygotsky, Bernstein, and the languaged body

John Shotter and Andy Lock

Human learning presupposes a specific social nature and a process by which children grow into the intellectual life of those around them.

(Vygotsky, 1978: 88)

Every culture specializes principles for the creation of a specific reality through its distinctive classificatory principles and, in so doing, necessarily constructs a set of procedures, practices, and relations from a range of such sets.

(Bernstein, 1981: 339)

[A] practice . . . is an instrument to be played upon, not a tune to be played.

(Oakeshott, 1975: 58)

Bernstein and Vygotsky wrote in very different times and circumstances (Bernstein being 10 years old when Vygotsky died in 1934). There are thus, necessarily, some difficulties in discussing *the* relation between their bodies of work: rather, we need to *construct* useful relationships. That said, it was very clear to the first author here (JS) in his personal contacts with Bernstein from 1959–62, and as Atkinson (1985) also makes clear, that in addition to being deeply influenced by Durkheim's emphasis on the importance of "the social bond" in the "structuring of experience" (Bernstein, 1971: 3), the works of Vygotsky, Luria (along with Whorf, Mead, and Cassirer) were also central in his attempts to set out *how* people's different ways of relating themselves to each other, and to their surroundings, give rise to different structures of experience, and types of relationship, which show up in our practical dealings with the others and othernesses around us.[1] We explore this interpenetration of ideas in three main ways here.

1 Basil Bernstein played a very important part in the intellectual development of one of us (JS). From 1959 to 1962, JS was a lab technician in the Phonetics Department at University College, London, while Basil was working with Frieda Goldman-Eisler there on hesitation phenomena. I (JS) often spent my lunchtimes with him. During that time

In the first part of this chapter, we situate ourselves inside the prevailing intellectual context within which both Vygotsky and Bernstein worked. While separated physically, culturally, and historically, both wrote when scientific modes of thought were taken to be at the pinnacle of human achievement, and thus motivated an almost neo-Darwinian struggle to express the one, true, final *theoretical* account of the *causes* of human behaviour. It was within this intellectual atmosphere that their fashioning of concepts, and arguments about the categorization and classification of things-in-the-world, flourished. This mode of thought is not extinct in psychology, and readers will note a compatibility between this part of the chapter and mainstream cognitive science: we work out the interpenetration of Vygotsky and Bernstein's ideas with respect to a disembodied, Cartesian "mind model". We will be a little controversial here by sliding away from the mainstream representational models of cognition to flirt with Gibsonian ideas, but by and large we will sit in the comfort of the "linguistic turn" (as termed by Rorty, 1967) initiated by Saussure (1916/1983). This is the notion that language is to be treated as a special kind of mental-object, as a mediatory instrument or organ, whose *structure* as such determines the uses to which it can be put.[2] There is an undeniable and seductive theoretical grandeur to this form of a Vygotsky–Bernstein synthesis.

Later in this chapter we consider what is coming to be called the "corporeal turn" (Johnson, 1987, 2007; Lakoff and Johnson, 1999; Sheets-Johnstone, 2009). There are many novel features to this new approach. But perhaps central to it is that those adopting it take it that our initial, living bodily movements in the world – as we try to relate ourselves to our surroundings in satisfaction of our need to be "in touch with [our] *circumstances*" (Todes, 2001: 66), our need for orientation – give rise to *pre-conceptual*, embodied "image schemas," i.e., to recurring, dynamic patterns of a distinctive nature, which function as "a means of structuring particular experiences schematically, so as to give order and connectedness to our perceptions and conceptions" (Johnson, 2007: 73).

Finally, we consider the possibility that there is a much more immediate, unreflective and bodily way of being related to our surroundings than the more conceptual forms of relation that have come to dominate our more self-conscious reflections on this matter. This possibility further calls into question the centrality of the *representational* role of language, and turns our attention to other possible uses of linguistic expressions. It is the distinct role of what we

he introduced me to Luria (1961), Mead (1934), Vygotsky (1962), Cassirer (1953, 1955, 1957), while all the time, of course, telling me about his post-office messenger boys and the meaning of their various turns of speech – recounting their utterances in such a way that I was transported into the social realities in which they lived.

2   Atkinson (1985), a major commentator on Bernstein's work, has placed it clearly within this tradition. This is the view that how we think about the nature of language, and its role in shaping our way or ways of being and behaving in the world, is of crucial importance in our coming to an understanding of what it is like for a human being to grow into the intellectual lives of those around them, with differently structured social surroundings giving rise to different subjectivities and mentalities.

will call these embodied *orientational* understandings that are, we shall argue, basic to the further development of both our everyday *and* our professional practices.

Concrete examples to introduce our perspective

> All the higher functions originate as actual relations between human individuals.
> (Vygotsky, 1978: 57)

Vygotsky's point here is at the heart of Bernstein's account of language as it is used in social situations. Consider tradesmen vs. yourself and spouse and/or friends in cooperative activities that cannot be completed alone – for example, getting a large piece of furniture upstairs, via a rather awkward staircase. Pulling this off requires professional movers and removers to have not only a clear grasp of their goal, but also a capability to judge their immediate situation with respect to that goal. There will certainly be some grunting, but judgements of width, balance, weight, momentum, and so on, will be accompanied by a bit of puffing, and a deal of appreciating mutually and tactilely how things are going. At any point in the exercise "Steady . . ." conveys, very explicitly but without saying it, what adjustment the partner needs to make. Tradesmen do this effortlessly: spouses and friends screw up and get very annoyed with each other when they try it. The point here is that where there is a high degree of shared, tacit understanding, language is largely unnecessary for the coordination of human interaction: bodies, their nudges and winks, reactions to each other's efforts, suffice for the completion of a *shared* project. Spouses and friends struggle to appreciate the significance of what they feel through their fumblings and struggles for the joint task; and consequently, even when one of them does have this appreciation, they lack the immediate ability to coordinate the enterprise through language: stating that "you up there need to back off a bit on your left hand load and shimmy your hips to the right while I make a step up onto the next stair to counterbalance that move of yours" doesn't come easily or economically in the heat of the moment. Why does it not? Why do the linguistic resources available to them not immediately provide a word that is appropriate for this moment?

These are important questions, because they bring us to the core of the two concerns that we find in both Vygotsky and Bernstein's work. First, in their goal of elucidating the character of the relationships that exist when people undertake joint activities (irrespective of whether these are cooperative, as in the case of shifting furniture or buying a beer; competitive, as in the case of playing tennis seriously; a weird mixture of both, as in professional wrestling; or perhaps even none of these, such as what is involved in hosting a successful dinner party, play-fighting, and practicing how to pack down a scrum in rugby). And, second, their concern with where language fits into these joint activities, and in what different ways it can fit. Thinking about the physical act of moving furniture is useful in setting the scene for our exploring how to shift some of the conceptual furniture around these two concerns, as is thinking about play-fighting and practicing. Moving furniture involves a goal that is mutually grasped, and which is pursued by mutually grasping a physical object, and then being able to sense tactilely the moment-to-moment shifts of weight, balance, and what is needed to be done, bodily-in-concert, to go forward. This is a multichannel activity, in which the embodied sensitivities of each participant become a shared experiential field, overlaid with facial expressions, eye contact, eye pointing, and so on, all structured around what they are jointly seeking to achieve: the agreed goal. Practising is interesting, because it is concerned with sensitizing and orienting towards sensitivity: a building up of a grasp of "what counts" with respect to "what is to be achieved". Play contributes here, because it is to do with all of this without there necessarily being a goal, *and hence*, provides a frame in which agreed goals can be constructed – which can subsequently be practiced – until they become joint skills.

Most of the above can be accomplished non-verbally; so where does language fit into all this? This is the question we pursue, within the classical framework, in the next section.

Language and interaction

Vygotsky and Bernstein have similar but different takes on these ideas. Both share the view that social structure is centrally important to understanding how language comes to be used, and how it subsequently comes to reorganize, for want of a better phrase, cognitive abilities. We can appeal to Voloshinov for a framework that underwrites their two sets of ideas:

> Every sign, as we know, is a construct between socially organized persons in the process of their interaction. Therefore, the forms of signs are conditioned above all by the social organization of the participants involved and also by the immediate conditions of their interaction . . . This is the order that the actual generative process of language follows: *social intercourse is generated . . . in it verbal communication and interaction are generated; and in the latter, forms of speech performances are generated; finally, this generative process is reflected in the change of language forms.* (1973: 21, 96)

Bernstein captures this relationship between language and social structure with his notion of language codes.

What is special about Bernstein's idea of a *code* is that he does not see it as a fixed scheme for translating patterns expressed in one symbolic scheme into another like, say, the Morse code. Rather, in his sense, a code functions more as a *formative tendency* or *principle*, in a way similar to the functioning of DNA in determining a person's bodily resemblances to other family members. As Bernstein (1971) himself suggests, "it is reasonable to argue that the genes of social class may well be carried in a communication code that social class itself promotes" (p. 143).

His essential point is that in a very close relationship, the parties to it have such intimate knowledge of each other and their skills that little needs to be said for them to effectively coordinate their activities. As relationships become less intimate – as shared presuppositionality declines – then more needs to be said to enable a shared understanding to be established. Thus, for example, in a shared visual environment, pronouns are quite adequate for coordinating activities. "Give me that one" is a sufficient directive in this case, but not sufficient when a common orienting framework is absent: "that one" needs to be specified more particularly – "the small red widget to the left of the green one". This framework need not be visual, but can be based in shared practices.

Consequently, there is no pressure in a small scale, low tech, social group to develop an elaborate language-based coding system for effective communication. Roles here are interchangeable: no one, bar the medicine man, has exclusive skills. In a differentiated society, the situation is different. Meaning needs explicit formulation when it is not able to fall back on shared contextual support. There is a large body of literature on parent–child interaction which is broadly compatible with this approach (see Light, 1983, for a review). Essentially, the claim is that culture comprises knowledge that may have an explicit or implicit form of coding; and that the cognitive operations of members of a culture operate with the symbols available within that culture. Consequently, analytic thought will be facilitated in cultures or subcultures which supply symbols that have resulted from a process of analysis, and hence explicitly code cultural knowledge in "elaborated chunks".

Put alternatively in a Vygotskian perspective, the point is that knowledge is reproduced in interactive situations. Those situations not only supply explicit symbols, but are also structured in ways that, being informed by an explicit symbolizer, present cultural knowledge to the novitiate in explicit, already analysed "chunks". If this is the case, then knowledge will readily make the transition from the implicit, tacit, intermental realm to explicit intramental ones. Conversely, where interactions do not exhibit such a structure, knowledge will remain implicitly coded, and its explicit intramental coding is less likely to be facilitated for those to whom the world is so transacted.

Implicit in these views is the claim that cognitive abilities and their development are inherently social practices (in contradistinction to the Piagetian paradigm, in which the knower constructs knowledge on the basis of his or her individual interactions with the world). Hence the notion of "scaffolding" is of crucial importance. Scaffolding refers to the way an adult structures the problem-solving contexts which provide the bedrock on which cognitive development is founded. Adults may set up problem-solving situations so that infants and children find it more or less difficult to extract the elements of problems, and master the principles that both underlie (and constitute) them. These principles are mastered because the data the child requires to formulate a solution to the problem is presented in a way that facilitates the extraction of the structure of the problem. Adults who themselves lack practice in explicitly coding such principles themselves will scaffold the interactive teaching situation differently, and make the abstraction of explicit knowledge from the interaction more difficult for their pupil.

This is clear in the following extracts from Hess and Shipman's study (1965), which describes the teaching techniques of three mothers who are showing their children how to solve a sorting problem. Here, we have reversed the order in which Hess and Shipman discuss these mothers, so as to convey a better "feel" for the difficulties facing the child who is being taught. They describe the interaction between the mother and child in a structured teaching situation. The wide range of individual differences in the linguistic and interactional styles of these mothers may be illustrated by excerpts from transcriptions of tape recordings of the "teaching" situations.

One mother introduces the task to her child as follows:

- *I've got some chairs and cars, do you want to play the game?*
- Child does not respond.
- Mother continues: *O.K. What's this?*
- Child: *A wagon?*
- Mother: *Hm?*
- Child: *A wagon?*
- Mother: *This is not a wagon. What's this?*

The conversation continues with this sort of exchange for several pages. Here, the child is not provided with the essential information he needs to solve or to understand the problem. There is clearly some impelling on the part of the mother for the child to perform, but the child has not been told what to do (*ibid.*: 881–2).

A second mother's style offers a bit more clarity and precision. She says in introducing the same task:

- Mother: *Now, I'll take them all off the board; now you put them all back on the board. What are these?*
- Child: *A truck.*
- Mother: *All right, just put them right here; put the other one right here; all right, put the other one there.*

This mother relies on non-verbal communication accompanying her commands to convey the task to her child; she does not define the task for the child; the child is not provided with ideas or information that she can grasp in attempting to solve the problem; neither is she told what to expect or what the task is, even in general terms.

The [final] mother outlines the task for the child, and gives sufficient help and explanation to permit the child to proceed on her own.

- Mother: *All right, Susan, this board is the place where we put the little toys; first of all you're supposed to learn how to place them according to colour.*

> *Can you do that? The things that are all the same colour you put in one*
> *section; in the second section you put another group of colours, and in the*
> *third section you put the last group of colours. Can you do that? Or would*
> *you like to see me do it first?*
– Child: *I want to do it.*

This mother has given explicit information about the task and what is expected of the child; she has offered support and help of various kinds; and she has made it clear that she expects the child to perform.

The overall results of this investigation show a strong correlation between each mother's social class, how she taught a problem, and her child's subsequent ability to solve it, and to explain the means of solution (that is, not merely succeed through uninformed imitation). In addition, Hess and Shipman report differences in speech style among the mothers on Bernstein's "elaborated–restricted" dimension which underpin these teaching styles, and a theoretically consistent difference in what they term "person vs. status orientation". Middle-class mothers legitimize their instructions to their children by appeal to personal responsibility; lower-class mothers to status roles and authority.

In a similar study, but one where the mother's style of teaching was assessed by having her teach a child other than her own, and the child's mode of learning assessed by the experimenter teaching a task to the child, Hartmann and Haavind (1981) found a strong relationship between maternal teaching style and child "educability": not only were children whose mothers presented the task to them in explicit form more likely to learn the task, they also showed a more "interested" and "cooperative" approach to being taught. Hartmann and Haavind claim, then, that what is being measured in such experiments is an enduring style of teaching on the mother's part, a characteristic mode of action which she exhibits over long periods of time. Further, children develop similarly enduring "traits" in their approaches to learning and problem-solving situations. But what, exactly, is being taught and learned here?

Attentional orientation

> It is contended that members of the unskilled and semi-skilled strata, relative
> to the middle classes, do not merely place different significances upon different
> classes of objects, but that their perception is of a qualitatively different order.
> (Bernstein: 1958: 24)

The Estonian ethologist and semiotician, Jakob von Uexküll, makes the notion of an *Umwelt* play a pivotal role in his effort (1957) to understand animal behaviour. Von Uexküll's *Umwelt* is a specification of an animal's environment in relation to the animal's sensory capabilities. Von Uexküll makes the important point that the perspectives and possibilities available to an animal are not things seen "from outside of" the evolving system, but are constituted within it, in an animal's perception of its environment, in its *Umwelt.*

His point is that animals provide "value-perspectives" that determine the way in which "the world" is presented to them. Sensory systems are not passive trans-ducers of information, but constitutive transducers. Some of these value-perspec-tives are given to animals as a result of their evolutionary histories; and some may be "imported" into the constitutive perceptual system by learning. Either way, the world is presented to an animal as possessing objects that are meaningful to it through the values that arise by its being in a particular relation to its environ-ment. It is in this sense that von Uexküll's *Umwelt* contains meaningful items:

> because no animal ever plays the role of an observer, one may assert that they never enter into relationships with neutral objects. Every action . . . that consists of perception and operation imprints its meaning on the meaningless object and thereby makes it into a subject-related meaning-carrier in the respective Umwelt (subjective universe). (1982 [1940]: 27, 31)

Thus, beginning to make sense of its world is not something any organism has to put a lot of work into. Organisms do not neutrally experience the world, and then have to build up massive interpretive skills so as to assign significance and meaning to events: significance in the sense of "what-to-do-next" is built directly into the way their perception is pre-structured; the world is "presented" to the organism as already containing many of its "interests". Or, put another way, relational knowledge has been sedimented into the *Umwelts* that organisms have on the world so as to inform the view their perceptual systems present to them. How does this "informing" come about?

This "informing" occurs, we suggest, in two ways. First, perceptual systems are selective in what, by way of their structure, they present to organisms as their view of the world. We might never know the answer to the philosopher Thomas Nagel's question (1974) "What is it like to be a bat?", but we can be quite certain that the landscape a bat navigates its way around is perceptually quite different from the view our perceptual systems present to us of that same landscape. This is the first way in which perceptual systems inform actions: by constituting the view an organism has of "what interests it in the world" – what it attends to. The second way is with respect to organisms – such as humans and probably most mammals – that have been equipped by evolution to be more reliant on knowledge they build into their perceptual relations with their world within their own lifetimes.

This *Umwelt* approach finds a resonance in Gibson's "ecological psychology" (1966, 1979), for, in a sense, many of the "affordances" that Gibson describes as being specified in the sensory arrays that organisms "pick up on" – especially as they move around in their worlds – are those parts of the organism's *Umwelt* that provide the organism with a direct presentation of the world as it is interested in it: they are attuned to pick up what they "need". Either objects stand out as meaningful to an organism because of what its biology brings to it as its perspectives, or by "an *improvement of perceiving with practice and the education of attention* – [by which means] – Differences are noticed that were previously not noticed. Features become distinctive that were formerly vague" (Gibson, 1979: 254, our emphasis).

Biology provides a perspective such that an organism's sense organs are selected so as to attune for it an appropriate *Umwelt*. *Individual learning* experiences provide an "improvement of perceiving with practice". And for humans, individual learning is inherently a *cultural activity*: an "education of attention" through providing the developing human with interactive experiences that involve body and mind in attuning his or her perceptions to a shared *Umwelt*, and thereby recruiting the process of human development into social practices in which orientations are generated and regenerated (rather than acquired) (cf. Bourdieu, 1988).

An example of how this leads to highlighting the difference between the traditional cognitive approach and the one we are moving to here is to consider placing two adults from different cultures, or an expert and novice from the same culture, in the "same" situation. These adults will regard their situation differently. On the one hand, the cognitive explanation would be that they bring different cultural knowledges or representations to their situation so as to handle the same sensory inputs differently. In our new perspective, these people are attuned to their environments differently, making them effectively living in different worlds that afford them different opportunities. The difference is not in their ways of representing their environment inside their heads, but in the ways they experience that environment as providing opportunities for their actions.

Vygotsky again: revisiting the decontextualization of mediational means

Vygotsky characterizes infant attention as involuntary: it is "captured" by "strong" stimuli. These can be external, such that the infant's attention can be captured by a bright light, a loud noise, or a human face. "Internal" stimuli also influence attention by narrowing down what external events can capture attention at any particular moment:

> Even in the youngest child, the state of hunger elicits a number of specific reactions. Instead of a non-differentiated state, that is, the state between sleeping and vigilance, some coordinated movements appear: a child reaches for his mother's breast, all the peripheral movements recede into the background, all the child's behaviour organizes itself in accordance with this dominant stimulus . . . This type of attention is characterized by its non-intentional, non-volitional character. Any strong and sudden stimulus immediately attracts the child's attention and reconstructs his behaviour. (Vygotsky and Luria, 1993: 187)

The task in development is first to find ways of organizing the direction of attention so that it can be sustained without continuous disruption from these "strong" stimuli, and, second, to develop planning skills that can be exercised "internally" so as to maintain a hold over attention, not so that it can just be held to "the task at hand", but also to "the task in mind". Vygotsky's claim is that "natural forms of attention cannot satisfy this condition and it is evident that alongside these forms there have to develop some other mechanisms. Artificial, voluntary, 'cultural' attention must emerge and is the most necessary condition for any work" (*ibid.*: 187–8).

Vygotsky characterizes the "education of attention" as beginning with its "natural" propensities, becoming a "cultural operation", and finally incorporating "specific cultural devices" that lead to the reconstruction and regulation of the child's given psychological functions. The general problem as framed by Vygotsky is this:

> The central characteristic of elementary functions is that they are totally and directly determined by stimulation from the environment. For higher functions, the central feature is self-generated stimulation, that is, the creation and use of artificial stimuli which become the immediate causes of behaviour. (1978: 39)

The general character of Vygotsky's solution is this:

> The inclusion of a sign in one or other behavioural process . . . reforms the whole structure of the psychological operation as the inclusion of a tool reforms the whole structure of a labour operation. (1982: 103; cited in van der Veer and Valsiner, 1991: 220)

A specific claim is that all people possess the same "lower", or "natural", or "elementary" psychological processes. But, depending on the degree of elaboration of the various symbol systems used in different cultures, people could vary widely in their mental functioning, in their "higher", or "instrumental", or "cultural" psychological processes. The ontological claim that results from Vygotsky's analysis of "human nature" is that

> The origin of all, specifically human, higher psychological processes, therefore, cannot be found in the mind or brain of an individual person but rather should be sought in the social "extracerebral" sign systems a culture provides. (*Ibid.*: 222)

The first stage in this process of "educating attention" is introducing cultural organisers into the child's natural *Umwelt* via gesture and speech:

> At first, a child takes in the picture of his surroundings in a diffuse manner; however, his mother only has to point out some object and name it in order for that object to stand out from its surroundings precisely in the way the mother pointed it out and in order that the child turn his attention particularly to it. For the first time, the process of attention begins to function as a

cultural operation . . . Attention becomes a real function only when the child himself masters the means of creating the additional stimuli that focus his attention on individual components of a situation and that eliminate everything else from the background. (Vygotsky and Luria, 1993: 189)

The crucial point that Vygotsky pursues is how, after mastering techniques for manipulating the environment, "the child at a certain moment begins to organize his psychological processes with the help of these manipulations. How does this complicated cultural activity of attention proceed?" (*ibid.*). Vygotsky essays his answer via a study conducted by Leontiev (see, for example, Leontiev, 1981) with 8–9-year-old children.

The problem the children were confronted with requires a deal of concentrated attention. The structure of the study was designed to provide insights into how the children accomplished this. First, the children are confronted with a specific and convoluted task. They are asked a set of questions, some of which can be answered by naming a colour:

"Do you go to school?" "What colour is your desk?" "Do you like playing games?" "What colour can grass be?", and so on. Answers are required to be given quickly, and with two conditions: a colour cannot be named twice, and two colours (for example, black and white) must never be used in an answer. The children found this an almost impossible task. They were then given a set of coloured cards that they could use as external markers to assist them in sustaining their attention and keeping things straight. The reasoning here was that if children tend to be dominated by external events, then providing them with cards that could function as external holders for their attention, they would find the task easier: "external actions help him organize his behaviour. Operating with the help of the cards, he organizes his inner processes in the same way". (Vygotsky and Luria, 1993: 190)

The first approach the children adopted was to lay out all the coloured cards they had been given, face up on the table, and take out the two forbidden colours, placing them face down on the table. This might seem intuitively sensible, because the array of cards now indicates, and keeps in front of them, only those colours that they were allowed to use in their answers. However, this approach doesn't work, because "in order to achieve success, the child should not remove the forbidden elements from the sphere of his attention, but *should make the process of attention mediated*; he must fix his attention specifically on the forbidden elements" (*ibid.*). That is, since untutored attention has a tendency to be dominated by what is in the environment, removing the wrong answers from one's view is counterproductive to wrenching attention away from the perceptual field. It might then seem that it would make better sense to turn over all the cards *but* the forbidden ones. However, this solution is not very workable either, because the child's attention is focused on a sign for the *wrong* answer, and there is no external prop as to an alternative, non-prompted, acceptable answer.

The children then devised a prompt system that both focused their attention on the unacceptable answer and prompted an acceptable one: place the forbidden cards face up in a row separate from the other cards, closer to oneself, and then when asked a question, do not answer directly but look at the forbidden card to check if the answer one was going to give is not allowed, and then select an alternative answer: "What colour can snow be?" . . . likely answer "white" . . . but white is forbidden, so answer after another look; "Brown after it turns slushy in the fields and people have walked through it": "forbidding one colour causes the inhibition of certain answers; turning to different, new situations a new roundabout path of thought" (Vygotsky and Luria, 1993: 191). To deal with the additional rule of not using the same colour in an answer twice resulted in the children then taking a colour card they had already named and putting it with the forbidden cards. Subsequently, the child who solves the problem in this way stops using the cards, and continues successfully without the external props.

> How are we to explain this change in behaviour? Under close examination we are convinced that the process of attention still remained indirect; only instead of externally indirect, it became *internally indirect*. Having learned to use auxiliary tools with the outer material cards, the child works out a series of inner auxiliary techniques. Instead of spreading out the forbidden cards in front of him, *he fixes in his mind* (visually or, even better verbally) on these two forbidden colours and then by means of these fixed colours gives all his answers. (*Ibid.*: 192)

Thus, via external support, the child develops a culturally skilled control of his or her attention: it becomes *mediated* through the training process so as to be controlled by the child, and not "captured" by the environment: instead, the child orients to his or her environment. Whichever way we might explain this transformation, Vygotsky captures here the important point that cultural activities have become incorporated into the developing processes and contributed directly to their elaboration, transforming the course of psychological development not by making given abilities more powerful – by augmenting them – but by changing them in their structural and functional characteristics as mind and cultural environment interact with each other in real time. This interaction is itself not one between an individual mind and objects in an inert environment, but with a cultural environment populated by other people who are already doing particular things: that is, development occurs in joint actions between people, whose minds are embodied, and whose bodies are likewise "enminded".

Speech genres, orientations, and the "sensing" of similarities

Both Bernstein and Vygotsky, in line with the presuppositions of their time, take it as a basic fact that living beings *categorize* things in relating themselves to their surroundings, that they act as if they can put the different things they encounter into bounded containers of a specific kind. More in accord with the corporeal turn we outlined above – in which the role of "recurring, dynamic patterns of a distinctive nature" (Johnson, 2007: 73) becomes central – we, however, want to suggest that *sensing similarities* is in fact more basic, and that our abilities to classify and categorize depend on it. Further, as William James (1890) noted long ago, such sensings are not of an *objective* (or representational) kind: "The truth is," he said, "that large tracts of human speech are nothing but *signs of direction* in thought, of which direction we nevertheless have an acutely discriminative sense, though no definite sensorial image plays any part in it whatsoever . . . Their function is to lead from one set of images to another . . . [they] must be described as in very large measure constituted of *feelings of tendency*, often so vague that we are unable to name them at all" (pp. 253–4).

In the light of these comments, we would now like to turn to Bakhtin's notion of speech genres, as a more "situated" or "grounded" alternative to Bernstein's rather abstract notion of codes. Basic to his notion of codes is the idea of their being realized by certain social categories of people (e.g., teachers) in specific practices: "Practices are the realization of categories . . . The practice can be regarded as the "message" of the category and is *the means of its acquisition*," he says (Bernstein, 1981: 334), and this leads him into making a clear distinction between "voice" and "message". "The positioning of the subject creates the 'voice' of the subject but *not* the specific message. The 'voice' sets the *limits* on what can be a legitimate message" (p. 338).

Making use of Bakhtin's (1986) notion of speech genres, Wertsch (1991) examines teachers' uses of what he calls the "speech genre of formal instruction" (p. 112). For instance, in asking such "instructional questions" (Mehan, 1979) as: "How many tens and how many ones are there in the top number (pointing at a number on the blackboard)?," a teacher is clearly working within a set of pre-existing, explicit schemes aimed at regulating the "students' mental processes (such as thinking or attention) in ways that are appropriate for the Socio-cultural setting of the classroom" (p. 112) – in which, of course, the power difference between the voice of the teacher and the voices of the pupils is palpable.

Bakhtin (1986) refines Bernstein's somewhat *monological* notion of a code by suggesting that to speak in a particular voice is to speak with a particular, *dialogically responsive* orientation or relation towards those whom one thinks of oneself as addressing – it is the situating of our utterances in a dialogically structured context that is missing in the notion of a code. As he puts it: "An essential (constitutive) marker of the utterance is its quality of being directed to someone, its *addressivity* . . . Each speech genre in each area of speech communication has its own typical conception of the addressee, and this defines it as a genre" (p. 95).

In saying this, Bakhtin introduces two issues of great importance – which we feel are not well expressed in Bernstein's use of the term "code". One is an emphasis on the fact that the main purpose of communication, of a speaker's utterance, is not the transmission of correct information, nor a matter of providing a true representation of an environmental state of affairs, but the *orienting* of an other towards a speaker's possible *future* intentions. Again, as Bakhtin (1986) puts it:

> The fact is that when the listener perceives and understands the meaning (the language meaning) of speech, he simultaneously takes an active, responsive attitude toward it. He either agrees or disagrees with it (completely or partially), augments it, applies it, prepares for its execution, and so on. And the listener adopts this responsive attitude for the entire duration of the process of listening and understanding . . . As we know, the role of the *others* for whom the utterance is constructed is extremely great . . . From the very beginning, the speaker expects a response from them, an active responsive understanding. *The entire utterance is constructed, as it were, in anticipation of encountering this response.* (94; our emphasis)

In other words, a crucial function of our utterances – what Vygotsky (1986) calls the "functional use" (p. 108) of words, and James (1890) alludes to in talking of our "acute discriminative sense" as functioning "to lead [us] from one set of images to another" (p. 253) – is to arouse anticipations in our listeners as to what next we might do or say. It is this anticipatory function that the notion of a code fails to depict.

The other important feature of our relations to the others and othernesses in our surroundings that Bakhtin's (1986) notion of a speech genre emphasizes is that these relations are not of a one-way, mechanical kind, in which two or more "things" of a fixed nature merely *inter*-act. To be involved in dialogically structured activities, is to be involved in two-way, living relationships of a mutually responsive kind, in which, not inter-actions but *intra*-actions occur. Like being "in" love, becoming truly involved in dialogue with others is to become involved "in" a dialogical space or reality with its own unique, contextualized character. "When one begins to hear voices in languages, jargons, and styles," says Bakhtin (1986):

> these cease to be potential means of expression and become actual, realized expression; the voice that has mastered them has entered into them. They are called to play their own unique and unrepeatable role in speech (creative) communication . . . Confidence in another's word, reverential reception . . . apprenticeship, the search for and mandatory nature of deep meaning, *agreement*, its infinite gradations and shadings . . . the layering of meaning upon meaning, voice upon voice . . . These special relations can be reduced neither to the purely logical nor to the purely thematic. Here one encounters *integral* positions, integral personalities (the personality does not require extensive disclosure – it can be articulated in a single sound, revealed in a single word), precisely *voices*. (p. 121)

To understand precisely what a person's utterance means, we need to under-stand not just the linguistic meaning of a person's words, but what the person actually meant in uttering them in a particular manner (intonation, pacing, pausing, etc.) – to understand it as a radically singular event, with its own unique dynamical shape, its own "vitality form" (Stern, 2004), at the time and in the context of their voicing.

It is difficult in such a short chapter as this to demonstrate how radical this claim is. But, in line with our corporeal turn, we must assume that, at first, we orient towards a speaker with certain embodied anticipations at the ready, so to speak, as to what their utterances *will* mean, and we then attempt to confirm that we have actually "got" their meaning by our responses to them. And in this process, in moving from a relatively indeterminate to a more determinate state of affairs, from a field of possible meanings to a speaker's actual meaning, we each help to "create" a meaning *uniquely* related to the context of its occurrence. This means, of course, that our thinking in relation to things, and our expressing those thoughts linguistically, are so bound up together that it is only as an abstraction that we can conceive of language as a pre-given system of possible signs from which a speaker can select a set of those relevant to his or her purposes. Signs as such are not the prerequisites for communication but its products.

Prior to our acquisition of language, children as young as two years old could – on the basis of, we presume, the embodied, preconceptual "image schemas" that Johnson (2009) describes in terms of "recurring dynamic patterns of a distinctive nature" (p. 73) – pantomime in a gestural manner the dynamic, relational features of objects portrayed in pictures (see Vygotsky, 1978: 32–3). It is this bodily, gestural aspect of speech, that can function in both a mimetic and indicative fashion, that others can make use of very early on in teaching us to judge what is of significance to us in our surroundings, and what is not. In other words, prior to language acquisition proper, it seems that even very young children can develop in their involved engagements with adults, a set of embodied anticipations which can function as what Todes (2001) calls a "ground floor of perceptually objective experience" (p. 100) which provides a basis for the later expression of more linguistically well organized expressions.

Conclusions: sixth sense, second nature, and our embodied ways of being in the world

Given our emphasis here, then, on what is involved, not in learning new facts, but in achieving a new orientation, we think it is now clear that, if the indeterminate "somethings" before us are new, never before encountered somethings that need to be identified uniquely "*as themselves*", then we cannot be told *about* them in terms representative of "things" already well known to us. We must first "introduce" ourselves to them, so to speak, to become acquainted with how they will respond to a range of our actions. We need to acquire some initial embodied anticipations in the course of practical involvements with them, if we are to "go on" with exploring their nature further. In other words, rather than treating ourselves as already having a complete mastery of our first language, and as learning to use theoretical talk like we learn to use a second language – to describe what is already well known to us, but now in terms that reveal aspects of it previously unknown to us – we must, even as adults, still treat ourselves as like *first-language learners*, as still having to distinguish, and to respond to the unique what-ness of previously unencountered, indeterminate "things" – that is, as still learning to make evaluative and contextualized judgments in determining what *in fact* they *should be* for us in ways that are intelligible (and useful) to the others sharing that context with us.

But as we intimated above, this is not easy. Achieving a new orientation entails our responding, not to representational (aboutness) uses of language, but to what Vygotksy (1986) calls its *functional* use, its use in directing our attention to certain distinctive features in our surroundings, and to "seeing" connections between them, i.e., to using language in a much more indirect, allusive fashion. The noun-language of Standard Average European (SAE), as Whorf (1956) terms it, is less than helpful, as it orients us towards "seeing" continuous processes only in terms of things and substances, i.e., as structures of already made things, and (mis)leads us into talking of things still-in-the-making in a similar way, i.e., again as already made things, and into a way of orienting to surroundings which, in fact, *reverses* the actual character of our relation to them.

In relation to our current concerns, this influence was blatant in the original mistranslation of the title of Vygotsky's (1962, 1986) final work as *Thought and Language*, with Norris Minick's later attempt (Vygotsky, 1987) to put this right as *Thinking and Speech*. But like Vygotsky, we have not been concerned with language as a substantive system, as a structure, or even a structurizing set of already spoken *forms*, but with the talk-intertwined nature of our bodily *activities*, and with the ways in which what *just happens to us* in such activities provides us with that sixth sense that is the basis of our judging the similarities between things – what both Vygotsky (1986) and Wittgenstein (1953) tried to capture in alluding to family relations and resemblances.

What is crucial, as we see it, is that it is only from within our living involvements with the others and othernesses around us that this kind of meaningful, anticipatory, responsive understanding can become available to us (Shotter, 1993, 2006, 2008, 2010). And this is what we think is so special about both Vygotsky's and Bernstein's inquiries into what is involved in children growing into the intellectual lives of those around them: it is not the nature of the actual knowledge children acquire that is of interest to them (and to us), but the nature of the orientations, the ways of relating to their surroundings, the attitudes that they learn to adopt to events occurring around them – which they learn implicitly in the course of their everyday practical involvements with those around them – that are of importance. For it is in these involvements that they (and we as adults) can learn to make the judgements of similarity that can enable them (and us), prior to categorizing and classifying things linguistically, to express these judgements in their (and our) actions.

As we have indicated above, treating "seeing the similarities" as primitive, requires a reconceptualization of the role of judgement in concept formation. As Michael Taussig (1993) suggests, in *Mimesis and Alterity* (1993), it is "that famous "sixth sense" . . . [which consists in] a formidable mimetic faculty, the basis for judging similitude" (p. 213), which is "the nature that culture uses to create second nature" (p. xiii). And what we have been trying to do in this all too brief exposition is to show how the work begun by Vygotsky and Bernstein can, in the light of recent work that is beginning to look in great detail into the capacities of what we might call the languaged body, be continued further.

References

Atkinson, P. (1985) *Language, Structure and Reproduction: An Introduction to the Sociology of Basil Bernstein*, London: Methuen.

Bakhtin, M. M. (1986) *Speech Genres and Other Late Essays*, trans. Vern W. McGee, Austin, TX: University of Texas Press.

Bernstein, B. (1958) 'Some Sociological Determinants of Perception', *British Journal of Sociology*, 9: 159–74.

—— (1971) *Class, Codes and Control*, vol. 1, London: Routledge & Kegan Paul.

—— (1981) 'Codes, Modalities, and the Process of Cultural Reproduction', *Language in Society*, 10: 327–63.

Bourdieu, P. (1988) *Homo Academicus*, Stanford, CA: Stanford University Press.

Cassirer, E. (1953) *The Philosophy of Symbolic Forms*, vol.1, *Language*, New Haven, CT: University of Yale Press.

—— (1955) *The Philosophy of Symbolic Forms*, vol. 2, *Mythical Thought*, New Haven, CT: University of Yale Press.

—— (1957) *The Philosophy of Symbolic Forms*, vol. 3, *The Phenomenology of Knowledge*, New Haven, CT: University of Yale Press.

Cavell, S. (1989) *This New Yet Unapproachable America*, Albuquerque, NM: Living Batch Press.

Gibson, J. J. (1966) *The Senses Considered as Perceptual Systems*, Boston: Houghton Mifflin.

—— (1979) *The Ecological Approach to Visual Perception*, London: Houghton Mifflin.

Hartmann, E. and Haavind, H. (1981) 'Mothers as Teachers and Their Children as Learners: Study of the Influence of Social Interaction upon Cognitive Development', in W. P. Robinson (ed.), *Communication in Development*, London: Academic Press, 129–58.

Hess, R. and Shipman, V. (1965) 'Early Experience and the Socialization of Cognitive Modes in Children', *Child Development*, 36: 869–86.

James, W. (1890) *Principles of Psychology*, vols. 1 and 2, London: Macmillan.

Johnson, M. (1987) *The Body in the Mind*, Chicago: University of Chicago Press.

—— (2007) *The Meaning of the Body: Aesthetics of Human Understanding*, Chicago and London: University of Chicago Press.

Lakoff, G. and Johnson, M. (1999) *Philosophy in the Flesh: The Embodied Mind and Its Challenge to Western Thought*, New York: Basic Books.

Leontiev, A. N. (1981) *The Development of Mind*, a reproduction of the Progress Publishers 1981 edition, plus "Activity and Consciousness," originally published by Progress Publishers, 1977, New York: Erythrospress.

Light, P. (1983) 'Social Interaction and Cognitive Development: A Review of Post-Piagetian Research', in S. Meadows (ed.), *Developing Thinking: Approaches to Children's Cognitive Development*, London: Methuen, 67–88.

Luria, A. R (1961) *Speech and the Regulation of Behaviour*, London: Pergamon.

Mehan, H. (1979) *Learning Lessons*, Cambridge, MA: Harvard University Press.

Nagel, T. (1974) 'What Is it Like to Be a Bat?,' *Philosophical Review*, 83: 435–50.

Oakeshott, M. (1975) *Of Human Conduct*, Oxford: Oxford University Press.

Rorty, R. (ed.) (1967) *The Linguistic Turn: Recent Essays in Philosophical Method*, Chicago and London: University of Chicago Press.

—— (1979) *Philosophy and the Mirror of Nature*, Oxford: Blackwell.

Ryle, G. (1949) *The Concept of Mind*, London: Methuen.

Saussure, Ferdinand de (1916/1983) *Course in General Linguistics*, ed. Charles Bally and Albert Sechehaye, trans. Roy Harris, La Salle, IL: Open Court.

Sheets-Johnstone, M. (ed.) (1992) *Giving the Body Its Due*, Albany, NY: State University Press.

—— (2009) *The Corporeal Turn: An Interdisciplinary Reader*, Charlottesville, VA and Exeter, UK: Imprint Academic.

—— (2011) 'The Imaginative Consciousness of Movement: Linear Quality, Kinaesthesia, Language and Life', in Tim Ingold (ed.), *Redrawing Anthropology: Materials, Movements, Lines*, Aldershot: Ashgate, 115–28.

Shotter, J. (1993) *Cultural Politics of Everyday Life: Social Constructionism, Rhetoric, and Knowing of the Third Kind*, Milton Keynes: Open University Press/Toronto: University of Toronto Press.

—— (2006) 'Understanding Process from Within: An Argument for "Withness"-Thinking', *Organization Studies*, 27(4): 585–604.

—— (2008) 'Dialogism and Polyphony in Organizational Theorizing: Action Guiding Anticipations and the Continuous Creation of Novelty', *Organization Studies*, 29(4): 501–24.

—— (2010) 'Inside Our Lives Together: A Neo-Wittgensteinian Constructionism', in S. R. Kirschner and J. Martin (eds.), *Socio-Cultural Perspectives in Psychology*, New York: Columbia University Press.

Stern, W. (1924) *Psychology of Early Childhood, up to the Sixth Year of Age*, trans. Anna Barwell from 3rd edn, London: George Allen & Unwin, originally published in 1914.

Stern, D. (2004) *The Present Moment in Psychotherapy and Everyday Life*, New York: W. W. Norton.

Taussig, M. T. (1993) *Mimesis and Alterity: A Particular History of the Senses*, New York: Psychology Press.

Todes, S. (2001) *Body and World*, with introductions by Hubert L. Dreyfus and Piortr Hoffman, Cambridge, MA: MIT Press.

Uexküll, J. von (1957) 'A Stroll through the Worlds of Animals and Men: A Picture Book of Invisible Worlds', in C. H. Schiller, ed. and trans, *Instinctive Behavior: The Development of a Modern Concept*, New York: International Universities Press, 5–80.

—— (1982 [1940]) 'The Theory of Meaning', *Semiotica*, 42: 25–82.

van der Veer, R. and Valsiner, J. (1991) *Understanding Vygotsky: A Quest for Synthesis*, Cambridge: Blackwell.

Voloshinov, V. (1973) *Marxism and the Philosophy of Language*, Boston: Harvard University Press.

Vygotsky, L. S. (1962) *Thought and Language*, trans. and ed. E. Hanfmann and G. Vakar, Cambridge, MA: MIT Press.

—— (1978) *Mind in Society: The Development of Higher Psychological Processes*, eds. M. Cole, V. John-Steiner, S. Scribner and E. Souberman, Cambridge, MA: Harvard University Press.

—— (1986) *Thought and Language*, trans. and ed. A. Kozulin, Cambridge, MA: MIT Press.

—— (1987) *The Collected Works of L. S. Vygotsky*, vol.1, *Problems of General Psychology*, includes the volume *Thinking and Speech*, trans. N. Minick, New York: Plenum.

Vygotsky, L. and Luria, A. (1993). *Studies on the History of Behavior: Ape, Primitive, and Child*, Hillsdale, NJ: Erlbaum.

Wertsch, J. V. (1991) *Voices of the Mind: a Socio-cultural Approach to Mediated Action*, London: Harvester Wheatsheaf.

Whorf, B. L. (1956) *Language, Thought and Reality: Selected Writings of Benjamin Lee Whorf*, ed. J. B. Carroll, Cambridge, MA: MIT Press.

Wittgenstein, L. (1953) *Philosophical Investigations*, trans. G.E. M. Anscombe, Oxford: Blackwell.

5 The concept of semiotic mediation: perspectives from Bernstein's sociology

Ruqaiya Hasan

Introduction

Over the last three decades, Vygotsky's work has become widely known among psychologists, social activity theorists and, above all, to an influential group of educationists. It is perhaps true to say that among the many brilliant insights provided by Vygotsky, he is best known for his richly productive concepts of *semiotic mediation* and the *zone of proximal development*. The present chapter focuses on the former, for reasons that will become apparent as I proceed. Simply paraphrased, semiotic mediation is concerned with the cultural mediation of mental development through acts of semiosis. The concept is set to become even more relevant to our ways of thinking about mental development as current trends in neurological research continue. Several well-known specialists have argued (for example, Edelman, 1992; Greenfield, 1996; Deacon, 1997) that both in the evolution of *homo sapiens* as well as in the development of any member of the species, the functioning of brain/mind cannot be dissociated from the experience of living with others. Susan Greenfield has described mind as a 'personalized brain' which develops the forms of consciousness that it does by virtue of what it experiences from day one of its inception. Since a large part of our experience of living is fashioned by our semiotic acts, i.e., by our acts of meaning and, because semiotic acts presuppose an 'other', both the social and the semiotic are crucially implicated in the processes of the formation of consciousness. My interest is based on the belief that the concept of consciousness is central to any code-based theory of sociology such as that of Bernstein. How consciousness is formed; how its distribution varies in form across different classes and groups in a society; what institutions contribute, and how, to such distribution; and what part variation in consciousness plays in the production and reproduction of society are all issues of importance to such a theory of sociology. In this chapter I will argue that Bernstein's 'take' on the issue of consciousness is of primary relevance to Vygotsky's concept of semiotic mediation. Not only do Bernstein's sociological insights contribute to the reach of the concept, but any application of it in official pedagogic sites that is not informed by such insights is simply likely to contribute to the reproduction of patterns of social injustices that have been long known to inhere in our educational systems. Before turning to this task, let me first present my understanding of Vygotsky's concept.

Semiotic mediation in the development of mind

Vygotsky postulated two lines for the genesis of human mental activity: (1) the 'natural', which was rooted in human biology, i.e., it had a bio-genetic foundation, and (2) the social, which was rooted in human culture and, thus, had a socio-genetic foundation. Human consciousness was seen as the product of the interweaving of these two lines of development. Mental activities, with their roots in biogenetic foundation, were referred to as *elementary mental functions* and they were said not to display the qualities that are specifically human – qualities which were to be found only in socio-genetically founded *higher mental functions*. Vygotsky (1978: 39; emphasis mine) maintained that:

> even at early stages of historical development, humans went beyond the psychological functions given to them by nature and *proceeded to a new culturally-elaborated organization* of their behaviour.

In the socio-genesis of such organization of human behaviour, the intervention of some variety of tool plays a crucial part. For example, in the practical sphere of physical labour, the use of *concrete tools* changes the very nature of human performance: not only does this mediation by *technical or concrete tools* alter the structure of human labour, but it also eventually affects the nature of the environment in which humans live. The same situation obtains in the sphere of mental labour, i.e., in making the human mind work. Here, too, mediation by tools changes the quality of mental functions and this:

> alters the entire flow and structure of mental functions. It does this by determining the structure of a new instrumental act just as a technical tool alters the process of a natural adaptation by determining the form of labour operation. (Vygotsky, 1981: 137)

In time, the alteration in mental functions will reveal itself also as changes effected in the human social and material environment.[1] But the tool that mediates mental activity is of a different order from concrete tools: it is *abstract, psychological* and *semiotic*. The *higher mental functions* mediated by this abstract tool display those qualities which Vygotsky considered to belong uniquely and specifically only to human mental life, representing a break from the biologically given to the culturally mediated. Below is one account of Vygotsky's views of these qualities (translation by Wertsch, 1985a: 26):

> [their] basic and distinguishing features are intellectualization and mastery, that is, conscious realization and voluntariness.

---

1 It is not fanciful to detect here the Bernsteinian theme of social subjects' internalization of the 'outside' and their modes of externalizing the 'inside'. Note also that this conceptualization of the relations between culture–mind–action–environmental change anticipate Popper's views on 'exo-somatic evolution' (1979).

At the centre of development during the school age is the transition from the lower functions of attention and memory to higher functions of voluntary attention and logical memory . . . the intellectualization of functions and their mastery represent two moments of one and the same process – the transition to higher psychological functions. We master a function to the extent that it is intellectualized. The voluntariness in the activity is always the other side of its conscious realization. To say that memory is intellectualized in school is exactly the same as to say that voluntary recall emerges; to say that attention becomes voluntary in school age is exactly the same as saying . . . that it depends more and more on thought, that is, on intellect.

Semiotic acts are acts of meaning and these can be construed in any semiotic modality, of which language is just one. But, although Vygotsky recognized the value of other modalities, such as gesture and image, he attached significantly greater importance to language. Thus, in the literature, by default, *semiotic mediation* has come to mean *mediation by means of the linguistic sign*. This was not because Vygotsky was bowing to the imaginary imperialism of linguistics (Bourdieu, 1991) it was because he had thought deeply about language and had actually worked with language, especially in relation to its development in children (Vygotsky, 1962). The study of the development of the mother tongue in children provides the best opportunity to appreciate the power of language, as the process of its acquisition mediates the transformation of a biological organism into a social person. Vygotsky's main interest in young children's acquisition of language, like that of Bernstein's in the context of early acquisition of coding orientation,[2] was not so much in the forms that were being learnt but in what the acquisition did psychically for the child:

> Prior to mastering his own behaviour, the child begins to master his surroundings with the help of speech. This produces new relations with the environment in addition to the new organization of behaviour itself. The creation of these uniquely human forms of behaviour later produce the intellect and become the basis for productive work: the specifically human form of the use of tool. (Vygotsky, 1978: 25)

Semiotic mediation: an analysis of the concept

The above account offers some indication of the centrality of the concept of semiotic mediation to Vygotsky's concern with the production of higher mental functions. Discourse around the concept grows daily (Cole, Engeström and Vasquez, 1997; Engeström *et al.*, 1999; Wells and Claxton, 2002) though has not been subjected to careful analysis. In my view this has had deleterious effect, stopping us from appreciating the full power of the concept as well as its

---

2 Though Bernstein paid meticulous attention to this aspect, because of his commitment to viable research.

need to be complemented by a theoretically sound linguistic and sociological foundation. In this section I will offer such an analysis of the phrase *semiotic mediation*.

The first thing to note is that the phrase represents what Halliday would describe as a grammatical metaphor, whose non-metaphorical form would be *mediate semiotically*. Here *mediate* is a process and *semiotically* refers to a quality of that process – a quality that pertains to semiosis, by means of which mediating is performed. The scenario to which the expression *semiotic mediation* refers is, thus, complex when both components are taken into consideration, as they should be. The point of using *semiotic* as a modifier of the nominalized process *mediation* is precisely that it is not an inherent characteristic of mediation as such: mediation by concrete tools does not have exactly the same character as that by the abstract tool of a meaning-making modality. Part of this has to do with the ubiquity of language: as a primary semiotic modality it pervades nearly all aspects of every single social being. Of course, both are cultural in origin and, of course, they are often not independent of each other. Nonetheless mediation by acts of meaning has specific characteristics which are not shared by mediation by concrete tools (Vygotsky, 1962, 1978; Hasan 1992, 2002). Acts of meaning call for someone who 'means' and someone to whom that meaning is meant: there is a 'meaner', some 'meaning' and a 'meant to'; so, underlying semiotic mediation are, in the last analysis, interactive events of meaning exchange. It follows that wherever there is discourse, i.e., verbal exchange, there is semiotic mediation; this is incontrovertible especially if the success/failure of the mediation is not at issue. Axiomatically, verbal interaction, being a variety of social practice, presupposes social context, and where there is a context for meaning, there also have to exist some relations between and within the components of the interactive events. Thus, when we talk about the semiotic mediation of concepts we are actually talking about concepts growing in and through the processes of meaning exchange between persons in some relation to each other as well as to the object of the interaction. A textbook in the official pedagogic site is as much a bearer of a range of social relations as is a casual conversation, a political discourse, a newspaper editorial or a soap opera on the TV screen.

So much for the term *semiotic*. I take *mediation*, on the other hand, as referring to a process that is inherently transitive, i.e., it calls for at least two participants: *something/someone mediates something*. So, summing up this brief analysis, it seems appropriate to suggest that *semiotic mediation* refers to *mediation by someone of something to someone by means of acts of meaning, typically by the modality of language, which entails a structure of socio-cultural relations*. When the phrase *semiotic mediation* is equated with *cultural mediation*, as it is sometimes, this elides two important aspects of the process: one, its essentially interactive character and everything that inheres in that fact; and two, the constant flow of mediation that inheres in the nature of semiotic action: wherever there is language in use, there is semiotic mediation.

Supposing this analysis to be correct, the fact of interaction by the modality of language in use takes on serious significance, with two consequences which need to be developed briefly. First, semiotic mediation is a logically ordered process, whose course in an analytical perspective may be shown as follows:[3]

> verbal interaction → meanings construing experience → experience construing mind

More specifically, harking back to Greenfield, if human mind is a personalized brain, shaped by what a person experiences then, in the above sequence we are referring to those aspects of human mind that are shaped through semiotic mediation. Following Vygotsky, let me refer to this as constituting (some aspects of) higher mental functions. Higher mental functions are the only functions that are said to have *specifically human characteristics*, from which it follows that anyone whose mental functions do not display these characteristics is at least sub-human, if not non-human. So what are examples of such mental functions? Most instances of semiotic mediation cited in Vygotsky and pursued by other scholars who turn to the concept pertain to areas of knowledge, such as technological concepts, logical/inferential reasoning, ability to form sets i.e., classification of objects/phenomena on some 'logical' basis, generalization, and so on. It is obvious that these mental functions are the ones most valued and nurtured in official pedagogic sites in 'progressive' western-type cultures. Now, these are precisely the mental functions that Luria's Uzbeki subjects were unable to perform successfully (Luria 1976) especially when the content of the tests was remote from the local base of their existence. It does not need to be added that these Uzbekis were not sub-human, nor was their language primitive, thus causing the mediation to be 'deficient' – in fact there are no such things as primitive languages (Hasan 1992). There can be no doubt whatever that they did engage in verbal interaction and, so, they had experience of semiotic mediation. Their minds, too, were socio-genetically formed, so presumably had some variety of higher mental functioning. We are, thus, driven to an inescapable conclusion: different forms of semiotic mediation entail different forms of higher mental function. True to the universal principle: if there is variation in socially rooted phenomena, there will be variation in their valuation. Thus we know that the form of mental function most often cited in the literature on semiotic mediation has a higher value in our culture than the form that Luria found in the Uzbekis which we dubbed 'practical wisdom' and, thus, damned. Given this situation, an adequate theory of semiotic mediation must answer at least two questions:

1   How should we describe the qualities of the various forms of semiotic mediation each of which mediates a distinct form of higher mental function? What does that variety of semiotic mediation have to be like to

---

3 The stages in this sequence are not necessarily temporally separated; however, conceptually they are distinct.

produce the best valued variety of mediation? What explains the difference in valuation?r

2   How can the theory establish some basis for the privileged and privileging status of one as against the other(s)?

To the best of my knowledge, there are no answers in the theory as it stands today; in fact, neither of these questions has ever been raised (but see Hasan, 1992, 1995).

The second conclusion that flows from the analysis of semiotic mediation concerns the nature of language in use and what that implies. As noted above, where there is verbal interaction, there is some social occasion for its occurrence. Language in use is typically responsive to the nature of the occasion, both in terms of legitimate meanings and in terms of their legitimate overall organization: there can be no semiotic mediation out of context. But even more important, participants in the interaction stand in some relation to every component of the context whereas, in the literature across the decades, they have remained faceless, *culturally non-specific* in Bernstein's terms. The upshot is that the socio-genetic process of semiotic mediation appears to occur in a social vacuum and the overall shape of the interaction or its context is never invoked as in any way consequential to the outcome. Of course, Vygotsky often mentions 'the school' but, in an avowedly socio-cultural theory of mental development, there seems to be no concern with the social significance of this critical site for interaction. These lacunae weaken the theory: under the label *semiotic mediation of mental life*, there lurks a complex structure of relations, none of which is probed, let alone integrated into the theory. Wertsch (1985b) did point out the absence of a theory of discourse, suggesting the importation of Bakhtin's approach to speech genres and language in general. However, I suggest this in itself will bring as many problems as it might resolve.[4] A comprehensive and adequate theory of semiotic mediation should provide frameworks at least for:

* understanding the relations of speaker and addressee to each other and to the elements of the occasion of interaction;
* analyzing the relation between the goal of semiotic mediation and the degree of achievement, which is particularly relevant to the evaluation of the variety; and
* identifying the linguistic properties of the different orders of semiotic mediation.

I suggest that such a theory of semiotic mediation does exist: it is Basil Bernstein's sociological theory, which goes a considerable distance in providing answers to many of the questions arising from a fuller understanding of the term. The rest of this chapter is devoted to an elaboration of this claim.

4 See my response (1992) to this suggestion; also see Axel (1997) on participants.

Basil Bernstein and the theory of semiotic mediation

Although Bernstein never used the expression *semiotic mediation* as a technical term in his own theoretical discourse, there is no question in my mind that he fully subscribed to the central thesis: the experience of social interaction is crucial to the formation of consciousness. Further, like Vygotsky, Bernstein, too, appears to attach a good deal of importance to language without ignoring other modalities of social practice. However, in some respects, these two seminal scholars are markedly different: for example, where Vygotsky appears to see homogeneity, Bernstein, from the very beginning, sees heterogeneity. The basic difference in their perspectives may be summed up this way: Vygotsky was a psychologist convinced of the centrality of the social; Bernstein was a sociologist convinced that no sociological theory could account adequately for the production and reproduction of society without taking into consideration the part played in the process by the social subjects themselves, which naturally implied, on the one hand, attention to forms of consciousness and, on the other, an account of how and why these forms coexist in most modern societies. The following extract, echoing these themes, occurred in Bernstein as early as 1965 (repr. 1971: 144):

> the particular forms of social relation act selectively upon what is said, when it is said, and how it is said . . . [they] can generate very different speech systems or codes . . . [which] create for their speakers different orders of relevance and relation. The experience of the speaker may then be transformed by what is made significant and relevant by different speech systems. As the child . . . learns specific speech codes which regulate his verbal acts, he learns the requirements of his social structure. The experience of the child is transformed by the learning generated by his own, apparently, voluntary acts of speech . . . from this point of view, every time the child speaks or listens, the social structure is reinforced in him and his social identity shaped. The social structure becomes the child's psychological reality through the shapings of his acts of speech.

This panoramic account of the mediation of consciousness through verbal interaction subsumes that particular form of mental functioning which is arbitrarily singled out in the Vygotskian discourse of semiotic mediation. To be more precise, it is provided with a cultural history: both Vygotsky and Luria do link the higher mental functions they cite so often to the experience of schooling. However, this does not answer any of the questions that the theory of semiotic mediation leaves unanswered; instead, it simply raises another question about the empirical basis of the claim. Is it, in fact, true that semiotic mediation in schooling always and invariably produces such consciousness? If not, what brings about the variation? Is the form of semiotic mediation different in those cases where such higher functions fail to be mediated? If so, why and how? This brings us back full circle to the issues raised earlier.

As the above extract makes clear Bernstein's theory recognizes the existence of distinct forms of semiotic interaction. In describing these distinctions at least two levels of abstraction have been recognized: that of code and that of the instance. Bernstein's theory offers an account of the system that underlies each of its instances, exhausting the entire array of interactions and their context type. The theory maintains that:

> The concept of code is inseparable from the concepts of legitimate and illegitimate communication . . . Code is the regulator of the relationships between contexts, and, through those relationships, a regulator of the relationships within contexts. (Bernstein, 1990: 15)

Thus, the more abstract level is that of coding orientation. Codes have this power for regulating relations and, therefore, regulating communication because they are directly related to what might be considered 'primitives' in Bernstein's sociological theory: 'the most primitive condition for the location of coding orientations is given by the location of agents in the social division of labour' (1990: 20). I can do no better than repeat Bernstein (1990: 20):

> *The simpler the social division of labour, and the more specific and local the relation between an agent and its material base, the more direct the relationship between meanings and a specific material base, and the greater the possibility of a restricted coding orientation. The more complex the social division of labour, [and] the less specific and local the relation between an agent and its material base, the more indirect the relation between meanings and a specific material base, and the greater the probability of an elaborated coding orientation.*

Herein lie the origins of social class and it is class relations that:

> generate, distribute, reproduce, and legitimate distinctive forms of communication, which transmit dominant and dominated codes, . . . subjects are differentially positioned by these codes in the process of acquiring them. (Bernstein, 1990: 13)

This account of what regulates interaction offers one way of distinguishing forms of semiotic mediation at an abstract level: discourse in society is not homogeneous and the most fundamental distinctions arise from subjects' positioning which is logically related to subjects' social positioning. It is here that subjects' orders of relevance are shaped, their sense of what is legitimate formed and psychic defences built and turned into second nature. This does not mean they are engraved in stone; simply that changing at this level is a major enterprise.

When, at a lower level, we examine the actual range of types of verbal interaction, two important facts emerge. In the description of the acquisition of codes, the theory has laid down the foundation for showing, first, that subjects with different social positioning will have access to a different range of evoking contexts. One manifestation of unequal distribution of power is precisely that the range of social practices in which subjects engage is itself differently positioned and differently valued. Second, even where, from some perspective, the evoking context might be regarded as the same, the sense of its identity and value is not the same across categories of differently positioned subjects. The point I am making may be perhaps better clarified by recontextualizing terms from another but related area of Bernstein's theoretical discourse: what the theory is claiming is that the 'reservoir' of contexts in any culture is always in excess of the 'repertoire' of contexts within which subjects positioned in specific social categories will move with confidence and comfort. Ergo, not everyone engages in the same form of semiotic mediation.

Since I have already tacitly invoked Bernstein's views on vertical and horizontal discourse (1999, 2000), this may well be the place to mention yet another vector of differentiation in verbal interactions and, hence, in semiotic mediation. There are in the life of the members of any society processes in common to all that have a common history because they arise out of 'the common problems of living and dying' (1999: 159). The sphere of knowledge pertaining to these processes is what sociology has recognized as 'common-sense' or 'everyday' knowledge, and the discourse associated with these activity types, Bernstein refers to as *horizontal discourse*. Typically, horizontal discourse is (i) oral (ii) local (iii) context dependent (iv) specific (v) tacit (vi) multilayered (vii) contradictory across contexts but not within and (viii) segmentally organized. The fact that the discourse is horizontal does not mean that 'all segments have equal importance' from the point of view of the subject engaged in the discourse. By contrast, vertical discourse pertains to what Hasan (1999) has referred to as specialized processes: by their nature these processes are not in common to all members of a society. In my understanding, vertical discourse has two distinct forms (i) where it represents 'a coherent, explicit, and systematically principled structure, hierarchically organized, as in the sciences' and (ii) where it represents 'a series of specialized languages with specialized modes of interrogation and specialized criteria for the production and circulation of texts, as in the social sciences and humanities' (Bernstein, 1999: 159). From the point of view of language, vertical discourse represents the space where the process is entirely semiotically constituted (Hasan, 1999): it is where disembedded knowledge flourishes. Thus I would expect vertical discourse to be concerned with what in the 1960s Bernstein referred to as context-independent meanings. Typically, also, vertical discourse, particularly since the advent of print, would involve a visual/graphic manifestation, which is, as it were, iconic of distancing from the local base of the participants. Note in particular Bernstein's emphasis on constraints on the circulation of knowledge construed in vertical discourse. Space does not allow further elaboration but, clearly, we will need to refer to the socially positioned categories of subjects that are highly relevant to understanding distinct forms of semiotic mediation. As I remarked elsewhere, language always mediates: the real issue is what and to whom.

Before leaving the discussion of codes, it should be pointed out that elaborated and restricted codes do not represent monolithic binomial categories imposing a rigid binary categorization on communication. The codes are known by the attributes of classification and framing and the theory offers vectors of variation in coding modalities by reference to whether classification and framing are internal or external as well as by the degree of their strength/weakness. Since strength and weakness are two end points of a continuum, in theory, variation can yield a large array of modes of mediation, particularly when applied to framing, which is itself a cluster of aspects of communicative practice each of which might vary independently (Bernstein, 1990, 2000).

I want to insert here another vector for the differentiation of forms of semiotic mediation (Hasan, 2002) which cuts across the horizontal–vertical distinction, though I think of it as code regulated. Speaking of pedagogy, Bernstein once remarked 'All experiencing carries a pedagogic potential but not all experiences are pedagogically generated' (2000: 199). I want to suggest here that mediation is, in one sense, different from pedagogy: things get mediated whether or not they are generated with mediation in mind. To reiterate, it is in the nature of any semiotic modality, and certainly in the nature of language, to 'mean' something to someone and, in the nature of things, meanings are what you construe experience with (see Halliday and Matthiessen, 1999).[5] Using conscious awareness of what is to be mediated, I suggested two forms: one mode that mediates mental dispositions, habits of the mind, or typical ways of responding to situations and one that targets some specific concept, some element of some vertical knowledge structure. The latter I would refer to as *visible semiotic mediation*, the former as *invisible semiotic mediation*. Visible semiotic mediation is pedagogically generated, whereas invisible semiotic mediation occurs without either party's awareness of what is being or has been mediated. For example, the component of pedagogic discourse that Bernstein refers to as *regulative* is normally invisibly mediated. It is hoped that putting it this way gives some idea of its power. I suggest that the mental disposition, the form of consciousness, that is mediated invisibly prior to schooling is a powerful determinant of how the pupil will respond to visible semiotic mediation of specific concepts, logical structures and elements of disembedded knowledge in official pedagogic sites. I hope this discussion shows how rich the concept of mediation of consciousness is within the framework of Bernstein's sociology; at the same time we note that those who participate in mediation are no longer faceless. Their social positioning offers some basis for understanding the nature of the results of Luria's research in Uzbekistan. Space does not permit me to show the relevance of Bernstein's analysis of the *pedagogic*

---

5 The fact that language always mediates, does not mean that it necessarily mediates what someone set out to mediate; if that were the case there would be no educational failures. What gets mediated depends a good deal on the mental disposition of the addressee. So something gets construed through meaning: successful mediation in pedagogic sites is that where the intended approximates the achieved.

device, where each component fills in what remains unsaid in the literature on semiotic mediation.

Moving to the question of valuation: why do some forms of consciousness (and their associated mediating discourses) have a privileged and privileging status in societies? This issue relates very closely to the genesis of variation in semiotic mediation. In one sense, of course, valuation, like authority, is always irrational. As Marx (quoted in Bottomore and Rubel, 1976: 93) pointed out, 'the ideas of the ruling class are, in every age, the ruling ideas'; and essentially, in my understanding, Bernstein's theory would explain the different valuation of different forms of consciousness and of their associated semiotic mediation by reference to dominating and dominated codes. Bernstein has argued that power and the strength of classification are proportionally related so that it would follow that the more clear cut, the more impermeable the categories of knowledge, the higher their valuation would be. It is well to recall here Vygotsky's view that the growth of specialized knowledge represents a form of human evolution: I doubt if seeing the results of our brilliant technological successes, we could be so very sanguine about the value of this evolution. I for one would agree with Whorf (1956: 81) that 'we do not know that civilization is synonymous with rationality'. Certainly what we call progress has not been synonymous with humanity! In Bernstein's sociology, these illusions do not exist; what exists is simply a description of what makes certain structures, certain behaviours, certain beliefs legitimate for whom, and why. This is the strength of the theory.

A word should be added, also, about the analysis of social subjects' relation to contexts in Bernstein's theory. In this respect, Bernstein is very definite that code regulated consciousness cannot be investigated piecemeal, concept by concept, word by word, fragment by fragment of activity. This element of the theory has relevance to the absence of a theory of discourse in Vygotsky. Bernstein's analysis of pedagogic discourse is a good place to ask questions about the operation of that variety of semiotic mediation which is concerned with scientific concepts, logical reasoning, inferential structures, mathematical concepts and other such phenomena. No learner comes face to face with *the* truth regarding any of these, because there is always the fact of selection and where there is selection there is room for the play of power and ideology.

Concluding remarks

It would seem quite obvious that the use of the expression *semiotic mediation* is in need of further reflection. One possibility is to limit the use of this term simply to those interactions that refer to the kind of communication which is instrumental in the creation, transmission and internalization of scientific concepts, of mathematical operations and of decontextualized reflections – in short, to the domain of vertical knowledge whose mediation is the specific, avowed goal of official pedagogy. To me this would pose a problem: it suggests that the line between, for example, scientific and everyday concepts is easy to draw; and I am not very certain that this is a viable proposition.[6] Besides, if this is how semiotic mediation were to be employed, then why not a better theorized term from Bernstein, namely official pedagogic discourse? One last point might also deserve attention: I have been emphasizing that mediation never fails to occur where semiotic acts are at issue: the trick is to know what it is that is being mediated. If the focus is on mental operations of the type that Vygotsky and Luria often cite as examples of semiotic mediation, this much needs to be said: semiotic mediation is definitely a necessary condition for the development of such mental activities but it is not a sufficient condition. This is because, as Vygotsky himself pointed out:

> children's learning begins long before they attend school is the starting point of this discussion. Any learning a child encounters in school has a previous history. (1978: 84)

Those who participate in the semiotic mediation of (components of) vertical knowledge come to the interaction with a mind – a mind that has already been socio-genetically shaped. This is not to claim that this shaped mind cannot be developed further and/or made to turn in different directions but it seems certain that this will be a difficult goal to achieve if we go on assuming homogeneity of coding orientation for all pupils and the myth of egalitarian education.

References

Axel, E. (1997) 'On Developmental Line in European Activity Theories', in M. Cole, E. Engeström and O. Vasquez (eds.), *Mind, Culture and Activity: Seminal Papers from the Laboratory of Comparative Human Cognition*, Cambridge: Cambridge University Press.

Bernstein, B. (1971) *Class, Codes and Control*, vol. 1, *Theoretical Studies Towards a Sociology of Language*, London: Routledge & Kegan Paul.

—— (1990) *The Structuring of Pedagogic Discourse*, vol. 4, *Class, Codes and Control*, London: Routledge.

—— (1999) 'Vertical and Horizontal Discourse: An Essay', *British Journal of Sociology of Education*, 20(2): 157–73.

—— (2000) *Pedagogy, Symbolic Control and Identity: Theory, Research, Critique*, rev. edn, Oxford: Rowman & Littlefield.

Bottomore, T. B. and Rubel, M. (1976) (eds.), *Karl Marx: On Sociology and Social Philosophy*, Harmondsworth: Penguin.

Bourdieu, P. (1991) *Language and Symbolic Power*, ed. J. B. Thompson, London: Polity.

Cole, M., Engeström, E. and Vasquez, O. (eds.), (1997) *Mind, Culture and Activity: Seminal Papers from the Laboratory of Comparative Human Cognition*, Cambridge: Cambridge University Press.

Deacon, T. (1997) *The Symbolic Species: The Co-evolution of Language and Human Brain*, New York: W. W. Norton.

6 See for example Lave (1988).

Edelman, G. M. (1992) *Bright Air, Brilliant Fire: On the Matter of the Mind*, New York: Basic Books.

Engeström, Y., Miettinen, R. and Punamaki, R. J. (1999) (eds.) *Perspectives on Activity Theory*, Cambridge: Cambridge University Press.

Greenfield, S. (1996) *The Human Mind Explained: The Control Centre of the Living Machine*, London: Cassell.

Halliday, M. A. K. and Matthiessen, C. M. I. M. (1999) *Construing Experience Through Meaning: A Language-Based Approach to Cognition*, London: Cassell.

Hasan, R. (1992) 'Speech Genre, Semiotic Mediation and the Development of Higher Mental Functions', *Language Sciences*,14(4): 489–528.

—— (1995). 'On Social Conditions for Semiotic Mediation: The Genesis of Mind in Society', in A. R. Sadovnik (ed.), *Knowledge and Pedagogy: The Sociology of Basil Bernstein*, Norwood, NJ: Ablex.

—— (1999) 'Speaking with reference to context', in M. Ghadessy (ed.), *Text and Context in Functional Linguistics*, Amsterdam: Benjamins.

—— (2002) 'Semiotic Mediation and Mental Development in Pluralistic Societies: Some Implications for Tomorrow's Schooling', in G. Wells and G. Claxton (eds.), *Learning for Life in the 21st Century: Socio-cultural Perspectives on the Future of Education*, London: Blackwell.

Lave, J. (1988) *Cognition in Practice: Mind, Mathematics and Culture in Everyday Life*, Cambridge: Cambridge University Press.

Popper, K. R. (1979) *Objective Knowledge: An Evolutionary Approach*, rev. edn, Oxford: Clarendon Press.

Vygotsky, L. S. (1962) *Thought and Language*, ed. and trans. E, Hanfman and G. Vakar. Cambridge, MA: MIT Press.

—— (1978) *Mind in Society: The Development of Higher Psychological Processes*, ed. M. Cole, V. John-Steiner, S. Scribner and E. Souberman, Cambridge, MA: Harvard University Press.

—— (1981) 'The Genesis of Higher Mental Functions', in J. V. Wertsch (ed.), *The Concept of Activity in Soviet Psychology*, Armonk, NY: Sharp.

Wells, G. and Claxton, G. (2001) (eds.), *Learning for Life in the 21st Century: Socio-cultural Perspectives on the Future of Education*, Oxford: Blackwell.

Wertsch, J. V. (1985a) *Vygotsky and the Social Formation of Mind*, Cambridge, MA: Harvard University Press.

—— (1985b) 'The Semiotic Mediation of Mental Life: L. S. Vygotsky and M. M. Bakhtin', in E. Mertz and R. A. Parmentier (eds.), *Semiotic Mediation: Socio-cultural and Psychological Perspectives*, New York: Academic Press.

Whorf, B. L. (1956) *Language, Thought and Reality: Selected Writings of Benjamin Lee Whorf*, ed. J. B. Carrol, Cambridge, MA: MIT Press.

6 Negotiating pedagogic dilemmas in non-traditional educational contexts

An Australian case study of teachers' work

Parlo Singh, Raymond Brown and Mariann Märtsin

The teacher's work is particularly complex because, in the first place, the teacher must be well oriented to the regularities of the child's personal activity, that is, know the child's psychology; in the second place, the teacher must know the particular social dynamics of the child's social setting; and in the third place, the teacher must know about the possibilities of his or her own pedagogical activity, consciousness and personality of his or her charges. This is why the work of a genuine teacher can never be stereotyped or routine; the teacher's work always carries a profoundly creative character.

(Davydov, 1995: 17)

Introduction

This chapter draws on the work of Vygotsky (see Daniels, 2001; van der Veer and Valsiner, 1991) and Bernstein (2000) to examine the pedagogic dilemmas in teachers' work as they attempt to re-engage learners with school knowledge in non-traditional education contexts. Mainstream schooling has failed the students who attend these educational contexts. Consequently, the emphasis on relevant curriculum, flexible implementation, inter-agency collaboration, life-skills development and readiness for work aims to provide an alternative or non-traditional context designed specifically to meet the needs of these students (de Jong, 2005; de Jong and Griffiths, 2006).

The educational context referred to in this chapter is situated within a system of non-traditional, flexible schools across Australia (to be referred to as the 'network'). The 'network' strives to promote authentic human development through an approach to education that is holistic and supportive of principles of social justice. The 'network' supports early school-leavers who have decided to re-engage with schooling and other young people who choose this educational option. A school site consists of between 50 and 80 young people, and is staffed by a multi-disciplinary team. These teams may include a combination of educators from a range of professions including registered teachers, educational support workers, youth workers, social workers, health workers, counsellors, community development workers, job placement workers, chaplains and administrative support staff. In the 'network', teachers, other adult workers and students commit to participate in learning environments that strive to be democratic, relational and to operate through key principles relating to 'respect', 'honesty', 'safety' and 'legality'. Relationships within the 'network' strive to show respect for personal dignity, to recognise difference, and emphasise the peaceful resolution of conflict.

Our starting point in this chapter is the conviction that teachers' work is inherently complex, for at the heart of it lies a myriad of pedagogic dilemmas that need to be constantly managed and negotiated. What constitutes a valuable and valued knowledge? How should this knowledge be taught and learned? Who should do it? And what are the criteria of success for teachers and learners? The ambivalence arising from those pedagogic dilemmas is particularly marked in the context of non-traditional schools that work with students from disadvantaged communities. In this chapter we are interested in exploring how two teaching professionals – a teacher and an educational researcher – work through these dilemmas in an interview encounter. We consider the interview to be a mediating device that both parties use to make an intervention into each other's orientations to meaning about the purpose of schooling in the lives of students in non-traditional educational contexts. By looking at three interview extracts we aim to examine the unfolding pedagogical relationship between the teacher and the researcher. Our analysis underscores the constant tension between the everyday and the scientific knowledge and the constant pull between both of these in the contradictory conception of educational equality, especially for students from disadvantaged communities, and in the meaning orientations of the teacher and the researcher as they are working through what constitutes valued and valuable knowledge for this group of students and how this knowledge should be taught, learned and assessed. Our analysis also highlights the mutuality of the interview experience as intervention, thus echoing the struggle of interweaving and integrating the everyday with the scientific knowledge in pedagogic encounters.

Pedagogic dilemmas: ambivalence, tensions and anxieties

Non-traditional education contexts, while setting themselves apart from mainstream schooling institutions, remain part of the machinery of the education bureau. The moral principles espoused by the 'network' are promoted by 'historically-invented political and intellectual technologies' (Hunter, 1993: 248) or socially, historically and culturally produced practices of the system (Daniels, 2010). Historically, the 'moral comportment and social capacities' of children of the 'lower classes' has been provided through the principles of pastoral pedagogy derived from Christian popular education (Hunter, 1994: 74). Pastoral pedagogy constitutes 'the organising routines, pedagogical practices, personal disciplines, and interpersonal relationships that come to form the core of the modern school' (Hunter, 1994: 56). Thus, the object of pastoral pedagogy has been to constitute socially, historically and culturally produced practices designed to enable individuals to 'comport themselves as self-reflective and self-governing persons' (Hunter, 1994: 57), that is, carry out 'work of the self on the self' (Hunter, 1993: 256).

Yet the pedagogic work of enhancing the 'moral comportment and social capacities' of children and young people is only one aspect of the work of schooling contexts. The other aspect relates to the dissemination of valued skills and disciplinary knowledge which will enable students to transition effectively into the world of work. As stated above, the 'network' of professionals striving to re-engage young people in learning operate within an overarching philosophy of education based on principles of educational equality and social justice. However, as Hunter (1993, 1994) has argued, the notion of equality within education bureaucracies has historically been characterised by an acute and arresting ambivalence, which operates at multiple levels. First, the very institution of schooling has historically failed a whole group of young people, mainly those from disadvantaged socio-economic backgrounds (see Ball, 2003; Bernstein, 2000). This historical failure can be traced to the ambivalent conceptualisation of equality at the heart of the modern school bureaucracy. On the one hand, equality has been conceptualised 'as the technical objective of government, to achieve a socially optimal distribution of trained capacities and lifestyles'; and on the other hand, it has been 'represented as an absolute moral right to self-realisation, claimed on behalf of our common humanity or universal moral personality' (Hunter, 1994: 95). The former requires re-socialisation, an active engagement and internalisation of school knowledge, as well as the gamut of moral, social capacities constituted through pastoral pedagogy. This necessitates a distancing from the everyday knowledge and moral dispositions, demeanours acquired in home and local community contexts. The latter entails acceptance and valorisation of difference – the difference between school and everyday knowledge, between the moral component and social capacities esteemed within pastoral pedagogy, and pedagogies of the home and local community. Second, ambivalence operates at 'the subjective level in the ambivalent relations of acceptance/rejection between majority and minority subjects' (Ang, 1996: 36); that is, teachers and students, or the 'network of professionals' and the cohort of 'disengaged young people'. Ambivalence at this subjective level may be realised in the ways in which teachers 'read' young people, and construct models of the 'normal' and 'other' school student.

Related to this ambivalent relationship between the school knowledge and pastoral pedagogy on the one hand and local knowledges and pedagogies on the other, is the dilemma of the differential distribution of valued and valuable knowledge to different cohorts of the student population. Indeed, as Bernstein (1996) has argued, the principles of power and control of a society are relayed through the pedagogic principles of who gets access to what types of knowledge? Bernstein (1996) suggests that school knowledge is a specialised type of knowledge, selected, organised, paced and evaluated by specific sets of principles or ensemble of rules. Thus, what knowledge gets selected, how it is organised, taught and evaluated to specific cohorts of students in school contexts is regulated by sets of rules or principles of power and control. Moreover, there are two components of school knowledge, the disciplinary skills, information and concepts, and the moral and social capacities that allow access to the disciplinary knowledge. Bernstein (2000) argues that the latter is often the dominant component as it regulates what skills, concepts, information are selected, organised, taught and evaluated for particular cohorts of students. It is the latter which contains within it a model or theory of the learner, the teacher and the pedagogic relation. In some privileged schooling contexts, the pedagogic practices allow students to internalise these necessary moral comportments and social capacities so that they can carry out 'work of the self on the self' (Hunter, 1993), in other words, conduct themselves as 'self-reflective and self-governing persons' (Hunter, 1994). In other schooling contexts, students are denied access to valued and valuable knowledge as the pedagogic practices constitute deficit models of the learner and the pedagogic relation deemed suitable for this type of learner.

The point here is that the acute and arresting ambivalence that lies at the heart of these pedagogic dilemmas makes the teachers' work inherently complex. The ambivalence refers to the difficult, unsettling state 'in which intrinsically contradictory or mutually exclusive desires or ideas are each invested with intense emotional energy' (Flax, cited in Ang, 1996: 44). Moreover, ambivalence suggests an emotional state of tension or angst as it is impossible to simultaneously hold contradictory ideas and desires, and it is unimaginable to let go or discard either (Ang, 1996). The constant pulls between the different conceptions and ideals about what should be taught, how, by whom and to who generates pedagogic anxieties and tensions that need to be continuously managed and negotiated. Teachers may, of course, choose to suppress or deny feelings of anxiety stemming from those perceived dilemmas, but even the act of denial and suppression is vested with intense emotional energy and requires active psychological and intellectual work.

Research interview as intervention to meaning orientations

Most analyses of pedagogic dilemmas in interview data (see Singh and Doherty, 2004) focus on the accounts of teaching/learning provided by the teacher in order to profile a range of pedagogic models or styles. Such analyses often logically lead to proposing an ideal pedagogic model or type that might improve educational outcomes for students who have previously been failed by schools.

Our analysis shifts the attention away from simply profiling the teacher, to examining the pedagogic relation constituted between the researcher and teacher in and through the interview. We are interested in analysing the ways in which meaning is 'mediated' in the interview encounter, where the interview encounter is viewed as an 'intervention' in making a difference to the interlocutors' orientations to meaning about the purpose of schooling in the lives of students in non-traditional education contexts. Building on Vygotsky's (1981) 'genetic law of cultural development', we view the evoking context of the interview as a mediating tool which affects the Socio-cultural organisation of mental functioning on the interpersonal plane, and also functioning on the intrapersonal plane. Along with Wertsch and Rupert's (1993) account of 'mediated agency' we emphasise the 'irreducible tension' manifested between agent/s on the one hand and the mediational means that they employ or have access to on the other, and argue that human action, including interpersonal and intrapersonal functioning, is fundamentally shaped and constrained by mediational means (Wertsch and Rupert, 1993: 230). However, we are interested in further unpacking what kind of knowledges are being mediated by whom to whom and in what ways and how these differing meditational means create variations in the formation of individuals' ways of thinking and being.

By looking at the research interview as a mediating tool with the potential to shift the interlocutors' orientations to meaning, and by placing this encounter in the context of non-traditional education we aim to move beyond the discussion about the fundamental tension between the personal and Socio-cultural. Vygotsky (1994) made a distinction between everyday and scientific knowledge and argued that everyday spontaneous concepts provide the necessary but not sufficient conditions for progress toward more powerful forms of thinking. He saw culture, for example, the systems of abstract concepts incorporated in school curricula, as being the driving force in development. The research of Bernstein (1996, 2000) provides further insight into what this intermingling of abstract and everyday has come to look like in formal education contexts. Bernstein proposed that the aim of formal contexts of education, such as schools, has evolved over time to focus on the apprenticeship of students into general, abstract, decontextualised ways of thinking free from personal, local, contextualised understandings (Rose, 1999). Additionally, Bernstein proposed that modern schooling aims to induct students into specialised modes of moral conduct. These two modes of knowledge (knowledge about abstract concepts and knowledge about moral conduct) are transmitted to students by teachers through the structures, processes and tools generated in and through pedagogic communication (Bernstein, 1990, 1996). Hasan (2004) further suggests that these different kinds of knowledges get mediated differently in pedagogic relationships and everyday communicational acts. She makes a distinction between visible and invisible semiotic mediation and suggests that much of the everyday knowledge of a cultural community, including school, gets mediated invisibly through ordinary and unselfconscious discourse, creating culturally appropriate and expected mental dispositions and habits of the mind.

This theoretical perspective focuses our analyses on pedagogic communication as it unfolds in an interview encounter as two teaching professionals – a teacher and an educational researcher – struggle towards a shared meaning of the complex dilemmas inherent in teacher's everyday work in non-traditional educational contexts.

One interview, one teacher, multiple dilemmas

The interviewee who is the focus of this article, is an experienced female teacher in the middle (students ranging in age from 12 to 16 years of age) phase of schooling and a long-term member (over ten years) of the 'network' of alternative education referred to above.

Before undertaking a pre-service teacher education degree, the interviewee worked in the 'network' as a teacher aide undertaking duties (e.g., cooking) relating to the care of students participating in outdoor education programs.

The interviewer is an experienced male teacher and researcher with extensive knowledge of the education system in which the 'network' is embedded. The interviewer is a chief investigator in the research project which formed the context of this interview. This research project was jointly funded by the education system responsible for the 'network' and the Federal Government of Australia. An overall aim of the research was to develop a 'values' approach to school renewal that could be employed by the 'network' when gathering evidence relating to the accreditation of the 'network' as a non-state school. The methodology of the research employed data gathering tools such as classroom observations, interviews and journal writing.

The interview reported in this chapter was chosen for analysis because it followed an observation of the interviewee's classroom practice, was deemed typical of the interviews conducted over the 'network', and captured the tension which became apparent as the research progressed between the people who worked within the 'network' and the 'institution' that administered the 'network'. This tension revolves around the need for educational institutions to ensure that their students attain national standards of literacy and numeracy deemed necessary to function in a democratic society and the need for people working in alternative education sites to ensure that their students are provided with alternative approaches to education that support the holistic development of the individual (see Trent *et al.* (1998) for a review of this tension as it relates to special education).

A language of description was developed to systematically analyse the interview transcript, centred on the following concepts: semiotic mediation – visible and invisible in the interview context, pedagogic dilemmas of schooling, valued and valuable school knowledge, pastoral pedagogy, including theories of the learner, the teacher and pedagogic relation, and value placed on institutional rituals of schooling.

The pedagogic dilemmas that we aim to highlight and discuss in this chapter emerged in the interview encounter on two separate planes (see Table 6.1). First, we can focus on the relationship between the teacher and the students as this is talked about by the teacher. The teacher's views about the relationship between scientific and everyday knowledge, her conception of educational equality and her acceptance/rejection of the local knowledges and pedagogies and pastoral pedagogy and knowledge of the school emerge from the way she talks about the students and their culture and community. Yet the same dilemmas emerge also when we focus on the relationship that is unfolding between the teacher and the researcher. Here the use of abstract and concrete knowledge and abstract and concrete language opens up a possibility to analyse how the researcher is seeking to shift the teacher's orientation to meaning in the research interview and how the teacher, in turn, seeks to shape the meanings that the researcher is constructing.

Table 6.1 Theoretical concepts–analytic questions

Theoretical concepts	Analytic questions to interrogate the data
Semiotic mediation – visible	What is talked about in the interview? What topics are introduced? Who introduces these topics? How are these topics sequenced, organised, reintroduced? With what effect?
Semiotic mediation – invisible	When and how does the researcher attempt to shift the teacher's orientations about school knowledge? How does the teacher respond to these challenges/interventions?
Ambivalence – pedagogic dilemmas about schooling	Are there points of contradiction/contestation in the interview? If so, when and about what? How are these contradictions negotiated in the interview? Does the teacher talk explicitly about tensions or difficulties in working out what to teach, how to teach, and the effectiveness of otherwise of teaching in these schools? Are there contradictory comments about curriculum, pedagogy and evaluation in the teacher's account of teaching/learning in this context?
Institutional rituals of non-traditional educational contexts	How is the educational context described? What institutional rituals or patterns of behaviour are valued? How are these patterns of behaviour similar to or different from what would be expected in mainstream schooling?
School curriculum, care for knowledge	What knowledge is considered valuable and valued for this cohort of students? Why? How does the teacher measure success? What do the students take away from this context?
Pastoral pedagogy, care for students	How is the learner described in the interview? What constitutes an effective pedagogic relation of care in this context? How does the teacher measure success? What does she expect to be internalised by the students? What do they take away from these contexts?

To discuss how these dilemmas emerge and are mutually negotiated in the interview encounter we focus on three extracts from the interview.

'Even though the place has gone, the space is still there in their minds'

Extract 1 begins with the researcher asking the interviewee about her roles and responsibilities as a teacher for students in this particular school community. Prior to this data extract the teacher has spent considerable time talking about the wealth of practical knowledge she has gained on the job: 'I've been here so long that I have gained a lot of skills here, and I have never really taken the time to name for myself or for others what those skills are.' She adds that, 'there are teachers that could benefit from what I have learnt on the ground.' The researcher then asks the interviewee the following question: 'Can you tell us what you do here at the "network" with young people?' and then when the teacher asks for clarification of the question he rephrases and says, 'can you tell me something that explains how you work with young people at the "network"?' The interviewee responds that it is difficult to answer the question because her role 'changes a lot of the time' because the school is a 'dynamic place', but then settles on the following response:

> I have always come to the place with the understanding that I teach kids not curriculum. So the content of what I teach is not of great importance to me, it's um, it's certainly not my priority, neither sometimes is actually teaching them skills. Initially, my priority is to make them feel like they are learning. So there's a lot of work, I think I put most of my energy into that, how to re-engage, how to help a young person experience success in some way. And that may be through addition or a piece of writing, or it may be through something curriculum type, but until they feel safe to take that risk, the rest is nothing.

Later the interviewee picks up a point that she raised at the beginning of the interview relating to her extensive experience in 'teaching young people who are either ascertained, verified or have quite specific special needs'. She states that 'one of the keys' to working in the 'network' is to be able to 'walk into the room and know where each one of them are, we know who's going to go off, we know who's in a bad place, we know who needs to be left alone, we know when to address an issue or when not to, that, that's crucial to what we do'.

This ability to make quick ascertainments/judgements about young people, she argues, can be achieved by developing a 'relationship to the young person', but it requires something else:

> but it goes beyond that, because we have to pick that up very quickly, we get a new young person in, we have to learn to read them very quickly too, so yeah, there's something about reading their body language and who they are and what they are doing.

The teacher then goes on to explain that this ability to know how things are and what to expect is not necessary only for the teachers working in this non-traditional context, but valuable also for the students:

Extract 1
Researcher: So this brings me to my next question, and you have probably answered it, but how does caring relate to what you do with young people at the 'network'? [pause 5 sec.] [Interviewee: caring] so you've got the accountability requirements, you've got the timetable and you can read people, you know who needs to be cared for and who doesn't in this particular moment in time, so how does caring relate to, can you tell me something that explains how caring works at the network?

Interviewee: [School] becomes for many of them I think it's the first place in their life they *feel safe in their life* and they *knew the rules,* they knew exactly *what they were* and they knew exactly *what they were going to be asked to do* and um, that's really important and they see, they come back, *they come back looking for that later in life when things are a little bit rocky* or they have been through a rocky time, they come back to *ground themselves* in that *safe place* or in that safe place where it was *okay to take risks* and okay to *make mistakes.* There are not many places in life where it is actually okay to make mistakes

Researcher: That's an interesting analogy . . . we [the Research Assistant and I] debrief after doing an hour here and capture that on tape and we were walking back to the car . . . and originally the Research Assistant wasn't going to come with me . . . but then she decided that she would come, and as we were walking there she called out 'my name' and then I turned. As I turned I put my foot down to the side, if I had put my foot down where I was walking I would have stepped on a brown snake. And we talked about this afterwards, and I said you know if you hadn't have come with me, because I wouldn't have seen it, I would have walked on the snake and I would have been bitten, and she said '*life is made up of those decisions you make in the instant*' and then we talked about the 'network' and how the 'network' *is actually extending, drawing out that instant for young people. Giving that space, that safe space in which to accept or reject*

Interviewee: And you know that, you know that saying, oh it's not a saying, *it's a strategy actually for coping with stressful situations* where you have a, you find *a place in your mind that's a safe place* and you imagine it, you visualise it. I think that becomes that for them sometimes. I have seen young people who have had awful things happen to them or they have gone to jail after here and they will come back, and I think there's a certain, I think they do it on purpose, they come back to get that sense again of, *this is the place where I knew what the 'go' was*

Researcher: Cause even though *the place has gone, the space is still there in their minds* [Interviewee: absolutely yeah] so they can come back and revisit it

Interviewee: Yeah and usually, there's at least one or two people that they know when they come back so you know [Researcher: staff wise]

In this data extract the researcher picks up the teacher's image of school as a safe place and links it to a metaphorical story about a snake. The story works as a semiotic device for lifting the teacher's thinking about the school, the students and her own teaching practice up from her ordinary ways of thinking and towards reflection and contemplation. It thus works as an invitation to move beyond the teacher's immediate experience with the students and towards a generalised notion of teaching/learning in non-traditional contexts. Yet the teacher rejects this invitation and instead brings the discussion back to her immediate experience, as the researcher's pause and space in the mind where a distance from here-and-now can be taken and a possibility to be otherwise can be imagined, gets interpreted by the teacher as a '*strategy for coping with stressful situations*'. The researcher tries to remain on the level of reflection, by referring to the difference between concrete places that cannot be returned to and mental spaces that are always available, yet the teacher rejects also this invitation and brings the discussion back to the concrete and to her image of the school that is safe because it is familiar.

Safety and safe place for the teacher then equates with the general institutional rituals of schooling; that is, the routines that govern consensual patterns of talking, walking, sitting, eating and so forth. These institutional rituals were aimed at governing a large population of young people placed in one space, so that the goal of educating the masses – compulsory education for all – could be achieved. For many students, particularly students from disadvantaged social economic backgrounds (working classes, unemployed classes) this mode of schooling has not worked. And yet this teacher continues to push the place of school and its institutional rituals and routines as a safe place. Throughout the interview exchange she reverts constantly back to the notion of a safe place – the physical space of school buildings and the cultural space of routines and rituals. It is this place that she encourages students to visualise and imagine when they might find themselves in stressful situations. At the same time, she does not talk about the moral and social capacities of self-reflection and self-problematisation which these students should be entitled to acquire through pastoral pedagogy. Instead, it is the researcher who alludes to this space in the mind that students (and the teacher) can go to do work of the self on the self, the space of self-reflection and self-problematisation. He talks about the space between the everyday local place, the contextualised knowledge of the local and the abstract knowledge of the scientific. He thus alludes to the different types of knowledges – everyday, commonsense knowledge and abstract, decontextualised, scientific knowledge.

From the teacher and researcher's discussion the image of the school as a special kind of place different from the students' everyday life-worlds thus emerges. Yet equally, the researcher's and teacher's contradictory views about the value of everyday, local knowledge and abstract and scientific knowledge become evident. According to Hasan, everyday knowledge is typically characterised as '(1) oral (2) local (3) context dependent (4) specific (5) tacit (6) multi layered (7) contradictory across contexts but not within, and (8) segmentally organised' (2004: 38). In contrast, abstract knowledge is typically characterised as decontextual, abstract and internally coherent, structured and hierarchical. Hasan's distinction echoes that proposed by Vygotsky (1994) between everyday or spontaneous concepts and academic or non-spontaneous concepts. While differentiating the two types of concepts Vygotsky, nevertheless, argued that the two are inevitably connected and intertwined in child's mental development:

> both types of concepts are not encapsulated in the child's consciousness, are not separated from one another by the barrier, do not flow along two isolated channels, but are in the process of continual, unceasing interaction, which has to lead inevitably to the situation where generalizations, which have a higher structure and which are peculiar to academic concepts, should be able to elicit a change in the structure of spontaneous concepts. (1994: 365)

He thus argued that academic concepts presented to students in general and abstract terms without connection to their concrete, empirical and personal experience must remain empty formalism (Vygotsky, 1987). Equally spontaneous concepts remain limited in their application and generality without being connected to more systematised concepts. Thus, the education of students requires the creation of social contexts of collaborative thinking where everyday concepts are brought together with the scientific concepts (Kozulin, 1990).

It is this possibility of bringing together the teacher's everyday concepts with the researcher's abstract concepts that interests us here. For by inviting her to interweave her knowledge with his, the researcher is trying to open up a space of self-reflection and self-problematisation for the teacher in this interview encounter as a form of pastoral pedagogy. For the researcher the abstract decontextualised knowledge about one's practice is valued and needed. He positions the teacher as someone who can, with appropriate guidance, access and engage with this knowledge. In seeking to disturb the teacher's everyday knowledge and thus push her to consider his abstract ways of thinking, the researcher talks about the importance of 'debriefing' with a colleague, engaging in semiotic mediation, in order to understand each local context of schooling in a more abstract/scientific way. He talks about the space that is needed to engage in this type of thinking, in this shift in orientation to meaning. And he stresses the importance of this space, not place, but space or gap between the everyday local context and abstract scientific knowledge that enables him to make informed choices from a number of possible options. He suggests that the spatial moving from the local to the abstract and back again provides him with the tools to step back and deliberate on whether to accept or reject a particular course of action. However, the researcher's efforts to construct this in-between space where a possibility to think otherwise can emerge, remain unnoticed by the teacher, as her settled position remains undisturbed. Furthermore, as we will see in the next interview extract, the teacher does not merely deny the possibility to open up a space in the mind for herself, but she renders it unnecessary also for the students.

'The kids that say sorry and mean it, is a huge success for me'

In Extract 2 the researcher attempts to refocus the interviewee on teaching and learning at the 'network'. The question is posed after a number of turns where the interviewee talks about the teaching population at the 'network', staff who have been at the 'network' for a long time, those that stay only a short while, some who return, the volunteers who work in the 'network' and so forth. She also talks about the recruitment strategies used to attract and maintain new staff to the 'network' and talks of the limitations of a resume and interview for ascertaining whether a teacher is likely to be effective in the 'network' environment. She argues that the key criterion for effective teaching is the ability to 'really need to read people' – and ascertaining this ability is only possible when you 'see . . . how the people work with young people that's what we need to see'.

Extract 2

Researcher: how does teaching and learning relate to what you do with young people at the network? Teaching and learning?

Interviewee: I think I have probably got a pretty broad view of what teaching and learning is, you know, I think *I learn as much as they do*, I learn everyday from them as well, and I acknowledge that to them, *they teach me*. I also think that um, we probably, most of us I would say have a broader view of what, ah what needs to be taught and what is teaching. I mean *sitting on that chair for longer than five minutes is teaching. Not swearing in public is teaching*, so our view of what teaching is, I think is [Researcher: or the outcomes of teaching] yeah and I think that *those things are as important as the academic teaching we do, socialising*

Researcher: So how do you gauge your successes in teaching?

Interviewee: um . . . I probably have *a much lower benchmark for success*, than mainstream teachers you know. *The kids that say sorry and mean it, is a huge success for me*. Um, when you see the lights go on, oh that's why the zero goes there, you know those little things or when they speak nicely to each other, those are the things that actually show me success and certainly give me a lot of joy.

Researcher: And the fact they come back tomorrow

Interviewee: Yes, I mean the amount of young people that come through with a tonne of excuses, now you have 90 – 100% attendance, that's success

The teacher starts her answer by referring to a mutual pedagogic relationship with the students: 'I learn as much as they do' and 'they teach me'. Yet very quickly this image of teaching and learning is abandoned as she moves towards an image of teaching that concentrates on 'socialising'– that is, inculcating the students into the institutional rituals of schooling. This shift in the image of teaching is accompanied by the shift from pronoun 'I' to refer to the teacher who has a mutually transformative relationship with students, to the pronoun 'we' to refer to teachers as those who institutionalise learners into schooling.

Later in the interview the teacher suggests that she never uses the term 'students'. 'There's a power thing with student/teacher isn't there?' she says.

Instead, she prefers to refer to learners as 'young people' or 'kids'. While her usage of 'young people' indeed evokes a symmetric relationship, her usage of 'kids' seems to instead construct a parental relationship – a relationship where her efforts towards inculcating students into institutional rituals of school can be easily foregrounded and justified, while not much space is left for the teaching of valued skills and disciplinary knowledge. On the one hand, this choice of words does resonate with the teacher's idea that this is not an ordinary school where scientific concepts and disciplinary skills are taught in an ordinary manner. On the other hand, however, she has translated the social and moral conduct of the world-out-there into a social and moral conduct of a school student. Paradoxically then, her teaching practice is explicitly aimed at constructing and normalising the 'school student', regulating them into the institutional rituals of schooling, although this mode of conduct is not needed for the transmission and acquisition of abstract knowledge, and indeed denies them access to the moral comportment and social capacities of self-reflection and self-problematisation, an integral component of pastoral pedagogy. Instead, the cultivation of specific manners and etiquettes (using a phone, sitting still) becomes the sole aim and purpose of schooling. Acquiring the habits and behaviours of a 'normal' school student does not function as a means for accessing the complex and abstract school knowledge, but becomes an end in itself – valued and praised by the teacher.

The complex pedagogic dilemma between school knowledge, pastoral pedagogy and institutional regulations in non-traditional education contexts thus gets foregrounded in this interview exchange. What should be taught in non-traditional schools? How are the resources that non-traditional schools provide similar or different to resources that traditional schools, that have failed these young people, provide? Should the non-traditional schools use the same kinds of rituals of consensus and differentiation as traditional schools? Or should the institutional order be different? And how should this institutional order be mediated and transmitted to students?

Daniels, (1989, 1995) research has demonstrated that students learn much more than the explicit, visible instructional relationships, pedagogical tools and processes allow for or aim to achieve in education contexts. Wertsch's (2007) distinction between implicit and explicit semiotic mediation is helpful in unpacking how this surplus mediation of meanings occurs. Wertsch suggests that explicit mediation refers to clearly defined pedagogical relationships designed to achieve the learning of schooled concepts, while implicit mediation refers to relationships embedded in the everyday discourses that people bring to schooling. In *explicit mediation* the purpose and intention of the mediation is clear and overt, and the stimulus means introduced to the situation are also obvious and nontransitory. In contrast, *implicit semiotic mediation* is less obvious, for it is not necessarily clear who is guiding whose learning, and what are the stimulus means that are mediating the meanings. In Wertsch's words they are instead 'part of a pre-existing, independent stream of communicative action that becomes integrated with other forms of goal-directed behaviour' (2007: 181).

Hasan (2004) too differentiates between two modes of the operation of semiotic mediation: 'one mode that mediates mental dispositions, habits of the mind or typical ways of responding to situations, and one that targets some specific concept, some element of some vertical knowledge structure' (p. 39). She refers to those two manifestations of semiotic mediation as *invisible* and *visible mediation*, respectively.

Hasan argues that although in the case of invisible mediation it is not immediately clear that any teaching and learning is going on, important elements of mental dispositions, identities and practices are still being mediated in those situations. In fact, she considers invisible mediation to be primary in human life, both in terms of time and pervasiveness. Yet she also claims that the two modes of mediation are not completely independent from each other, but rather work in tandem to create and reproduce the culture and provide individuals with the sense that they belong to a community.

What is relevant for our current discussion is Hasan's suggestion that invisible semiotic mediation is effective in creating certain mental dispositions or habits of the mind exactly because it is ordinary. That is, the culture of the community, with its appropriate ways of being, tendencies to respond and beliefs about the world becomes learned precisely because it is normal and unquestionable to the degree that it becomes invisible: 'This does not mean that culture is irrelevant to these encounters; it is simply that it goes underground: sayings that pertain to everyday activities and seem to be "of no great importance" depend largely on taken-for-granted "truths" whose validity is treated as self-evident' (Hasan, 2002a: 116). Along with Bernstein (1990), she argues that the contexts of human action offer different possibilities for different people, depending on their social location in that specific context. Thus if we are to understand how variations in human consciousness and identities are shaped by differences in social structures then we need to take into account the different ways individuals position themselves and are positioned by others in social contexts (Hasan, 2002b).

In this and the previous interview extract the teacher presents a particular reading of learners and teachers. In this reading the learners are positioned as bruised and hurt by their previous schooling and other life-experiences and therefore not anymore ready to fully engage in academic activities. Later in the interview she says: 'I mean we are dealing with young people that are maybe third generation unemployment, how do they know what they want to be or want to do'. In relation to this reading of the learner, the teacher appears as someone who should not spend her energy on transmitting abstract school knowledge, for the learner is not ready to receive this, but should rather aim at teaching the learners some basic social skills and appropriate moral conduct that will allow them to function effectively in the world-out-there. The pedagogic relationship that the teacher envisions between these bruised learners and teachers as socialisers is the one of *knowing* oneself and each other. As discussed above, she values the teachers' ability to quickly read the students, place them into appropriate categories and deal with them as if they are reified and fixed into these. The same principle of security and familiarity, of knowing what is expected and what to expect applies to students too. There is thus not much room for surprises or unexpected outcomes, for questioning, problematising or reflection in this pedagogic relationship. People and their roles are clear, familiar and secure. And the teacher is free to work with what these young people are today and what they should be from the perspective of the school, instead of helping them to move across the boundary between the everyday–concrete and abstract–imaginative safely, and thus work with what they could be in the future.

The teacher's particular way of reading the students, their world and the world-out-there thus becomes evident. In the teacher's reading the world-out-there is eclipsed into the world-of-schooling. It is not equal to the world-of-school, which gives young people access to abstract school knowledge and the art of self-reflection, self-problematisation, but to the world-of-schooling, where certain institutional behaviours are expected and accepted. It is a kind of fantasy world cut off from the young people's everyday experiences and realities and from the world of work that the teacher is imagining for those young people.

The teacher's image of the learners and teachers and their pedagogic relationship thus cuts wide open the dilemma about acceptance and rejection of local and abstract knowledges. How to translate the everyday or real life relations of signification into those of abstract disciplinary knowledge? How to help the disadvantaged students to cross the boundary between their everyday knowledge and abstract school knowledge without committing symbolic violence? It also raises questions about the explicitly and implicitly learned knowledge for these young people. How does the teacher's positioning of the young people shape their ways of thinking about themselves and their position in the world? What do these young people learn in school above being model students who know how to sit still and talk nicely?

'What use is this education if he goes into the world unable to communicate?'

Our last interview extract follows directly from the extract that was presented and analysed in the previous section. The researcher asks the teacher how she gauges her success in teaching and the teacher explains that she has 'a much lower benchmark for success' and measures her success by noticing little improvements in the students' behaviour and conduct. She then asks for confirmation that she is not 'talking too much' and having received a confirmative answer shares the following story with the researcher:

Extract 3

Interviewee: There's a story I have that I think is a real example of that and I think this young man is quite a bright kid, um academically, and older, I think he was almost fifteen and I get a phone call in the office one day and I answered the phone, and this um, it didn't sound like a young person actually, he had quite a deep voice and he said 'is John there?' John was a teacher at the time and he was in class and I said 'can I take a message?' and he said 'when does he come out of class?' and I said such and such a time, and he said 'can you just tell him that 3,000 is nowhere near enough, I have to have at least 5, I can't possibly do it on 3,000' and I said 'who is this?' He said it's Pete, this kid, 'oh right, what are we talking about Pete?' and then he went on to explain to me. He was doing this assignment where he had to plan for a trip with a budget of $3,000, it really struck me. It was actually one of those things that I took away and reflected upon, and I thought he is going to pass that assignment and *he is going to get a good mark for that assignment, and yet he couldn't use the phone properly*, he couldn't say to me, it's Pete here can I speak to John, you know *have we succeeded?* You know *I just had a different view of the grade he'll get for that assignment and that it really doesn't reflect what he has learnt or needed*

Researcher: So Pete was the student? [Interviewee: yeah] and he was talking to John the teacher?

Interviewee: Oh the message was for John, $3,000 was not enough I need, I mean it was just the most bizarre conversation. *What use is this education if he goes into the world unable to communicate?*

Researcher: Yeah, but I mean the very fact that he was able to, he was able to see that 3,000 wasn't enough

Interviewee: Oh academically great. You know there was academic success in this kid ringing up at school to finish the assignment yeah. But what about socially? How are you going to ever use that if you can't go, it's Pete here can I speak to John? [Researcher: mm] so you know *I just have a very different view I think of what's important*, I think both are important and I think one without the other

Researcher: But I think also too, there's that bond of trust too, he wouldn't have told you his name unless he trusted the people at the network

Interviewee: He did though, and he would have, but he didn't know to, *he did not know how to use the phone appropriately*. And the presumption that teachers have that a kid knows how to hold a book up the right way, that they know how to turn to the left. I mean the presumptions that we have hit me in the face every day here at the network

Researcher: They bring a different set of prerequisite knowledge don't they?

Interviewee: Absolutely, totally, *it's a different culture* and it requires the *teaching of some of the things that we take so for granted*, and that we take them so for granted is half the [problem]

In the beginning of this chapter we suggested that the pedagogic tensions between abstract and everyday knowledge and between the pastoral pedagogy and knowledge of the school and local knowledges and pedagogies, emerge in this interview on two planes – in teacher–students relationship and teacher–researcher relationship. In this extract the dilemmas on those two planes become intertwined as the teacher rejects and disregards the abstract scientific knowledge that the researcher advocates and offers on two different levels. First, she rejects it as something that she can use as a practitioner to improve her own practice and lift herself off the everyday towards a more reflective view of teaching and learning. In this extract and before, the researcher invites the teacher to consider the art of self-reflection and use it to undertake the work of the self on herself. He thus invites her to step out from her fixed and clear perspective and put herself in the vulnerable position of ambivalence, unfamiliarity and confusion, where her pedagogic anxiety can release the intense emotional energy and create a space between familiar everyday and strange abstract knowledge and thus renew her understanding of her students and their life-worlds, but above all of herself as a teacher. Second, the teacher refuses to use abstract knowledge in her classroom and does not seem to believe that it should be taught to young people in non-traditional educational contexts so that these young people too would have the semiotic tools to move beyond their everyday worlds. By contrast to the teacher's focus on the transmission of institutional rituals of schooling, the researcher continues to advocate the abstract scientific knowledge of schooling both in terms of its disciplinary content, but also in terms of the moral components and social capacities it creates. He invites the teacher to consider the relevance and importance of this kind of knowledge in the lives of young people from disadvantaged communities.

Vygotsky insisted that abstract and everyday concepts cannot be treated and assimilated in 'ready-made or pre-packaged form', but instead need to be brought into 'forms of relationship within which they both develop' (Daniels, 2001: 54). He thus argues that aiming for a direct pedagogic transmission of abstract concepts is fruitless, but instead there is a need for creating spaces of learning where the two can be actively explored and intertwined. An example of integrating everyday and scientific concepts comes from the work of Newman, Griffin and Cole (1989). They argued that creating conditions for conceptual change necessarily required a divergence in understandings. They elaborated their case on the basis of the pervasive indeterminacy of the meaning of speech. Any word or utterance has a number of meanings, depending not only on the relative levels of development of the communicative partners (as Vygotsky had argued), but also on differences in personal experiences, or interpretations of the present situation. To coordinate their actions and regulate joint attention, the student and teacher necessarily speak and act in ways that are responsive to the words and actions of the other. In such dialogues teachers will expand the contributions of students, paraphrase, reinterpret, and substitute more general concepts for the student's everyday forms of speaking and acting. In this manner, collaborative interaction with teachers enables students to enter into new more abstract and general ways of speaking about, and acting towards objects – that is, it opens up a zone of proximal development (Vygotsky, 1978). To encapsulate their view of such interaction, Newman, Griffin and Cole (1989) describe the partners as entering into 'a strategic fiction' – a space of productive misunderstanding where students are assisted to transform their everyday understandings through the words and actions of more advanced students and teachers.

What is implicitly apparent, but not emphasised in Vygotsky's theorising and in Newman, Griffin and Cole's account is the idea that interweaving of everyday and abstract necessarily entails bidirectional movements. That is, it is not only the everyday concepts that develop through their relationship with abstract concepts, but the opposite also applies. In the interview extract above, the teacher's story works as a semiotic device which invites the researcher to consider the teaching in non-traditional contexts from her point of view. By bringing his abstract question to her concrete level of everyday practice, she encourages the researcher to intertwine his abstract knowledge with her everyday understanding. The intervention to the meaning orientations is thus mutual. Yet, just as the teacher refused to make a move from her everyday to his abstract in the first interview extract, so the researcher here rejects the invitation to move from his abstract to her everyday. He thus refuses to consider the world from her perspective, adopt her particular reading of the students, their world, the role of education and the world-out-there. Instead, he reacts by trying to change the teacher's point of view, by suggesting that there might be other ways of interpreting the student's behaviour. These invitations to consider the situation from another perspective are, in turn, rejected by the teacher who insists that she 'has a very different view . . . of what's important'. The teacher's and researcher's conceptualisations of what counts as appropriate teaching/learning in non-traditional contexts, what constitutes valued and valuable knowledge and how to measure success in teaching thus clash and collide and the interlocutors need to continue navigating and negotiating their opposing meanings and the pedagogic dilemmas that arise from this divergence.

Discussion

In this chapter we have sought to highlight the complex pedagogical dilemmas that surface from the unfolding research interaction between a teacher and a researcher as they struggle towards making an intervention into each other's orientations to meaning. In particular, we have been interested in exploring how the interlocutors negotiate the interrelated contradictions between pastoral pedagogy and disciplinary knowledge of the school and the knowledges and pedagogies of the local disadvantaged communities, and bring these together with the tensions between everyday and abstract knowledge in the context of non-traditional schooling.

Our concern in this analysis has not been the existence of these pedagogic dilemmas, for these are ordinary and ever-present in teaching practice. Instead, our worry here is the fact that the teacher does not seem to notice or recognise these tensions and dilemmas as something that requires her attention. The dilemmas seem to become visible for the researcher, yet remain undiscovered for the teacher. It is thus not the teacher's negotiation of these dilemmas in her everyday work, but the negotiation of these dilemmas in the interview encounter, prompted by the researcher's awareness, that is highlighted by our analysis. The teacher's 'blindness' seems important for us, for if we aim at moving students from the everyday and concrete to the abstract and imaginative, then teachers have to be able to make that move too. Yet the example here indicates that the shift to a position where reflection is possible and possibilities to be otherwise can be imagined is not always easy, even if the opportunities for it are offered intentionally and repeatedly.

What is also of interest from the analysis reported in this chapter is the mutuality of the experience of the interview. Having set out to simply record a particular teacher's view of teaching and learning at a non-traditional education context, the interviewer found himself offering an alternate view of teaching and learning to the interviewee, elaborating his alternate view through the use of metaphor and juxtaposition of views. As such, the interview may be construed as an intervention where the interviewer is attempting to influence the interviewee's orientation toward the purpose of schooling in the lives of students in non-traditional education contexts. However, as evidenced in the above extracts the interview may also be construed as an intervention where the interviewee is attempting to influence the interviewer's understanding of the meaning of teaching and learning in non-traditional education contexts. This mutuality of the interview experience in many ways echoes the relationship between the everyday and the scientific where the scientific does not simply replace the everyday during the process of development, but develops out of a reciprocal influence of growth where scientific understandings grow downward through everyday under-standings, while everyday understandings grow upward through scientific understandings (Vygotsky, 1987, 1994).

This mutuality of experience expresses the dialectical tension within the interview, a tension that portrays future zones of proximal development that researchers may negotiate with teachers and others so that talk about the practice of teaching in alternative education contexts and how to improve it may become accessible to those beyond the interview. In this way, the interview becomes a mediating tool with the potential to shift teachers' and researchers' orientations to meaning in non-traditional education contexts. What these future zones of contact may be and where they may be negotiated provides fertile ground for further study.

Acknowledgements

Raymond Brown's research was supported by the Australian Research Council Linkage scheme project LP0882566 (Brown *et al.*, 2008–10).

Parlo Singh's research was supported by the Australian Research Council Linkage scheme project LP0990585 (Glasswell *et al.*, 2009–12).

References

Ang, I. (1996) 'The Curse of the Smile', *Feminist Review*, 52(spring): 36–49.

Ball, S. J. (2003) *Class Strategies and the Education Market. The Middle Classes and Social Advantage*, London and New York: RoutledgeFalmer.

Bernstein, B. (1990) *Class, Codes and Control*, vol. 4, *The Structuring of Pedagogic Discourse*, London: Routledge.

—— (1996) *Pedagogy, Symbolic Control and Identity: Theory, Research, Critique*, London: Falmer Press.

—— (2000) *Pedagogy, Symbolic Control and Identity: Theory, Research, Critique*, 2nd, rev. edn, Oxford: Rowman & Littlefield.

Brown, R., Hirst, E., Woods, A. F. and Heck, D. A. (2008–10), *The Development of a Values Approach to School Renewal*, Australian Research Council Linkage 2008–10: LP0882566.

Daniels, H. (1989) 'Visual Displays as Tacit Relays of the Structure of Pedagogic Practice', *British Journal of Sociology of Education*, 10(2): 123–40.

—— (1995) 'Pedagogic Practices, Tacit Knowledge and Discursive Discrimination: Bernstein and Post-Vygotskian Research', *British Journal of Sociology of Education*, 16(4): 517–32.

—— (2001) *Vygotsky and Pedagogy*, London and New York: RoutledgeFalmer.

—— (2010) 'The Mutual Shaping of Human Action and Institutional Settings: A Study of the Transformation of Children's Services and Professional Work', *British Journal of Sociology of Education*, 31(4): 377–93.

Davydov, V. (1995) 'The Influence of L. S. Vygotsky on Education Theory, Research and Practice', *Educational Researcher*, 24: 12–21.

de Jong, T. (2005) 'A Framework of Principles and Best Practice for Managing Student Behaviour in the Australian Education Context', *School Psychology International*, 26: 353–70.

de Jong, T. and Griffiths, C. (2006) 'The Role of Alternative Education Programs in Meeting the Needs of Adolescent Students with Challenging Behaviour: Characteristics of Best Practice', *Australian Journal of Guidance and Counselling*, 16(1): 29–40.

Glasswell, K., Singh, P., McNaughton, S. and Davis, K. L. (2009–12), *Smart Education Partnerships: Testing a Research Collaboration Model to Build Literacy Innovations in Low Socio Economic Schools*, Australian Research Council Linkage 2009–12: LP0990585.

Hasan, R. (2002a) 'Semiotic Mediation and Mental Development in Pluralistic Societies: Some Implications for Tomorrow's Schooling', in G. Wells and G. Claxton (eds.), *Learning for Life in the 21st Century: Socio-cultural Perspectives on the Future of Education*, Oxford: Blackwell, 112–26.

—— (2002b) 'Ways of Meaning, Ways of Learning: Code as an Explanatory Concept', *British Journal of Sociology of Education*, 23(4): 537–48.

—— (2004) 'The Concept of Semiotic Mediation: Perspectives from Bernstein's Sociology', in J. Muller, B. Davies and A. Morais (eds.), *Reading Bernstein, Researching Bernstein*, London and New York: RoutledgeFalmer, 30–43.

Hunter, I. (1993) 'The Pastoral Bureaucracy: Towards a Less Principled Understanding of State Schooling', in D. Meredyth and D. Tyler (eds.), *Child and Citizen. Genealogies of Schooling and Subjectivity*, Brisbane: Griffith University, Institute of Cultural Policy Studies, 237–87.

—— (1994) *Rethinking the School. Subjectivity, Bureaucracy and Criticism*, Sydney: Allen & Unwin.

Kozulin (1990) *Vygotsky's Psychology: A Biography of Ideas*, Cambridge, MA: Harvard University Press.

Newman, D., Griffin, P. and Cole, M. (1989) *The Construction Zone: Working for Cognitive Change in School*, Cambridge: Cambridge University Press.

Rose, D. (1999) 'Culture, Competence and Schooling: Approaches to Literacy Teaching in Indigenous School Education', in F. Christie (ed.), *Pedagogy and the Shaping of Consciousness*, London and New York: Continuum, 217–45.

Singh, P. and Doherty, C. (2004) 'Global Cultural Flows and Pedagogic Dilemmas: Teaching in the Global University "Contact Zone"', *TESOL Quarterly*, 38(1): 9–42.

Trent, S. C., Artiles, A. J., and Englert, C. S. (1998) 'Deficit Thinking to Social Constructivism: A Review of Theory, Research, and Practice in Special Education', *Review of Research in Education*, 23: 277–307.

van der Veer, R. and Valsiner, J. (1991) *Understanding Vygotsky: A Quest for Synthesis*, Oxford: Blackwell.

Vygotsky, L. (1978) *Mind in Society: The Development of Higher Psychological Processes*, ed. and trans. M. Cole, V. John-Steiner, S. Scribner and E. Souberman, Cambridge, MA: Harvard University Press.

—— (1981) 'The Development of Higher Forms of Attention', in J. V. Wertsch (ed.), *The Concept of Activity in Soviet Psychology*, Armonk, NY: M. E. Sharpe, 189–240.

—— (1987) 'Thinking and Speech', in R. W. Rieber and A. S. Carton (eds.), trans. N. Minick, *The Collected Works of L. S. Vygotsky*, vol. 1, *Problems of General Psychology*, New York: Plenum Press, 243–85.

—— (1994) 'The Development of Academic Concepts in School Aged Children', in R. van der Veer and J. Valsiner (eds.), T. Prout and R. van der Veer (trans.), *The Vygotsky Reader*, Oxford: Blackwell, 355–70.

Wertsch, J. V. (2007) 'Mediation', in H. Daniels, M. Cole and J. V. Wertsch (eds.), *The Cambridge Companion to Vygotsky*, Cambridge: Cambridge University Press, 178–92.

Wertsch, J. V. and Rupert, L. J. (1993) 'The Authority of Cultural Tools in a Socio-cultural Approach to Mediated Agency', *Cognition and Instruction*, 11(3–4): 227–39.

7 Modalities of authority and the socialisation of the school in contemporary approaches to educational change

David H. Eddy Spicer

Introduction

Recent educational reforms in England have emphasised school-to-school relationships as the cornerstone of school improvement initiatives in a radically devolved system of schooling (Department for Education, 2010; Hargreaves, 2010). These shifts reflect an emphasis in new public management more broadly on organisational autonomy within overarching frameworks of 'light touch' institutional regulation by the state (Mulgan, 2009). Such devolution highlights linkages among organisations as a means of systemic improvement in lieu of centralised initiatives (e.g., King, 2010; OECD, 2003; Rashman, Withers, and Hartley, 2009). Critical perspectives have pointed to the ways in which organisational autonomy has structural features that maintain dominating discourses, particularly in terms of the distribution of power and the ways in which 'professional' is defined. According to these critiques, beneath the velvet glove of 'light touch' lies not the fist of the state, but the ever more elusive networks of control of advanced capitalism (Apple, 2009; Ball, 2007; Bourdieu, 1998). A fulcrum of both sides of this debate concerns modalities of authority in public-sector institutions, and a frequent contrast is the distinction between hierarchical authority characteristic of bureaucracies and the professional authority of those at work within.

In the institution of schooling, national systems of education have seen huge changes in enrolment, accompanied by ever more complex and differentiated bureaucratic structures over the past six decades. Forms of instruction, however, remain strikingly similar, across levels of the educational system and even across national systems (Bernstein, 2003 (1990): 169; Bidwell, 2001). Anyone who has been educated in a modern system of schooling will find similar features of teacher, teaching and school in the Congo and China, in villages and cities. Systems of schooling have undergone massive change; yet the instructional core remains resilient, relatively undifferentiated in comparison with the bureaucratic complexity wrought by shifts in demography and scale.

The question of this relative stability of the instructional core merits the close attention of those concerned with the social formation of mind. Conceptualising the school as a context for the socialisation of students has long been of central concern to post-Vygotskian theories, as it was to Vygotsky himself, who wrote of the "essential difference" between the process of instruction that takes place before school age and that which occurs within schools (Vygotsky, 1956: 445, cited in Wertsch, 1985: 74). This central insight concerning the ways in which social, historical and cultural processes at the level of the institution condition the interpsychological functioning of individuals has inspired deep understanding of the instructional core – the relationship among teacher, student and subject matter – *as it should be*. Despite this, relatively little attention in post-Vygotskian theories has gone towards the institution of schooling that shapes the instructional core *as it is*, the processes of structuring the organising context of the school itself. This issue is particularly salient given recent policy emphasis on school-to-school relationships that aim to shift two crucial dimensions of the school, the organisation of the instructional core and the management of that organisation, the governance and administration of the school.

This chapter asserts that devolution has introduced a new phase in the institution of schooling in which ever more articulated, complex and differentiated forms of administration accompany increasing complexity, but not necessarily transformation, of the instructional core. The chapter explores the connections between modalities of authority in the school as organisation and schooling as a societal institution. I describe this as a process of socialisation at the level of the organisation. The emphasis here is on the organising context and the processes of socialisation structuring that context. This implies the socialisation of those who work and learn within but shifts the angle of sight from the person to the processes of structuring the context itself.

Organisational socialisation in these terms emphasises the link between institution and the organisational contexts doing the work of that institution, the institution of schooling and the organising context of the school. The term highlights the organising context itself as a cultural, historical product conditioned by underlying relations of power and principles of control and regulating the social relations produced within that context (Daniels, 2008b: 154). Following Bernstein (1977, 2000, 2003 (1990)), whose sociology of cultural transmission finds roots in Vygotskian notions of speech as an orienting and regulative system (2000: 177), this process of regulation is viewed as fundamentally pedagogical, not in the limited sense of teacher and student but in a wider sense. The basic image that I elaborate further is of a pedagogic discourse that involves an institutionalised transmitter, an agency recognised as a legitimate purveyor of the texts deemed 'thinkable' by the institution, and an acquirer, an agency in the process of being recruited into the dominating discourse, one whose access to privileging texts is constrained.

The line of approach taken in this chapter builds on work inspired by Bernstein that explores the school as organising context in the work of Daniels (1995, 2008a), Tyler (1988), and Gamble and Hoadley (2008). The chapter begins with an overview and examples drawn from the literature of explanations of authority in the organising contexts within and across schools. I then move on to the alternative perspective offered by Bernstein, which suggests, "at the deepest level of social organisation the relations between the organisation of the curriculum, the methods of teaching and the patterns of governance and supervision are tightly related" (Tyler, 1988: 154). The aim is to produce generative models that explore the underlying principles that produce and reproduce structure, as a means of illuminating alternative pathways towards change.

Modalities of authority

The form, but not the formation, of schools as organising contexts for teaching and learning has been a topic of intensive research and debate in sociological and organisational studies of education, particularly in light of the rapid expansion of state systems of schooling in the post-war years (Lauder *et al.*, 2006: 1–70). In the following, I review several studies that have aimed to explain modalities of authority in the organising context of schools by examining the relationship amongst educational goals, teaching and learning, and governance and administration. This is in the service of understanding what constitutes the *social* in schools as institutionalised workplaces. The review lays the foundations for an approach to understanding the *social* in terms of connections amongst institution, organisation, and persons; and discerning from this how new institutional arrangements, such as school-to-school relationships, create new institutional possibilities or serve to reproduce the status quo.

School-to-school relationships offer special insight into the process of an organisation being acquired by an institution, or organisational socialisation. This is the process through which the institutionalised practices, knowledge, and criteria that are legitimated by the wider system are transmitted by one organisation and acquired by another. Typically, systems of authority are invoked in articulating the sculpting of the school as an institutionalised organisation. Traditional sociological and philosophical perspectives view authority relations as the means through which power and control are exercised. The explanatory framework explored here views systems of authority as the *outcome* of patterns of institutional control that select and organise what is taken as legitimate knowledge in particular contexts. A view of patterns of authority as historical, societal, and cultural products highlights how the acquirer comes to recognise, evaluate and reproduce phenomena which the transmitter takes to be of legitimate concern. As Daniels (1995, 2008b) has highlighted, Bernstein provides a grammar for parsing how "institutional structures themselves are cultural products that serve as mediators in their own right" (2008b: 168).

I characterise the debate around the modalities of authority in the school in terms of three dimensions of authority. Broadly, these three consist of vertical relations of control through hierarchic or managerial authority, horizontal relations through the collective ascription of operative authority, and epistemic authority in terms of acknowledged expertise that draws on what is taken to be the knowledge base of the education profession. Following McLaughlin (2007), these types of authority can be characterised as managerial, operative, and epistemic (pp. 72–3). The first two, managerial authority and operative authority, have to do with obedience to one *in* authority. The third, epistemic authority, corresponds with deference to one considered *an* authority. Both managerial and operative forms of authority depend on formal and informal roles, either formally constituted through the institution or, with operative authority, provisionally defined by the collective. Epistemic authority is commonly defined as an authority in a field of knowledge in contrast to hierarchical authority within an institution or within a collective. To paraphrase de George (1985), epistemic authority is that one person holds a proposition "to be true or more probably true" after someone or something taken as an authority enunciates that proposition (p. 33). De George elaborates that a 'de facto' epistemic authority is one considered to be an authority, "by another or by others with respect to some field or area of knowledge" (*ibid.*: 27). Wilson (1983) identifies epistemic authority more simply as that which arises from collective perceptions of those who "know what they are talking about" (p. 13).

This section advances the argument that, in looking closely at the processes of how schools as organisations come to be recognised as legitimate, these are not contrasting systems but deeply interwoven and that the underlying principles of their interconnection cannot be traced following the surface features of authority. This points to a methodological orientation towards structuralist explanations. This argument also raises the substantive conjecture that increasingly complex systems of authority along any of the three dimensions require equivalent sophistication in the others. However, we have not yet forged a grammar capable of interrogating these developments. A proposal for this awaits in the section following this review, in which I put forward a tentative framework for such an understanding.

Bureaucratic, artisanal, and professional control

The interrelationship of organisational socialisation and modalities of authority in schools has occupied social theorists, educational researchers, policymakers, and educators particularly since the post-war boom in state education and consequent perennial calls for comprehensive change in the system of schooling (Berman and McLaughlin, 1975; Levin, 2010). Modalities of authority have most frequently been portrayed as split at the root between an outward-facing administrative sphere and an inward-looking technical sphere controlling the instructional core. In the following I look at two influential reviews that aimed to characterise patterns of authority in the institutionalisation of schools as organisations. The first review (Lortie, 1969) came at the crest of the initial wave of studies of large-scale educational change; the second review (Rowan, 1990) arrived two decades later as attention began to turn towards comprehensive school reform through formalised relationships among schools, a trend that has culminated in the emphasis on school-to-school relationships. I conclude with an alternative perspective on the distribution of power in schooling from a recent study of modalities of authority in the English educational system (Gunter and Forrester, 2007, 2009) before going on to develop an alternative analysis.

Lortie's tangle

Lortie (1969) drew on over a decade of research to explore the disconnection among educational goals, teaching and learning and the organisation of the school. Lortie identified what he termed the "tangled and complex" strands of bureaucracy, professional control, and individual autonomy at play (p. 1). Bureaucratic control, a hallmark of modern national systems of education worked through a vertical and formal structure of accountability enshrined in positions within the organisation and operating through powers of allocation, the ability to direct resources. However, Lortie and others observed that, although schools and school systems exhibited high degrees of vertical structure through a clearly articulated bureaucracy, those in charge had few means to influence directly the actions of those they were meant to oversee. School leaders, in actuality, could do little to constrain the work of teachers. Lortie attributed this to the state of the profession; teachers, in general, and primary teachers in particular, were not part of a unified occupational group that maintained its own professional standards. They were more like artisans, with individual craft prized above standardisation of practice. Moreover, schools were organised in ways that protected teachers' autonomy as artisans, respecting their apparent claim to knowledge based on close understandings of their students. Status as a craft meant that any individual teacher could agree in principle with superordinates' directives while "feeling certain that the principle does not apply to her particular circumstances" (1969: 9). Lortie, along with other researchers at the time, pointed out the lack of connection between the administrative sphere of school organising and the vague and imprecise technical sphere of the work of teachers and students. His research into the organisation of primary schools had led him to conclude that the field lacked any firm basis for professional authority. If such a foundation existed, Lortie asserted, "supervisors could, through mastery of that consensus, assert the right to prescribe for subordinates" (p. 9). By invoking the oxymoronic term 'mastery of the consensus', Lortie asserted that managerial authority alone would never prevail if it were not fused with the epistemic authority of a commonly agreed upon foundation of professional knowledge.

Lortie's work, rooted in the symbolic interactionism of George Herbert Mead and Herbert Blumer, seeks to explain the constitution of identities and selves in terms of social interaction, particularly with those most influential. Lortie (1969) posited that the bipolar structure of schools was rooted in the socialisation of teachers through their long sojourn in the institution of schooling (p. 26ff.). This sojourn included their own schooling, their preparation in teacher training, and their subsequent interactions with colleagues. Such an arrangement meant that tight bureaucratic controls were unnecessary, as the socialised conservatism of teachers maintained the existing order. Lortie and other researchers at the time (Cohen *et al.*, 1972; Meyer and Rowan, 1977; Weick, 1976) perceived two social orders, the externally facing administrative sphere and an insulated and insular technical sphere.

Building on Lortie's research as well as a wide range of other studies, these insights were encapsulated in the formulation of 'loose coupling', which posited that the lack and incoherence of tight bureaucratic and professional controls over teaching meant that schools were "loosely coupled systems" (Weick, 1976). 'Loose coupling' viewed the social order as a negotiated settlement between the halves of the school, one imbued with managerial authority but lacking means of enforcement and the other under the operative authority of the artisan but lacking the wider legitimacy that a professional knowledge base would bring.

Professional commitment and bureaucratic control

While illuminating in many aspects, the notion of two incommensurate halves comprising one stable whole failed to account for the "deep-seated stability and relative simplicity" in the organisation of instruction at the classroom level (Bidwell, 2001: 101). This was especially so in light of the increasing differentiation and specialisation of administration aimed specifically at instruction, which accounted for much of the development of school bureaucracy in the post-Sputnik push for educational reform. Lortie's tangle took on a different, pro-fessionalised form, especially in light of policy shifts towards more comprehensive models of tightening controls on the technical sphere through the promulgation of standards along with closer specification and supervision of curriculum, teaching practices and student outcomes.

For example, Rowan conceptualised and then tested empirically two contrasting approaches to systems of authority in the organising context of the school, that of what were termed 'mechanistic controls' and that of 'collective commitment'. In a review of a wide body of research, Rowan (1990) portrayed mechanistic controls as derived from a clearly delineated hierarchical social order, accompanied with a parallel structuring of knowledge that included prescriptive curriculum and the close monitoring of educational outcomes through standardised measures. Rowan concluded from his review that competency-based instructional management and intensive evaluation did lead to increased alignment among teaching and the content of tests, the pace of instruction, student behaviour and improvement in test results (p. 368). Moreover, such mechanistic controls, when applied intensively, increased teachers' perceptions of efficacy and feelings of cohesiveness rather than increasing alienation, as Lortie's tangle might suggest. The nature of efficacy and of teachers' conception of the task of teaching, however, was tightly constrained. Mechanistic controls resulted in teachers' instru-mentalisation of the task of teaching and of their view of learning, with the artisanal reduced to freedom to use "a different worksheet or create a worksheet of my own, as long as it meets the objective" in the words of one interviewed teacher (Bullough *et al.*, 1984: 349, as cited in Rowan, 1990: 362). In this characterisation, supervisors had achieved the 'mastery of the consensus' suggested by Lortie, combining managerial authority with epistemic authority, resulting in a constrained rather than expansive professionalism.

Rowan (1990) contrasts this pattern of authority with collective commitment, which hinges on professional collegiality in the teachers' immediate environment. Collective commitment, in Rowan's summary of the research, requires decen-tralised management and adaptive approaches to instruction that hinge on shared educational values and the development of 'professional learning communities'. Such professional groupings assumed local, collective responsibility for specifying locally adapted innovations (p. 369ff.). The premise to this approach of socialising the school was one that posited a coherent ideological orientation to the profession of teaching, serving as anchor in an environment with high levels of uncertainty. Such an emphasis on values above scripts had as its premise that no pedagogical doctrine could "provide procedural templates of sufficient specificity to guide a teacher's day-to-day practice effectively" (Bidwell, 2001: 106). In such an environment of uncertainty, the operative authority of the collective legitimises the professional knowledge base, the epistemic authority of the teacher.

In essence, Rowan's review and subsequent work clarified two sources of epistemic authority. The first, mechanistic controls, required high levels of differentiation and specialisation in the administrative sphere while the professional knowledge of teachers was closely constrained. In this approach to the socialisation of schools, hierarchical managerial authority comes fused with *prescriptive* epistemic authority. The second system of authority, collective control, entails a qualitatively different fusion of the operative authority of the collective with a *discursive* epistemic authority. This resonates with a range of other studies that identified similar dichotomous patterns of authority, either oriented towards complexity in the organisation of instruction or complexity in the management of that organisation. Daft and Becker (1978), for example, note:

> Low formalisation, decentralisation and high complexity (professionalism) are suited to both initiation and adoption of innovations within the technical core. The opposite structural conditions facilitate innovation in the administrative domain. High formalisation, centralisation and low complexity (professionalism) fit the initiation and adoption of innovation which pertain to the organisation itself. (pp. 146–7)

Lortie's 'mastery of the consensus' shifts from autonomous halves to a teeter-totter between the complexity of the instructional core versus the complexity of the management of that core. In these terms, a dominating managerial authority necessarily invokes constraints on professional knowledge and, conversely, an expansive operative authority entails elaboration of the professional knowledge base but only when managerial authority and the formal structure that supports it are kept at bay. Epistemic authority, in this view, serves as the pivot, veering either towards administrative elaboration or differentiation and complexity in the instructional core, but not both.

Increasing complexity

A multi-year study by Rowan and colleagues set out to explore the juxtaposition of control and commitment as organising principles in 'chains' of schools, a form of inter-organisational relationships in which a template for both the organisation of instruction and governance and administration is introduced as schools join the chain (Miller and Rowan, 2006; Rowan *et al.*, 2009a, 2009b). Two familiar patterns of mechanistic and organic were evident, the former relying on highly specified instructional and managerial routines and the latter emphasising shared values and the development of 'professional learning communities'. The study also highlighted a third modality that combined elements of both. Researchers characterised the approach as using 'professional controls' (Rowan *et al.*, 2009a: 29). This pattern involves carrying forward targeted initiatives within the framework of a curriculum that has been developed through broad professional consensus on effective pedagogy. The approach involved close attention to strategic local adaptation and rapid dissemination of successful adaptations to others. In terms of the management of teachers and students, implementation of the strategy in schools was overseen by two new leadership positions each school adopted that included a design coach who worked with school leaders and a literacy coordinator who worked directly with teachers. Professional expertise was also available through programme coaches and facilitators that worked across schools. The study found that the strategy of 'professional controls' had strong effects both in the development of teacher leadership and in the development of teaching practice. Ultimately the third strategy proved to have the most sustained effect of any of the three strategies (or a control group of schools) on accelerating growth in students' mastery of literacy across their primary years.

The findings of this study are corroborated by a recent longitudinal case study of design-based whole school reform that identified a 'differentiation strategy' as a key and often tacit step in implementing designs for secondary school reform (McDonald *et al.*, 2009). A differentiation strategy allows those developing a design and those carrying it out in schools to maximise both fidelity and adaptation through an iterative process of differentiating principles and practices that are central to the design from those that can be adapted to particular settings. Such complex forms of organisation, when underpinned by explicitly framed professional values, had the greatest effect overall.

These studies point towards the conjoined complexity of all three dimensions of authority resulting in the most generative modality for teaching and learning. The dichotomous halves, these findings suggest, are part of a larger whole, rather than tangle or teeter-totter. As Tyler (1985) notes, "The much celebrated tension between hierarchical and professional control could, in other words, be more a symptom of a certain maturity in organisational development rather than a deep-seated structural tendency" (p. 55). Generative epistemic authority, it would seem, corresponds with the complexity of both managerial and operative authority, which, "presupposes an administrative apparatus of considerable sophistication and complexity, with the capacity to adapt the patterns of governance, administration and surveillance to changing demands at the workflow level" (Tyler, 1985: 60).

Sources of epistemic authority

That professional autonomy should depend at some crucial point on bureaucratic sophistication and complexity appears to be a contradiction. If the increased sophistication of the instructional core entails the increased sophistication of governance and supervision structures, what shapes such sophistication? In other words, what are the sources of legitimacy for modalities of authority that rely on 'professionalised' epistemic authority, if not rooted in the managerial authority of bureaucratic structure or the authority of the collective, operative authority? Such questions cannot be answered by looking at systems of authority alone. To understand the interconnections requires a broader framework.

In the English context, Gunter and Forrester (2007, 2009) bring an analytic perspective drawn from Bourdieu to an exploration of the sources of legitimation of professional knowledge in the English system of schooling. Their analysis draws on critical policy sociology and its critiques of the past quarter century of large-scale shifts in educational policy in England, North America, Australia and New Zealand (Apple *et al.*, 2003; Ball, 2007, 2008; Whitty *et al.*, 1998), policy initiatives that undergird the push towards school-to-school relationships. There is broad agreement about features of such policy shifts, features that include devolution of powers to local schools accompanied by greater involvement in the educational agenda by central government. Schools are granted greater autonomy, while the state tightens control over specification of the definition of quality at all levels in terms of educational standards, systems of examination, and criteria used for inspection. In England, specialised units within the Department of Education, such as the Standards and Effectiveness Unit and, most recently, the National College of School Leadership promulgate officially sanctioned definitions of 'professional'.

Gunter and Forrester (2009) explore how the articulation of professional knowledge in education came to be a state project. They trace how knowledge from one field, that of business and management, in particular, has been inserted into the field of education. They document this process through an extensive analysis of primary (e.g., government policy) and secondary (journal articles) documents, as well as 116 purposively sampled interviews with a broad range of those involved in various facets of policy formulation, implementation, evaluation, and critique. Close readings of the documentary data and interview transcripts led to the identification of two distinct 'regimes of practice'. The dominant regime, 'school leadership policy network', generates overarching policy. This multi-dimensional and multilayered network both promulgates and enacts official policy. The result is that the local autonomy of schools, according to Gunter and Forrester, parallels the autonomy of the teacher cited earlier in Rowan's research whose freedom extended to the design of one's own worksheet. Gunter and Forester (2009) assert, "Local autonomy is framed around the tactics of delivery in regard to local context (e.g. pace of reform implementation), and to building on [governmental] policies and strategies rather than creating alternative agendas and models" (p. 498).

This perspective on the state legitimation of professional knowledge appears to be Lortie's 'mastery of the consensus' writ large, wherein a policy elite come to define what is taken as legitimate meanings for the profession. This is accomplished not through hierarchical control but through the more pervasive control of a dominating discourse that invokes epistemic authority. Here we have a compelling explanation of the construction of epistemic authority absent from earlier analyses. Gunter and Forester offer the clear portrayal of the formation of the state classification of knowledge and a plausible mechanism for its diffusion into schools through regimes of practice. The process through which schools as organisations and those who work within come to acquire such a discourse is not explored. The immediate concern of their study is the identification of the policy elite itself, not the articulation of the processes through which official policy becomes local practice. However, the processes of transmission and acquisition are of central concern in the effort to understand how the epistemic authority woven into the dominating discourses of the state might be taken up from one location and take root in another.

Authority and pedagogic discourse

The processes of dislocation and relocation are integral to what Bernstein (Bernstein, 2003(1990): 165–218) defines as characteristic of *pedagogic* discourse. The use of the term 'pedagogic' in the context of schooling is potentially confusing. Bernstein (2003(1990)) uses the term to denote a pedagogic process at work, not that the content of the discourse concerns teaching and learning. The pedagogic process is one of symbolic control, the transmission and acquisition of legitimate meanings. Thus, the state classification of professional knowledge identified in Gunter and Forrester's analysis serves as a form of official pedagogic discourse, the official legitimation of what is 'thinkable' in the institution of schooling.

The power of Bernstein's analysis towards an understanding of devolved systems of schooling lies in its articulation of how schools as organisations are recruited into the official pedagogic discourse. Bernstein makes clear that there is not one official discourse but several discourses. Pedagogic discourse is multidimensional in systems of schooling, with each dimension insulated in varying degrees from others. There is the dimension of the 'thinkable' in official policy and political practice; there is the dimension of the 'thinkable' in the training for school leaders and another dimension of legitimate meaning in the work of school leaders with teachers and teachers with students, local pedagogic discourses (2003(1990): 205–6). I use the term dimension rather than level here to emphasise that these planes are not embedded in the sense that classrooms add up to school, schools add up to state system. These planes are interdependent but the dependencies are more or less strong as a result of the distribution of power. The autonomy of alternative discourses, the possibility for different forms of practice to influence official pedagogic practice depends crucially on the constitution of the dominating discourse (2003 (1990): 196). Bernstein asserts that, "Official pedagogic discourse regulates the rules of production, distribution, reproduction and interrelations of transmission and acquisition (practice) and the organization of their contexts (organization)" (*ibid.*).

However, the patterns of practice that constitute a particular dimension do not depend solely on a deterministic distribution of power (Atkinson, 1985: 172). Bernstein (2003(1990): 165–218) repeatedly emphasises that any given set of principles of order also relays principles of disorder, challenge and contradiction. Distributive rules based in the social division of labour provide the 'grammar' of pedagogic discourse. This grammar is further elaborated by two additional rules embedded within distributive rules. Recontextualising rules provide the principles that structure pedagogic discourse, that is to say the principles that realise the 'thinkable' in official and local sites of pedagogic practice; and evaluation rules define legitimate realisations of that practice, what forms the 'thinkable' can take (2003(1990): 180–7).

These underlying principles provide a way for examining the earlier analyses of systems of authority in schooling through a different lens. Rowan *et al.* (2009) locate their analysis of systems of authority in schooling at the level of evaluation rules, in that they are primarily concerned with explaining the constitution of legitimate realisations of practice across different organisations. Gunter and Forrester (2009), on the other hand, are concerned with distributive rules, as their focus is on the correspondence of the social division of labour to the dominating discourse of schooling. The concern of this chapter is to develop an understanding of the interrelationship of official and local pedagogic discourses and the legitimation of practice across organisations. For this reason, I focus on recontextualising principles.

Recontextualising principles are akin to transcription rules in the creation of recombinant DNA. Transcription takes bits of genetic material from one context and inserts it into an entirely different context, generating a variant life form. The recontextualising field takes bits of knowledge, practices, criteria from their original sites of production and recombines these in an entirely different context. Recontextualising rules operate on semiotic material, material for making meaning, and transcribe texts from one field and position them in another field, from the context of production to a context of reproduction. Within the system of education, pedagogic discourses specialised to each plane dislocate texts – knowledge, practices, criteria – from elsewhere, and reconstitute these as texts, elements of ongoing practice, within that plane.

The term 'texts' is used in the broadest sense as language that is serving a function in a context. Bernstein writes:

> It is important to note that we are here using 'text' both in a literal and in an extended sense. It can refer to the dominant curriculum, dominant pedagogic practice, but also to any pedagogic representation, spoken, written, visual, postural, sartorial, spatial. (2003(1990): 175)

The recontextualising rules of pedagogic discourse act to interrupt the connection between the text and its primary context and appropriate the text to another, secondary context (Bernstein, 2003(1990): 191ff.). In the constitution of the instructional core, recontextualising has to do with taking disciplinary knowledge from the sites of its production in academia and weaving it into the discourse of the classroom. These transformed texts might appear as textbooks or as patterns of action that have been borrowed from their original practices, like biology labwork or studio art. The recontextualising field of the management of the instructional core appropriates texts, knowledge, practices, criteria for evaluation, from business management and educational research to constitute the 'thinkable' for managing instruction. These relocated texts are part of the pedagogic discourse that specifies how schools as organisations are socialised into a particular system of schooling.

Recontextualising rules operate both backwards and forwards. Recontextualising reaches back to appropriate text from its primary context. In this process, the text shifts fundamentally through changing its position in relation to the primary context, repositioning and refocusing it in a secondary context. Such dislocation modifies the text through selective appropriation, condensation, and elaboration (Bernstein, 2003(1990): 192). A recent example of this process is the notion of 'distributed leadership'. The term arose through observations of leadership practice drawing on theories of activity to view leadership as 'stretched over' persons, tools, and activity settings. The term has been taken up in official pedagogic discourse as a normative approach to differentiating the management of the organisation of instruction. For example, distributed leadership is a guiding principle of the National College of School Leadership's 'Leading from the Middle' programme for 'middle leaders', department heads and specialists. In this dislocation and relocation, certain attributes were amplified that were consistent with a dominating discourse around managerialism and professional values, while other aspects from the primary context, such as the theoretical framing of the term, were elided (Hall *et al.*, 2011; Mayrowetz, 2008).

Recontextualising also reaches forward, entailing a second-order transformation of the text. The transformed text is appropriated by the acquirer, a pedagogic process that introduces yet another transformation. This realisation of the text in the secondary context is of great interest to an understanding of the dynamics of change in schools, where we begin to see how the organisation of contexts and pedagogic discourse mutually shape one another.

How does recontextualising operate when one school establishes a pedagogic relationship with another? The curious matter in school-to-school pedagogy is that the reaching back entails a recontextualisation of texts from the transmitter itself. Among the primary contexts from which the lead school, the transmitter, draws its texts are its own sedimented practices, knowledge, and criteria that have come out of its socialisation as an organisation. Recontextualising rules operate here to appropriate selectively and reposition the texts that are taken up as part of the relationship with the supported school, the acquirer. That is the backwards glance of recontextualising. There is also the forward motion of how these dislocated texts are then relocated in the secondary context of the school-to-school relationship itself. The lead school, for example, may draw on its existing practices around distributed leadership in attempting to shift the organisational context of the supported school. Relationships between peers across schools working at similar levels, say those addressing special educational needs, will appropriate texts from the existing practice and introduce these into the relationship. The texts are realised as the specialists in the supported school take up these texts, these recontextualised practices, as part of their ongoing work in the secondary context of the supported school. The forward movement of recontextualisation may also reshape the lead school. As noted before, recontextualising generates disorder and dilemma in the process of dislocation and relocation at the same time as it is generating principles of order, relation, and identity (2003(1990): 196).

Interpersonal and ideational meaning

The example above demonstrates how the official pedagogic discourse may loom large but not in a deterministic sense. Recontextualising in the context of school-to-school relationships offers underlying principles for the ways in which systems of authority are recognised and realised as legitimate. Specifically, recontextualising constitutes the 'what' and 'how' of the rules of specialised communication between schools, the pedagogic discourse. The 'what' indicates the contents, categories and relationships among these to be transmitted. The 'how' specifies legitimate order, relation, and identity of transmitters, acquirers, and contexts. That is, the 'how' regulates the rules for 'what a context is a context for', social relations and social identity (Bernstein, 2003 (1990): 184).

The distinction between 'what' and 'how' of pedagogic discourse resonates with the distinction between the field of discourse and the tenor of discourse in the social semiotics of Halliday and Hasan, which draws on Bernstein's theory of pedagogic communication (Halliday and Hasan, 1989; Halliday and Matthiessen, 2004). The field of discourse is the topic or focus of the action and refers to what is happening, to the nature of the social action that is taking place: what is it that the participants are engaged in, in which the language figures as some essential component? The field of discourse regulates ideational meaning. The tenor of discourse encompasses role relations of power and solidarity, referring to who is taking part, to the nature of the participants, their statuses and roles: what kinds of role relationship obtain among the participants, including permanent and temporary relationships of one kind or another, both the types of speech role that they are taking on in the dialogue and the whole cluster of socially significant relationships in which they are involved. The tenor of discourse regulates interpersonal meaning (Halliday and Hasan, 1989: 12).

Ideational meaning associated with the 'what' of pedagogic discourse, its field, varies along a cline that ranges from closed to open. Tightly bound categories and relations encode texts that are condensed and in which meanings are implicit through an assumed collective understanding. An open orientation of ideational meaning implies permeable boundaries that encode texts which demand explication and the elaboration of meaning within the text itself. At the open end, there is a continuing negotiation of ideational meaning; at the closed end, meaning is not 'up for grabs'.

A similar cline for interpersonal meaning associated with the tenor of pedagogic discourse exists between highly structured relationships to relationships that are apparently flexible, in which social order does not appear to be prescribed and speech roles are distributed. Thus, at one end of the cline of interpersonal meaning, a tight correspondence exists between interpersonal meaning and an explicit social order; interpersonal meaning is positional. At the other end, interpersonal meaning appears to be negotiated between and attached to persons, not positions; it is apparently personal.

Institutional modalities

Bernstein (2000: 102) states that the tenor of pedagogic discourse, interpersonal meaning, embeds the field of discourse, ideational meaning. By this, he indicates that the content of the discourse, the categories that define and legitimate knowledge and render the relations among ideas depends fundamentally on social relations, the relations among persons, which he labels the regulative component of pedagogic discourse. The roots of the legacy of Vygotsky and Luria are clear at this juncture, that social interaction regulates meaning and orients forms of consciousness. Bernstein extends this insight to reveal how meanings are institutionalised; both social relations and relations amongst ideas derive from the distribution of power in society, the social division of labour, as recontextualised within various organizing contexts. The varieties of those organising contexts that are recognised as legitimate and realise practices judged to be legitimate, describe the modalities of authority sustained by a given distribution of power.

The intersection of interpersonal and ideational meaning provides a tool for describing those modalities. The embedding of ideational in interpersonal meaning suggests two already familiar modalities, one which privileges managerial authority and another which privileges the collective. With managerial authority in the foreground, interpersonal meaning orients to the positional and ideational meanings are correspondingly constrained. Such a modality, as Bernstein (1977) writes, implies the following:

> Knowledge . . . is dangerous, it cannot be exchanged like money, it must be confined to special well-chosen persons and even divorced from practical concerns. The forms of knowledge must always be well-insulated from each other: there must be no sparking across the forms with unpredictable outcomes. Specialisation makes knowledge safe and protects the vital principles of social order. (p. 74)

In the term specialisation, we recognise interpersonal meaning oriented towards the positional and ideational meanings that hinge on well-protected boundaries. Neither ideational nor interpersonal meaning is open for negotiation. Here we have a crystallisation of the 'mechanical control' strategy described by Rowan *et al.* (2009) earlier, one in which we can imagine a clear hieratic order of both ideas and persons at work, displayed through patterns of authority that emphasise the importance of managerial authority. We might contrast this with what Rowan *et al.*, portrayed as the opposing construct, the organic controls of professional commitment. Rowan *et al.* (2009) describes the template for the organisation of instruction put forward in one chain of school, in which:

> the kinds of changes teachers were expected to make as a result of parti-cipating in Accelerated School Project, or ASP, were not formally specified, and instead, each schools (and each teacher within a school) was asked to 'discover' the most appropriate means to producing powerful learning within his or her own particular context. (p. 28)

Here, the apparent negotiation of both interpersonal and ideational meaning serves as the organising principle. Knowledge is viewed as lodged in the person, in discovery, and contingent on the situation. Nonetheless, it is important to emphasise that there are underlying principles at play. It is not that a coherent pedagogic discourse dissolves into autonomous discourses, based on the construction of each teacher. It is that an implicit order is at work; the pedagogic discourse of skills and competences is replaced by one that prizes performance. 'Discovery' hinges on a diffuse amalgam of skills and competences but it is the act of discovery, its performance, that is highlighted here. This is made clear in the articulation of the pedagogic discourse that animated the Accelerated Schools Project, or ASP approach, which Rowan *et al.* (2009) describe as: "a normative commitment among school leaders and faculty to the program's abstract vision or ideal of 'powerful learning' for all students" (p. 27). With 'powerful learning' defined as "constructivist in nature, with an emphasis on authentic, learner-centered, and interactive forms of instruction" (p. 28).Here the text, as it were, the pedagogic practice of 'powerful learning' has to do with the performance of authenticity to which interactive forms of instruction are oriented. The instructional discourse of authenticity eschews categorical specialisms, just as the overarching regulative discourse of authenticity denies fixed positions in favour of 'discovery'.

The key is ideological consensus. When the pattern of organizing gives priority to operative authority, "The co-ordinating framework shifts from standardised practices of supervision to those of socialisation" (Tyler, 1988: 155). This kind of control must then proceed through a relatively shared negotiation of the interpersonal 'who' and the ideational 'what'. The apparent absence of authority, or masking of authority in the collective, is a distinguishing feature of this 'commitment' approach. It involves a regulative discourse that is person-oriented embedding an instructional discourse that is open. No single participant or group of participants maintains explicit, positional control, nor are categories of ideational meaning fixed.

The negotiation entailed by such a pedagogic discourse does not imply that control is absent; control is implicit. Person-oriented discourses grant the non-dominant participant more *apparent* control. Hasan (2001) emphasises that such fluidity in social relations is not the same as the absence of control; it indicates "a qualitatively different kind of power and a different mode of control" (p. 65), one that is potentially totalizing. Practice reaches far deeper into the construction of self, as order, relation, identity are bound not by external constraint but by internal ideological alignment. Under mechanical controls, a teacher who fails to master the expected skills dictated by the privileging text of a prescribed curriculum is merely an incompetent professional. In an ASP school, the teacher who fails to adhere to its basic humanistic values, might be found morally corrupt, inauthentic. In this latter case, the 'bandwidth' of the dominating discourse encompasses the fused identity of professional and person.

But what of the socialisation process that showed the congruent differentiation and complexity of all three dimensions, the professional modality? This was identified as the most promising in terms of enduring influence on the instructional core by Rowan *et al.* (2009) and as the most enmeshed in the machinery of advanced capitalism by Gunter and Forrester (2009). The professional strategy of control at the level of organisation relies on a similar correspondence of a pedagogic discourse that hinges on the positional in its orientation to interpersonal meaning and yet orients towards elaborated ideational meanings. I expand on this in the following.

Re-examining modalities of authority

Pedagogic discourse provides the means for viewing what have been taken as dichotomous halves of forms of organising in the school – the administrative sphere and the instructional core – as a coherent whole. Moreover, the device as relay provides the means for relating the process of formation of pedagogic discourse to organisational form, text to context. We can now use the notion of pedagogic discourse and corresponding orientations to ideational and interpersonal meanings to characterise variations in the modalities of authority in the socialisation of schools as organisations. The example of school-to-school relationships helps to make this concrete. Figure 7.1 presents the view from the supported school, the acquirer, of its relationship to the supporting school, the transmitter.

The vertical axis portrays the line of the tenor of discourse from positional on the top to personal on the bottom. This corresponds to patterns of interpersonal meaning that vary from social relations closely tied to hierarchical structure to ones that emphasise the autonomy and unique value of the person. The horizontal axis portrays the field of discourse, the potential range of ideational meanings, from those that are highly contextualised, and as a result are tightly condensed, prescribed or closed to negotiation to those that are decontextualised, open to negotiation and entail elaboration. This delineates four realms or characteristic modalities of authority in the recruitment of schools into the dominating discourses of schooling.

1   *Bureaucratic*: The bureaucratic pattern of socialisation emphasises hierarchical order both in terms of the base of knowledge as well as ascribed position. The

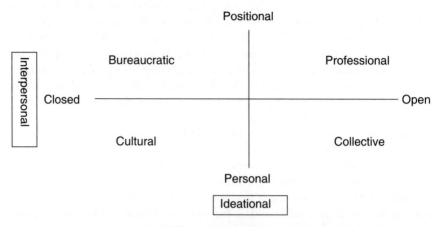

Figure 7.1 Modalities of authority based on orientations to interpersonal and ideational
   meanings

examples cited earlier have referred to mechanistic control and the privileging
of managerial authority.

2   *Cultural*: The cultural pattern of socialisation assumes a tight-knit and closed
    system of ideational meaning coupled with an orientation to the personal.
    This might exemplify interorganisational relationships in a chain of schools
    connected by a faith that emphasised personal salvation. The moral order
    privileges the transcendence of the person over the constraints of society,
    within a universe of shared and, hence, condensed meanings (e.g., Douglas,
    2003 (1996): 32).
3   *Collective*: The collective pattern of socialisation emphasises autonomy both
    in terms of person and of the categories of knowledge that comprise the
    profession. Here lies the 'authentic' of 'deep learning' mentioned earlier
    relating to the organisation of instruction by one of the chains of schools
    studied by Rowan *et al.* Operative authority results in that the acknowledged
    expert emerges from the collective, highlighting the importance of the
    collective, with patterns of epistemic authority shifting with changes in
    interpersonal and ideational relations.
4   *Professional*: This modality provides for the negotiation of ideational meaning
    within ascribed positions, one in which there is increasing complexity and
    differentiation in all three dimensions of authority simultaneously.

We see in these contrasting examples how pedagogic discourse yields patterns
of institutional positioning that establish, in Bernstein's words, "specific relations
to other subjects and the creating of specific relations within subjects" (2003
(1990): 13). I have advanced a view here of organisations as subjects, positioned
within the wider educational field, with those deemed legitimate, 'outstanding',
in a pedagogical relationship with those deemed illegitimate, 'in need of im-

provement'. Socialisation into the dominating discourses of school is akin to organisational repositioning, a recalibration of social relations and relations among categories of professional knowledge. The ways in which organisations position themselves and one another in the system of education thus shapes the possibilities for the range of meanings that may be conveyed within any particular organising context.

The emphasis on the professional modality in a devolved system is not merely a matter of discerning the most effective relationship of transmitter and acquirer. The process of recontextualisation brings to the fore the fundamental question for research posed by Bernstein (2003 (1990)), "Whose ruler? What consciousness?" (p. 195). This is a struggle over the "ideological constitution of the subject" (Gamble and Hoadley, 2008). The professional modality provides highly differentiated roles and the elaboration of ideational meaning, which as Douglas (2003 (1996)) points out, 'in so far as it is used to sustain role patterns, reduces ambiguity' (p. 157).

The emergence of the professional modality in devolved systems of schooling demonstrates a novel elaboration of Lortie's 'mastery of the consensus' and a fulfilment of Tyler's (1988) hunch that the system of schooling was evolving towards "a novel set of 'tight' correspondences between the organization of the knowledge (the technical core) and the bureaucratic forms of organisation (the administrative core)" (p. 154).

Conclusion

The institution of schooling has long been a central emphasis of the elaboration of post-Vygotskyian theories, with insights around the ways in which the social, cultural, and historical processes that shape social institutions influence forms of consciousness. The relative stability of forms of instruction despite widespread change in systems of schooling merits close scrutiny for those who would employ post-Vygotskian theory to understand the role of the institution of schooling in the mutual shaping of society and individual consciousness. This chapter focused on the formation of professional consciousness through processes of organisational socialisation, which I put forward not as the socialisation of persons but as the socialisation of the organisation itself, the recruitment of the school as organisation into the dominating discourses of the institution of schooling. Earlier literature has focused on the ways in which modalities of authority organise the processes of socialisation. This analysis, adapted from Bernstein who himself found inspiration in Vygotsky and Luria, takes modalities of authority as the outcome of underlying principles of pedagogic discourse rooted in the societal distribution of power. I extended Bernstein's notion of the twinned aspects of interpersonal and ideational meaning in the constitution of pedagogic discourse to identify four characteristic modalities of authority through which organisational socialisation might proceed: bureaucratic, cultural, collective and professional.

Available literature on interorganisational support derives from private sector studies that fit awkwardly with the systemic dynamics of education (Rashman *et al.*, 2009). Understanding how power and control condition the distribution, recontextualisation and evaluation of professional knowledge in national systems of schooling offers a way of revealing how patterns of institutional control operate in the pedagogic relationship to enforce compliance, catalyse resistance, or permit adaptability. The explanatory framework put forward views relations of power and control as central to the construction of a pedagogic relationship operating between schools, establishing one organisation in the role of transmitter and another in the role of acquirer. This is a novel application of Bernstein's work which has hitherto been constrained to analyses of pedagogic formation within schools rather than between them. The conceptualisation of these developmental relationships between schools as pedagogic relationships is also novel and opens a pathway to generalisable explanation rather than local description. Puzzles around institutionalised modalities of authority are rooted in the fundamental questions of the social sciences, the role of the professions in society, the nature of modern bureaucracy and wider questions of structure and agency, as well as enduring questions around the connections between social order and orders of consciousness.

References

Apple, M. W. (2009) *Changing Teacher Professionalism: International Trends, Challenges and Ways Forward*, London and New York: Routledge.

Apple, M. W., Aasen, P., Cho, M. K., Gandin, L. A., Oliver, A., Sung, Y.-K. *et al.* (eds.), (2003) *The State and the Politics of Knowledge*, New York: RoutledgeFalmer.

Atkinson, P. (1985) *Language, Structure, and Reproduction: An Introduction to the Sociology of Basil Bernstein*, London; New York: Methuen.

Ball, S. J. (2007) *Education plc: Understanding Private Sector Participation in Public Sector Education*, London; New York: Routledge.

—— (2008) 'The Legacy of ERA, Privatization and the Policy Ratchet', *Educational Management Administration Leadership*, 36(2): 185–99.

Berman, P. and McLaughlin, M. W. (1975) *Federal Programs Supporting Educational Change*, vol. 4, *The Findings in Review*, Santa Monica, CA: Rand Corporation.

Bernstein, B. B. (1977) *Towards a Theory of Educational Transmissions*, 2nd edn, vol. 3: *Class, Codes and Control*) London: New York: Routledge.

—— (2000) *Pedagogy, Symbolic Control, and Identity: Theory, Research, Critique*, rev. edn, Lanham, MD: Rowman & Littlefield.

—— (2003 (1990)) *The Structuring of Pedagogic Discourse*, vol. 4, *Class, Codes and Control*, London: New York: Routledge.

Bidwell, C. E. (2001) 'Analyzing Schools as Organizations: Long-term Permanence and Short-term Change', *Sociology of Education*, 74: 100–14.

Bourdieu, P. (1998) *Practical Reason: On the Theory of Action*, Stanford, CA: Stanford University Press.

Cohen, M. D., March, J. G., and Olsen, J. P. (1972) 'A Garbage Can Model of Organizational Choice', *Administrative Science Quarterly*, 17(1): 1–25.

Daft, R. L. and Becker, S. W. (1978) *The Innovative Organization: Innovation Adoption in School Organizations*, New York: Elsevier.

Daniels, H. (1995) 'Pedagogic Practices, Tacit Knowledge and Discursive Discrimination: Bernstein and post-Vygotskian research', *British Journal of Sociology of Education*, 16(4): 517–33.

—— (2008a) 'Institutions as historical products: analyzing communicative action as it brings about change', paper presented at the the Fifth Basil Bernstein Symposium (available at: www.cardiff.ac.uk/socsi/newsandevents/events/Bernstein/papers).

—— (2008b) *Vygotsky and Research*, London; New York: Routledge.

de George, R. T. (1985) *The Nature and Limits of Authority*, Lawrence, KS: University Press of Kansas.

Department for Education (2010) *The Importance of Teaching: The Schools White Paper*, London: HMSO.

Douglas, M. (2003 (1996)) *Natural Symbols: Explorations in Cosmology*, London and New York: Routledge.

Gamble, J. and Hoadley, U. (2008) 'Positioning the regulative', paper presented at the the Fifth Basil Bernstein Symposium (available at: www.cardiff.ac.uk/socsi/newsandevents/events/Bernstein/papers).

Gunter, H. M. and Forrester, G. (2007) *Knowledge Production in Educational Ladership (KPEL) Project: Full Research Report ESRC End of Award Report*, RES-000-23-1192, Swindon: ESRC.

Gunter, H. M. and Forrester, G. (2009) 'School Leadership and Education Policy-Making in England', *Policy Studies*, 30(5): 495–511.

Hall, D., Gunter, H. M., and Bragg, J. (2011) 'The Discursive Performance of Leadership in Schools', *Management in Education*, 25(1): 32–6.

Halliday, M. A. K. and Hasan, R. (1989) *Language, Context, and Text: Aspects of Language in a Social-Semiotic Perspective*, 2nd edn, Oxford and New York: Oxford University Press.

Halliday, M. A. K. and Matthiessen, C. (2004) *An Introduction to Functional Grammar*, 3rd edn, London: E. Arnold.

Hargreaves, D. H. (2010) *Creating a Self-improving School System* (pdf) Nottingham, UK: National College for Leadership of Schools and Children's Services.

Hasan, R. (2001) 'The Ontogenesis of Decontextualised Language: Some Achievements of Classification and Framing', in A. Morais, I. Neves, B. Davies and H. Daniels (eds.), *Towards a Sociology of Pedagogy: The Contribution of Basil Bernstein to Research*, New York: P. Lang, 47–79.

King, R. (2010) 'Policy Internationalization, National Variety and Governance: Global Models and Network Power in Higher Education States', *Higher Education*, 60(6): 583–94.

Lauder, H., Brown, P., Dillabough, J.-A., and Halsey, A. H. (2006) (eds.) *Education, Globalization, and Social Change*, Oxford and New York: Oxford University Press.

Levin, B. (2010) 'Governments and Education Reform: Some Lessons from the Last 50 Years', *Journal of Education Policy*, 25(6): 739–47.

Lortie, D. C. (1969) 'The Balance of Control and Autonomy in Elementary School Teaching', in A. Etzioni (ed.), *The Semi-Professions and Their Organization: Teachers, Nurses, Social Workers*, New York: Free Press, 1–53.

McDonald, J. P., Klein, E. J., and Riordan, M. (2009) *Going to Scale with New School Designs: Reinventing High School*, New York: Teachers College Press.

McLaughlin, P. (2007) *Anarchism and Authority: A Philosophical Introduction to Classical Anarchism*, Aldershot and Burlington, VT: Ashgate.

Mayrowetz, D. (2008) 'Making Sense of Distributed Leadership: Exploring the Multiple Usages of the Concept in the Field', *Educational Administration Quarterly*, 44(3): 424–35.

Meyer, J. W. and Rowan, B. (1977) 'Institutionalized Organizations: Formal Structure as Myth and Ceremony', *American Journal of Sociology*, 83(2): 340–63.

Miller, R. J. and Rowan, B. (2006) 'Effects of Organic Management on Student Achievement', *American Educational Research Journal*, 43(2): 219–53.

Mulgan, G. (2009) *The Art of Public Strategy: Mobilizing Power and Knowledge for the Common Good*, Oxford: Oxford University Press.

OECD (2003) *Networks of Innovation: Towards New Models for Managing Schools and Systems*, Paris: OECD Publishing.

Rashman, L., Withers, E., and Hartley, J. (2009) 'Organizational Learning and Knowledge in Public Service Organizations: A Systematic Review of the Literature', *International Journal of Management Reviews*, 11(4): 463–94.

Rowan, B. (1990) 'Commitment and Control: Alternative Strategies for the Organizational Design of Schools', *Review of Research in Education*, 16: 353–89.

Rowan, B., Correnti, R., Miller, R. J., and Camburn, E. M. (2009a) *School Improvement by Design: Lessons from a Study of Comprehensive School Reform Programs*, Philadelphia, PA: Consortium for Policy Research in Education.

Rowan, B., Correnti, R., Miller, R. J., and Camburn, E. M. (2009b) 'School Improvement by Design: Lessons from a Study of Comprehensive School Reform Programs', in G. Sykes, B. L. Schneider, D. N. Plank and T. G. Ford (eds.), *Handbook of Education Policy Research* New York and London: Routledge; American Educational Research Association, 637–51.

Tyler, W. (1988) *School Organisation: A Sociological Perspective*, New York: Croom Helm.

Weick, K. E. (1976) 'Educational Organizations as Loosely Coupled Systems', *Administrative Science Quarterly*, 21(1): 1–19.

Wertsch, J. V. (1985) *Vygotsky and the Social Formation of Mind*, Cambridge, MA: Harvard University Press.

Whitty, G., Halpin, D., and Power, S. (1998) *Devolution and Choice in Education: The Choice, the State and the Market*, Buckingham and Philadelphia, PA: Open University Press.

Wilson, P. (1983) *Second-Hand Knowledge: An Inquiry into Cognitive Authority*, Westport, CT: Greenwood Press.

8 Semiotic mediation, viewed over time

Gordon Wells

> Who we become depends on the company we keep and what we do and say together.

Semiotic mediation is at the heart of learning and development, as is clear in the work of both Vygotsky and Bernstein. Yet their applications of this concept are so different that, initially, I was not sure how to bring them into dialogue with each other. However, when I began to think about my own intellectual trajectory, I realized that, in quite different ways, they have each played an important part in it. I hope, therefore, that, by reflecting on some of the key issues concerning the relationship between language and learning, I shall be able to show that my opening aphorism could have been arrived at from either Vygotsky's cultural theory of semiotic mediation or Bernstein's sociological theory of pedagogy.

The Bristol Study of Language Development

Detailed studies of language development really only started in the 1960s, in part as the result of the advent of the tape recorder, which made it possible to capture and transcribe speech verbatim. A second impetus, of a theoretical nature, came from the desire to test Chomsky's (1965) claim that language learning was driven by an innate "language acquisition device," which was equipped with knowledge of universal grammar (Brown, 1973). The 1960s also saw the rise to prominence of the concept of linguistic and cultural deprivation as the explanation for the scholastic underachievement of lower-class children (Hess and Shipman, 1965).

It was in this context that, in 1969, I was charged with the design and conduct of a naturalistic study of the language development of a large, representative sample of children, 128 in all. Half of the children were 15 months at the start of the study and half 39 months. Each child was recorded in his or her home for a whole day every three months over two and a half years, with short samples being selected at random intervals throughout the day for a total of 27 minutes on each occasion. Since no observer was present during the recordings, we were confident that the samples of conversation would be completely spontaneous, and this was confirmed when we came to transcribe them.[1]

The first questions we asked concerned the pattern of development: Did all the children follow the same sequence of development? And, if so, did they all develop at the same rate? Both questions yielded clear-cut answers. Across the three systems of utterance functions, semantic relations and syntactic structures, the sequence of development was significantly the same for all children. However, with respect to rate, there was substantial variation; at the age of 42 months (at which all 128 children contributed data), the slowest developing child was functioning at the level of the average two-year-old, while the most advanced was above the level of the average five-and-a-half year-old.

Naturally, we were intrigued by these results and keen to test alternative possible explanations. As far as sequence of development was concerned, two candidate hypotheses were entertained: the first was that the sequence corresponded to increasing complexity within each of the three major systems, and the second was that it corresponded to the relative frequency of the items within each system in the speech addressed to the children. Statistical tests yielded a high rank order correlation ($r \leq .75$) in support of each hypothesis, so no decision could be made between them. However, the most plausible explanation is that the two predictions are themselves related: the sequence in which children learn the items within each linguistic system is related to the items' relative complexity and the same applies to the same items' frequency in the speech input. It seems, therefore, that adults increase the frequency with which they use particular items in response to the evidence their children demonstrate of comprehending them. In other words, children "teach" their caretakers how to help them learn.[2]

While the results concerning sequence of development were of interest to other researchers in the field, those concerning rate of development attracted attention from a much wider audience. Did the great variation found in our representative sample provide support for the "deficit" hypothesis? Since the children had been selected to give equal representation to four intervals on a scale of "family background," calculated on the basis of the education and occupation of both parents, it was possible to investigate the relationship between the children's rate of language development and various characteristics of their home backgrounds.

Not at all coincidentally, this possibility was of considerable interest to Basil Bernstein, as he had been appointed a member of the Social Science Research Council (SSRC) steering committee for the project and had provided considerable help in the design of the maternal interview in particular, allowing us to use several instruments from his own research at the Sociological Research Unit (SRU) at the University of London Institute of Education.

The first analysis tested the relationship between the children's rate of development and the score assigned to them on the scale of family background.

1 A full account of the methods employed in this study, as well as the results obtained, can be found in Wells (1985, 1986/2009).
2 This is a corollary of Vygotsky's (1978) zone of proximal development.

Although there was a trend for children who were at the two extremes of rate of development to have low or high scores on the scale of family background, the overall correlation was not significant. When this result was first made public it met with quite strong statements of rejection from some of those who were associated with the deficit hypothesis. The results we subsequently obtained from analyses of the responses from interviews with the mothers of all 128 children when the children were three-and-a-half years old were also inconclusive with respect to a relationship with family background.

When I spoke to Bernstein about this he was surprised at the lack of observed relationship between mothers' answers in the maternal interview and their family background. In particular, he was concerned at the lack of observed correlation between family background and a schedule that was designed to measure the family's orientation to "personal" or "positional" forms of control. However, it emerged that, in the interval between making the instruments available to us and my reporting the results, Bernstein had developed a different analysis of the social division of labor. In place of the binary division between "working" and "middle" class, he now proposed a tripartite division in terms of three forms of relationship to the material base of society: "production", "symbolic control" and "power". In order to test the predictive utility of this revised index of social class, he offered to work with one of his students to reanalyze some of the data from our maternal interview.

Using this more refined index, several interesting results were obtained. With respect to their use of positional or personal control, the difference between mothers in households where the male head was either middle or working class was highly significant, with those in working class households being more likely to use positional control ($p < 0.0005$). A further analysis within the middle class, comparing households where the male head had an occupation in either production or symbolic control, also produced a significant result, with mothers in production households being more likely to use positional control ($p < 0.01$).[3]

Bernstein was obviously very satisfied with this confirmation of the utility of his revised conception of social class and its relationship to maternal modes of control, for it was the first to be derived from data collected outside the SRU. A quarter of a century later, he wrote:

> When the mothers' mode of control was related to occupational position, Holland found that mothers located in the field of symbolic control were more personal in their mode of control than mothers in families located in the field of production, who were more positional. Further, "white collar" mothers within the working class tended to have personal modes of control. Thus there was indirect evidence from Wells's study . . . that socialization practices vary in their classification and framing according to field location of parents. (1996: 112)

3 The section reporting these results in Wells (1985: 313–14) was written by Bernstein.

The quality of parent–child interaction

Vygotsky's ideas, on the other hand, played no part in the design of the Bristol Study, for *Mind in Society* (Vygotsky, 1978) was not even on the horizon when we were deciding on the methods of data collection and analysis. In retrospect, that was unfortunate for, had I been familiar with his theory of semiotic mediation, I should certainly have arranged to take longer samples from the continuous recordings in the children's homes. However, by the time we began to analyze the data in terms of their interactional quality, I had become very interested in Vygotsky's ideas about children's development. At about this time, too, "motherese" had become a topic of interest in the field of child language development (Cross, 1977).

The fact that we had regular observations over a period of more than two years made it possible to investigate whether the variation in the children's rate of language development could be at least partially explained by the speech they were hearing and the quality of the interaction they had with their parents and other family members. In order to test this hypothesis we selected the recording in which each child's mean length of utterance was as close as possible to 1.5 morphemes and measured the gains made on a number of linguistic variables by the time of the recording nine months later. Next we analyzed the input to the child on the first occasion for the frequency of features that had been proposed as likely to facilitate children's language development; we then correlated these results with the measures of gain made by the children in the following nine months. Space does not permit a detailed report of the results of the analysis but, overall, there was considerable evidence that the children's progress was significantly affected by the quantity and quality of the interactions in which they engaged at the time of the initial recording (Barnes *et al.*, 1983).

Looking more closely at the interactions involving the faster developing children, it became clear that they shared similar characteristics: the talk often arose out of ongoing shared activity; the adult showed attention to the child's initiations and frequently checked to make sure she or he understood the child's meaning intention; the adult built on the child's contributions more often than developing their own. Moreover, this type of supportive interactional style on the part of the adult was found in lower-class as well as middle-class homes.

Reading *Mind in Society* (Vygotsky, 1978) at about this time, I was struck by the relevance of Vygotsky's metaphorical construct of the zone of proximal development (zpd) as a theoretical explanation of the findings concerning the "high quality" interactions that I have just described. Such interactions provided occasions for "good learning" because, through their involvement in them, the children were enabled to do and say more than they could have achieved without the adult support. The zpd also suggested an explanation for the strong correlation between the sequence of the children's language development and the relative frequency of the same items in the speech addressed to them.

The transition from home to school

In a second stage of the project (1976–82), thirty-two of the younger cohort were selected for a follow-up study of the transition to school. Each child was recorded twice at around the age of five years, just before and immediately after starting school. These children were then observed regularly at school until age 10, when a wide range of assessments was made. Here, though, it is the initial comparison between home and school that is relevant.

Based on seven 5-minute samples spread over the morning of each recording, a comparison was made between the two occasions of the characteristics of the child's speech and the speech addressed to him or her by an adult. Not surprisingly, given the very different adult–child ratio in the two settings, the opportunity for one-to-one interaction was much less at school. However, it was not simply that the children spoke less with an adult at school; they also initiated a smaller proportion of sequences of talk and expressed a narrower range of meanings than at home. There was also a significant difference in the ways in which the speaking turns of the adults in the two settings were related to those of the children. As can be seen from Table 8.1, teachers made more requests and asked far more display questions than parents; they were also significantly less likely to show uptake of the children's contributions by extending their meanings or inviting them to do so themselves; by contrast, teachers were much more likely than parents to develop the meanings that they themselves had introduced.

Overall, the results of the comparison showed that children were less frequently treated as conversational partners at school than at home and were thus less able to display their competence as language users. This was particularly consequential for the children from the lower end of the scale of family background, since the children's restricted range of language use in school only served to confirm their teachers' low expectations for them. Significantly, in their case (but not in that of those from the higher end) there was a clear tendency for the estimate of their oral language ability made by the teacher at this age to be lower than that obtained from analysis of their speech in the recordings made at home in the preceding weeks.

Although not directly involved in this comparison, a series of tests of knowledge of literacy was also administered on entry to school and a measure of frequency

Table 8.1 Comparison of parents' and teachers' speech to children

Proportions of adult turns	Home	School
Requests	22.5	34.1
Display questions	2.1	14.2
Extends child's meaning	33.5	17.1
Develops adult's meaning	19.1	38.6

Source: Wells (2009)

The differences in Table 8.1 were in all cases statistically significant (p < 0.001).

of shared book reading was calculated based on all the home recordings. Both these measures proved to be strong predictors of subsequent academic achievement at seven and ten years of age and were significantly correlated with family background; it seems probable, therefore, that the teachers' estimates of the children's oral language at the point of entry to school were also influenced by their differential familiarity with stories and written language more generally.

Search for an explanatory theory

The previous sections have provided a brief description of the patterns of development that were derived from the recorded observations of spontaneous interaction in the children's homes. These were used to construct a scale of language development which allows the progress of individual children to be measured (Gutfreund *et al.*, 1989). However, what was missing was a theoretical explanation of the findings – although this could largely be explained by the state of the field when the study was being planned. By the end of the study, however, a considerable amount of development had taken place in a number of fields relevant to an interpretation of the results summarized above and it was in this context that I discovered the work of Vygotsky and recognized its relevance.

One of the most important of Vygotsky's contributions was his methodological insistence on the adoption of a "genetic" approach: to understand development, he argued, it is necessary to study the history of development. And, as he recognized, history exists on more than one timescale. In addition to the ontogenetic – that of individual development – the culture in which the individual is growing up also has a history, as does the human species as a whole. In fact, there are four levels of genetic development: phylogenetic, cultural historical, ontogenetic, and microgenetic, each influencing and being influenced by the level(s) "above" and "below" (Cole, 1996).

Most students of human development ignore the phylogenetic and cultural-historical levels. However, both are important in accounting for the course taken by ontogenetic development in different contemporary societies. Phylogenetically, since the first emergence of human-like primates some six million years or so ago, there have been major developments that, unlike those that can be attributed to biological evolution, can only be the result of intergenerational transmission of skills that are both cumulative and unique to humans (Tomasello, 1999). The increasing pace of this "cultural evolution" has been to a large degree made possible by the sequential emergence of progressively more "abstract" forms of semiotic mediation – first gesture, then speech, then writing and, most recently, computer-mediated communication – that have, each in turn, greatly enhanced the possibility of thinking and acting together to solve new challenges and of passing on the solutions to future generations (Donald, 1991). However, as a result of migration to different geographical regions, and settlement in varied ecological environments, each presenting its own challenges and resources, every cultural group has its own history, which, in turn, provides a unique set of affordances and constraints that influence the ontogenetic development of its individual members. Such variation also occurs within societies as a result of the different activity systems in which they participate (Luria, 1976).

At the same time, while each more encompassing level of historical development affects the levels below by setting the parameters within which it can occur, it is the actions and interactions that occur at the microgenetic level of situated events in the present that create possibilities for change. In particular, it is the invention, modification and appropriation of artifacts and activities, both material and semiotic, that changes the potential for future action and, if such changes become diffused across many activity systems, for the cultural evolution of society as a whole as well as of its individual members (Wells, 1999).

Vygotsky did not expand in his theoretical writings on this broader aspect of what has come to be called cultural-historical activity theory. However, its potentially revolutionary implications have since been widely recognized (Newman and Holzman, 1993; Stetsenko, 2010); they have also been operationalized in recent years in such projects as those carried out by the Center for Activity Theory and Developmental Work Research in Finland (Engeström, 2007) and in the various realizations around the world of the after-school program known as the Fifth Dimension (Cole, 2006).

Semiotic mediation

On the other hand, Vygotsky did give a great deal of attention to the relationship between the cultural, ontogenetic and microgenetic levels, as enunciated in the "general genetic law of cultural development."

> Any function in the child's cultural development appears twice, or on two planes. First it appears on the social plane, and then on the psychological plane. First it appears between people as an interpsychological category, and then within the child as an intrapsychological category. (1981: 163)

On the cultural plane are the resources that have been created, improved and accumulated over the history of the culture: the material and semiotic artifacts, the practices in which they are used, and the institutions that sustain and organize them. Our daily lives, and the activities in which we engage, are dependent on these resources and our actions and interactions only have meaning because of them. This remains the case even when we are physically alone, for our solo activities still make use of the same resources.

Each infant is born into a family that is part of a wider culture and, from birth, is increasingly involved in the range of cultural practices that make up family life.[4] Initially, an infant's involvement is largely in physical routines that are controlled by a caregiver but, as they become familiar with the constituent parts of these

---

4 Families vary enormously in size from members of several generations living together to a single parent. Whatever the size, the family acts as the main agent in the infant's enculturation.

activities, they can take a more reciprocal role, gradually initiating as well as responding. While similar reciprocity is seen in caregiver–infant activities in other primates, in the case of humans, the infant seems quick to attribute intention to the adult's behavior and to imitate, rather than just copy, that behavior in order to fulfill the same intentions (Tomasello, 1999). However, it is equally the case that caregivers attribute intentions to infants, and it has been argued that it is by being treated *as if* their behaviors were intended to communicate that infants come to have intentions and to attribute intentions to others (Newson, 1978). Either way, such intentionality is essential to the development of intersubjectivity, first in the achievement of mutual attention in the early months and then, by the end of the first year, in the establishment of joint attention directed to some object that one or other of them initiates (Trevarthen and Hubley, 1978).

Notice that the child's first interactions are non-verbal; facial expressions, vocalizations and gestures are sufficient to communicate affect and to coordinate attention and action. Then, by the end of the first year, most infants begin to produce idiosyncratic "words", which they use with contrastive intonation to distinguish between assertions and questions/requests about their environment. Halliday (1975) refers to this as "protolanguage." By the end of the second year, most children have taken the crucial step of beginning to appropriate the language of their community, in which meanings are related to vocalizations through the intermediary of a lexico-grammar (Halliday, 1993).

This stage certainly depends on the availability for imitation of the language model provided by the child's interlocutors. But while imitation plays a crucial part, it is not a matter of the child simply filling a preexisting store with others' words; rather, as Leontiev (1981) makes clear, what is involved is the creation of new psychological processes that are only made possible by the child's taking over and making her own the semiotic resources of the community's language. In particular, in learning the language of their community, children are also learning how to make sense of their own experiences. For, as Halliday puts it, "Language has the power to shape our consciousness; and it does so for each human child, by providing the theory that he or she uses to interpret and manipulate their environment" (1993: 107).

Spontaneous speech in the context of ongoing activity is the most frequent medium in which young children's understanding is mediated by more expert members of the culture, but as they grow older mediation can take many different forms, from explicit spoken definitions of new concepts, through written texts of all kinds, to diagrams, maps, and other forms of representation. It is by engaging with the various semiotic representations that he or she encounters that the individual appropriates more and more of the culture's meaning potential and transforms it for personal use.

Vygotsky also saw the appropriation of social speech as gradually creating a medium for individual thinking, which he termed "inner speech". While the extent to which all the various modes of thinking are dependent on the "internalized voices of others" is not clear, what is quite generally agreed is that the various kinds of symbolic resources that we use in solo problem solving, reasoning, and reflecting are taken over from our encounters with them in interaction with others. As Vygotsky put it:

> In the process of development, children begin to use the same forms of behavior in relation to themselves that others initially used in relation to them. Children master the social forms of behavior and transfer these forms to themselves. (1981: 157)

Similar ideas about individual mental activity were also developed in the same period by the Bakhtin circle. As Voloshinov (1973) argued, it is only through the construction of inner signs in the course of interaction with others that consciousness itself can arise.

However, unlike Vygotsky who, intent on exploring the relationship between speaking and thinking, chose the "word" as the primary unit of analysis, Bakhtin and his colleagues treated "utterance" as primary, since it is the minimal unit of linguistic interaction. However, even an utterance does not stand alone; it always and necessarily occurs as part of an ongoing interaction in some sphere of activity. In this way, it functions as a link in an ongoing chain of dialogue and, as such, both responds to what has gone before and anticipates a further response. Thus, although he was not specifically concerned with children's language development, Bakhtin's emphasis on dialogue shines a further light on the ways in which each person's ways of speaking are related to and taken over from others.

Because they focused on language in interaction, the Bakhtin circle also drew attention to the affective aspects of language use, together with the values and attitudes that nearly always accompany the ideational content of utterances. For not only do participants have to identify what is being referred to; each in turn also has to decide on the position they wish to adopt to that content and to their interlocutor(s), and equally to recognize and respond to the ways in which they themselves are positioned (Voloshinov, 1973). These affective features of utterances are particularly salient in the interactions in which young children take part and constitute an important part of their learning; they also play a significant role in the mediation of the cultural patterns of behavior that parents want their children to adopt.

Taken together, then, Bakhtin's and Vygotsky's insights create a powerful theoretical account of how each individual child is enabled to appropriate the language of the community into which he or she is born and how, through the everyday use of that language to organize, interpret, and reflect on the activities in which they engage with family members and other people in the community, they gradually take over those ways of thinking and feeling and use them in the dialogue of inner speech.

Semiotic mediation and social structure

Although, in principle, Vygotsky recognized the possibility of cultural differences within a community, this was not an issue that he explored in any detail. Since his major interest was in individual (ontogenetic) development, he tended to pay little attention to cultural diversity, treating the population from which he drew his research subjects as essentially homogeneous. However, from the point of view of his theory as a whole, this must be seen as a serious limitation.

As many studies have shown, in all the capitalist democracies there tend to be important cultural differences between subgroups within society based on the relative social status, wealth and occupation of group members and, in some countries, on their ethnolinguistic origins. Since these differences create inequities, which tend to be repeated within families over successive generations, it is necessary to understand their nature and causes so that progress can be made towards achieving the egalitarian goals that these societies profess. It was to this task that Bernstein devoted his career.

For Bernstein (1981), the most important group differences were best explored in relation to social class, which he conceptualized in terms of the different categories of role that people play in the division of labor. His initial hypothesis was that different roles in the labor force (e.g. unskilled worker or work manager) orient their holders to different orders of meaning; these differences give rise to different forms of socialization of their children; the children subsequently experience differences in the form of educational provision to which they have access, resulting in their leaving school with different qualifications with respect to finding employment within the labor force. In this way, the cycle of differential opportunity and achievement is perpetuated across the generations.

Bernstein's first attempt to get some purchase on this issue – which he later recognized to have been undertheorized – was to distinguish two codes of language use, "restricted" and "elaborated". Use of restricted code assumed shared experiences and thus little need for verbal explicitness; by contrast, use of elaborated code was based on the opposite assumption, giving rise to much greater lexical and grammatical explicitness. It was proposed that both codes would be selected, as appropriate for the occasion, by members of the middle class, whereas the working class would typically use the restricted code in all situations. Illustrated by examples that seemed to many to epitomize the general inferiority of the restricted code, this first attempt was immediately denounced as embracing a "deficit" theory of linguistic variation by educators and social scientists alike.

By 1971, Bernstein had abandoned a specification of the codes in terms of performance features and retheorized the codes as "regulative principles" which selected the meanings to be communicated and the form of their realization according to the speaker's classification of the situation. At about the same time he introduced the distinction between "positional" and "personal" family types and related these to his more finely differentiated categorization of occupation. As described above, this was a major step towards explaining how the different forms of linguistic socialization in the home prepared children differentially for what would be expected of them in school.

This line of research was further developed by Hasan (1986, 2002) who, in the 1980s, compared the ways in which Australian middle and working class mothers talked with their preschool-aged children in the course of their everyday activities. As Bernstein had predicted, she found systematic differences, which, she suggested, would be consequential in the context of the children's subsequent formal education. Based on her analysis of the recorded data, she proposed a distinction between two modes of semiotic mediation. The first she termed "invisible". This mode of mediation typically occurred on the fly, in the course of some other activity, and such sequences of talk were so brief and apparently insignificant that they hardly merited being called discussions. The second mode of mediation, termed "visible", tended to extend over a longer period and be much more explicit in the information conveyed. In this visible mode, the talk became more verbally explicit and was the joint focus of attention.

Nevertheless, because invisible mediation occurs earlier in the child's life and is more pervasive, Hasan argues that it creates "habits of the mind," that is to say, the predisposition to treat some situations rather than others as relevant and worthy of attention and involvement. Furthermore, as she illustrates with examples, one of the habits of mind that is fostered in some children more than in others on the basis of the invisible mediation that they experience is the predisposition to elicit and engage enthusiastically in semiotic mediation of the visible kind and, in this way, to start making connections between what Vygotsky called everyday and scientific concepts.

Summing up her findings, Hasan considers the likely consequences of the different mental dispositions that children develop from the forms of semiotic mediation experienced in the preschool years:

> The pre-school learning history of the first group of children [those who engage in more visible mediation] favours an easier engagement with the specialised discourses of the school; by contrast, for those of the second group, it favours easier adjustment to the regulatory aspect of the pedagogic discourse. To the extent that the real aim of education is to enable pupils not to reproduce knowledge, but to produce it, not simply to replicate but to create, this appears to place the first group in an advantageous position. (2002: 125)

Unlike the Bristol Study, Hasan's work was explicitly designed to test Bernstein's theory of the social reproduction of social class. However, in reporting her results she refrained from putting class labels on the two groups she identified. This was an important decision, since – as we found in the Bristol Study, the social class membership of a particular family does not determine the forms of semiotic mediation that the children will experience. Parents are not defined by their occupation or level of education, although these are certainly significant. Had we been able to carry out the same analyses on the Bristol data as those performed by Hasan, we should almost certainly have found examples of each of the two types of mediation she identified occurring in families right across the spectrum of family background.

However, both studies provided confirming evidence for Bernstein's basic argument that:

> as the child learns his speech . . . he learns the requirements of his social structure. The experience of the child is transformed by the learning generated by his own, apparently, voluntary acts of speech . . . The social structure becomes the child's psychological reality through the shaping of his acts of speech. (1971: 144)

I suspect that Vygotsky would also be in agreement.

Language, learning, and schooling

Space does not allow me to discuss in any detail the second phase of the Bristol Study, in which we followed thirty-two of the original sample through their elementary schooling until they were 10 years old. Most relevant here is the relationship between their preschool experience and their academic achievement at age 10. Table 8.2 shows the longitudinal rank order profiles of six children chosen to represent the distribution of family background. (The ranks were computed for all thirty-two children.)

One of the most striking features of Table 8.2 is the large change between the rank positions on the early measure of oral language at age three and a half and overall school achievement at age ten in the cases of three of the children: Anthony, Gary, and Penny. While Anthony was a slow developer who became successful in school, Gary and Penny, by contrast, were early developers who were not nearly as successful in school. Jonathan and Rosie, on the other hand, maintained their respective high and low positions throughout the study. From these results, it seems that there is little relationship between rate of early language development and later school achievement. Nevertheless, there was one preschool measure that strongly predicted achievement at 10: children's familiarity with written language at age 5, as measured by Clay's (1972) test of *Concepts about*

Table 8.2 Six children's longitudinal rank order profiles

	Abigail	Anthony	Gary	Jonathan	Penny	Rosie
Oral language at 3½	7.5=	23	7.5=	1	3	29
Freq. of story reading	5	13.5=	13.5=	1.5=	26=	32
Oral language at 5	4=	6	20.5=	4=	12.5=	29
Knowledge of literacy at 5	7.5=	3	29	1.5=	10	31.5=
Oral language at 10	2	11	6	1	8	32
Reading at 10	2	3	26	1	21.5	31.5=
Vocabulary at 10	2.5=	2.5=	22	2.5=	5.5=	30.5=
Overall achievement at 10	2	3	22	1	13	32

Source: Wells (2009: 186)

Print. And this was quite significantly related to their oral language at the same age. Since no observations of the children were made between three-and-a-half and 5, there are no data on which to base an explanation of the changes that took place in the children's relative positions on the measure of oral language during that period. However, it seems likely that the amount of attention to written language in the home that is indicated by the children's relative ranks on the *Concepts about Print* test also led to differential gains in oral language.

At this point it seems appropriate to ask whether the theories considered earlier might further elucidate the developmental patterns represented in Table 8.2, and particularly those of the children whose later school achievement was least well predicted by their early rate of oral language development. Here, Vygotsky has little to contribute, since his work did not include longitudinal research and, as mentioned above, he gave little attention to social demographic differences between individuals. On the other hand, Bernstein's sociological research seems to be potentially quite relevant, particularly to the investigation of possible relationship between the social class and school achievement of the Bristol children.

For the cohort as a whole, there was not a significant correlation between class of family background and early oral language development; however, by the age of 5 there was a substantial correlation, r = 0.58, which remained more or less constant through age 10. The possible influence of social class is most clearly seen in the cases of Anthony and Gary. Anthony was the only child of professional parents, who took positive steps to ensure that he succeeded in school despite his slow start in learning to talk; by the end of the study, he had been accepted into a prestigious private school. Gary, on the other hand, was an early starter, but this did not help him to succeed in school. He was the second child in a family headed by an engine mechanic; by age 10, Gary's greatest interest, supported by his father, was to go "scrambling" on his motorbike. Abigail's and Rosie's backgrounds were also important in their relative success. Abigail was the daughter of professional parents; in her early years, as the last in a family of four children, she was often overshadowed by her older siblings but, as she grew older, she was encouraged to join in their literary pursuits and, at school, she excelled in story writing. Rosie, on the other hand was the youngest of five children; both of her parents were relatively uneducated and were unemployed throughout the duration of the study. There was little about her family life to stimulate her intellectual development and, unfortunately, the same was true of her experience in school.

The trajectories of the remaining two children, on the other hand, do not conform so well to class-based predictions of educational achievement. In both cases, the head of the household was a skilled worker – Jonathan's father was a mechanic in a factory, and Penny's a fire-fighter. Both children enjoyed rich conversations with their parents and made rapid oral language development in the early years. However, based on the social class of the family, neither would have been expected to excel academically. Nevertheless, Jonathan remained at the top of the rank order throughout the study and Penny was doing better than average at the age of 10. Both families were supportive of their children's school learning;

the major difference was in the much greater emphasis given to story reading and other literate activities in Jonathan's home.

From the overall results of this follow-up study, I conclude that there is considerable support for Bernstein's theory of the effect of social class on children's readiness to benefit from schooling. However, it is equally clear that predictions of children's educational achievement based on class, where this is measured in terms solely of parental education and occupation, are not very reliable. Many other characteristics of the children and of their home environment can play a significant role in determining the outcome.

Theoretical perspectives on learning in school

Bernstein spent practically the whole of his academic career on the construction of a sociology of pedagogy that would explain the relationship among social class, primary socialization in the family, and schooling, within a theory of power and symbolic control in society as a whole (Sadovnik, 1995). Quite early in his theorizing about this complex of concepts, Bernstein (1977) made a distinction between "visible" and "invisible" pedagogies, defined in terms of the extent to which the rules pertaining to the hierarchical relationship between transmitter and acquirer(s), the sequencing of transmission of the curriculum, and the criteria for acceptability of performance are made explicit. Critical to the difference between the two is that, in a visible pedagogy, the learner knows what is expected because it is explicitly set out and adhered to; in an invisible pedagogy, by contrast, the learner has more freedom to be creative but less awareness of what is ultimately required for success in the wider society.

At the time of the Bristol Study, the schools that the children attended were generally towards the centre of the continuum from visible to invisible, with the practice in individual classrooms depending more on the training and personal beliefs of the teacher than on strong district policy. In general, there was a tendency for the pedagogy to become more visible as the children got older.

Unfortunately, Bernstein argued, neither form of pedagogy is likely to overcome existing class inequalities. Visible pedagogy favors the middle class because parents are more knowledgeable about the academic curriculum and more willing and able to supplement it in various ways; it disfavors the working class because the children are less well prepared to deal with the decontextualized curriculum and the literate mode in which it is largely transmitted, and also because their parents are less equipped to provide support. But invisible pedagogy is no more favorable to the working class because the school's middle-class assumption of personalized authority relations is likely to be in conflict with the more positional expectations of the home. Furthermore, an invisible pedagogy requires more time for the required content to be acquired, which is in conflict with increasing governmental actions to reduce any spending on education that is not seen as meeting the demands of the labor market.

In his later work, Bernstein (1996/2000) further developed his theory, attempting to integrate the various levels from the institutional to the interactional by means of the "pedagogic device". Continuing to use the concepts of classification and framing, he also developed a more abstract system for distinguishing different modes of pedagogic discourse and the contexts in which they occur. To simplify greatly, power is realized through classification – decisions about what counts as legitimate knowledge and how it is organized in terms of boundaries – while control is realized through framing – decisions about the discourse in which knowledge is transmitted, its sequencing and pacing, and about who makes these decisions. In this later work, he elaborated the basis on which the earlier distinction between visible and invisible pedagogies depended and introduced a number of subcategories.

However, recognizing the complex interplay of power, class, and symbolic control, Bernstein did not attempt to propose a solution to the practical problem of overcoming social inequalities. Instead, his aim was to provide a sophisticated theoretical framework that would allow possible solutions to be systematically investigated and tested. However, as he himself recognized, many readers find his theory to be too abstract, overly given to nested binary distinctions and lacking in illustrative examples; for these reasons it has rarely been accepted as the basis for empirical research. Nevertheless, it has been widely recognized as a ground-breaking attempt to explain the role of education in cultural reproduction.

While Bernstein approached the nature and function of pedagogy from a sociological perspective, Vygotsky approached these issues from the perspective of a psychologist concerned to explain the genesis of human development. And as Bruner (1962) observed in his introduction to *Thought and Language* (Vygotsky, 1962), "Vygotsky's conception of development is at the same time a theory of Education" (p. x). This is also implied in Vygotsky's general law of cultural development as well as in the following passage from the chapter he wrote with Luria, *Tool and Symbol in Child Development*.

> The entire history of the child's psychological development shows us that, from the very first days of development, its adaptation to the environment is achieved by social means, through the people surrounding him. The road from object to child and from child to object lies through another person . . . [Furthermore] speech lies at the very beginning of the child's development and becomes its most decisive factor. (Vygotsky and Luria, 1934/1994: 111)

Moreover, as Bruner later pointed out, if the higher mental functions, as he called them, are first encountered in, and taken over and transformed from, speech in social activities, it is clear that those activities must be organized in such a way as to facilitate their appropriation.

Vygotsky considered "mediation" to be the key to an explanation. Initially, in the context of joint activities, the adult both models the relevant actions and facilitates the learner's increasing participation. Later, by also engaging in spoken interaction with the learner in and about the activity in which they are jointly involved, the discourse they create together provides the learner with the opportunity to appropriate both the language used and the cultural "theory of experience" that it encodes.

It was in relation to this essentially dyadic mode of joint activity that Vygotsky introduced the idea of the zone of proximal development (zpd). The zone, as he conceived it, was a sort of window of opportunity between what the learner could manage on his or her own in a particular situation and what he or she could manage with the assistance of a more capable other. Providing this assistance was an essential aspect of Vygotsky's view of pedagogy, as was argued earlier when discussing early language development.

However, when one compares the two settings – home and school – in which the zpd is typically considered to be relevant, it is clear that the latter is more formal and systematically organized than the former. Moreover, although Vygotsky used the term "instruction" with reference to both, his description of instruction in school clearly assumes that, as compared with the situation at home, the one providing the instruction has a clear, sequential plan of what is to be addressed over a period of time and is capable of providing a theoretical justification for that plan. Furthermore, at home, the child is for the most part learning "spontaneous", or everyday, concepts, while at school the emphasis is on "scientific" concepts, that is to say, concepts that are semantically related to each other in systematic ways and at a higher level of generalization (Vygotsky, 1987: 224–8). For these reasons, it can be argued that Vygotsky considered the two settings to call for different kinds of instruction.

What characterizes the learning of scientific concepts, according to Vygotsky, is that they require conscious awareness and volition. Everyday concepts, he argued, are appropriated from "spontaneous, situationally meaningful, concrete applications, that is, in the sphere of experience and the empirical" (1987: 220). Scientific concepts, on the other hand, require the teacher's active participation:

> The teacher, working with the school child on a given question, explains, informs, inquires, corrects and forces the child himself to explain. All this work on concepts, the entire process of their formation, is worked out by the child in collaboration with the adult in instruction. (pp. 215–16)

This, then, was the way in which Vygotsky envisaged the teacher's role when working in the zpd at school: to identify the extent to which a child could cope with a problem arising in a conceptual area of the curriculum and to provide assistance that would enable him or her to solve the problem and thereby to gain a better grasp of the relevant concept and its relationship to other concepts in the same domain. Moreover, the overall aim of instruction was for the student to continue to master new and more inclusive structures of generalization that would "create the potential for his thought to move to new and higher planes of logical explanations" (p. 232).

Taken on its own, this view of pedagogy may seem unacceptably narrow, with its strong focus on cognitive development and its apparent lack of attention to social and emotional development. On the other hand, it should be recognized that Vygotsky's aim in this text (1987: ch. 6) was to expound his theory of conceptual development and the role that instruction played in that process, whereas his concern with social and emotional aspects of human development is clearly apparent in other works (Mahn and John-Steiner, 2002), including the final chapter of *Thinking and Speech*. Nevertheless, in the light of the very different social, economic and political challenges that face us a century later, it is important to recognize that there are aspects of his theory that need to be reconsidered in order to build upon his legacy to create a pedagogy appropriate for the education of young people today.

Conclusion

Interpersonal semiotic mediation must be as old as the species *homo sapiens*, as has been cogently argued by Donald (1991) and Tomasello (1999). But we owe to Vygotsky the recognition of the central part it plays in enabling both individuals and cultures to develop in the first place and to change in response to changes in their environments, often themselves brought about, at least in part, by semiotic mediation.

Vygotsky gave the greater part of his attention to elucidating how interpersonal meaning making between the more and the less capable and knowledgeable members of a community enables the latter to become increasingly competent members of the community and at the same time to appropriate the community's semiotic practices as the means for their *intrapersonal* mental activity. In propounding this theory, Vygotsky made a universal claim about human development, while also recognizing that each individual inevitably follows a unique trajectory of participation in time and space and therefore has a unique contribution to make to any particular activity or interaction. Seen in this light, the diversity that exists in any society is not only inevitable but also important for the development of individuals and productive in the improvement of society as a whole; knowledge building, effective problem solving, and wise decision making almost always benefit from the collaboration of multiple participants, each contributing from their own unique perspectives.

To fully understand learning and development, however, it is not sufficient to focus only on interpersonal interaction. As Rogoff (2003) argues, when investigating any event:

> it should be recognized that it is the *ensemble* of "the interpersonal, personal and cultural–institutional aspects of the event [that] constitute the activity". (p. 58)

However, as she recognizes, it is difficult to keep all three aspects in focus at the same time and so, in practice, each tends to be studied independently and even to become a field in its own right. This has certainly proved to be the case with respect to the "cultural–institutional" aspect of education, which has received much less attention from those working in the Vygotskian tradition.

Bernstein, on the other hand, as a sociologist of education, has certainly made an important contribution to our understanding of the school as an institution and of its role in reproducing the structure of power and opportunity in the larger society through the different expectations of, and provision for, students' education, on the basis of their presumed social class membership. Equally important is his explanation of how educational achievement or underachievement is transmitted from generation to generation through class-based styles of socialization, particularly those realized through the use of language codes that foreground different orientations to meaning.

From my perspective as a teacher educator, however, his theoretical work is problematic in its pedagogic value. While it is important for teachers to understand why they should not accept a deficit explanation of class differences in educational achievement, the stark binary distinctions from which Bernstein's theory is constructed are likely to reinforce any tendencies teachers may have to assign children to class-based categories and to act on expectations of their ability based on category membership rather than on the evidence gained from working with them individually. Most of the new teachers with whom I work are entering the profession with the intention of changing the world – one student at a time. For them, principles derived from the work of Vygotsky and those who have developed his ideas provide a more useful toolkit than a theory that does not offer guidance as to how to help individual children.

Ultimately, of course, we need both perspectives, since they make complementary contributions to an overall explanation of the many ways in which semiotic mediation sustains a culture across generations while also contributing to its evolution. However, from a genetic perspective on development, it is apparent that, while change takes place on every level from phylogenetic to microgenetic, it takes place at different rates. Changing the institution of public education can only be achieved over the long haul; nevertheless it takes particular individuals in their various roles – as policy makers and managers, theorists and researchers, elected representatives and voters – acting together on particular occasions to bring about that change. And for that to happen, it is necessary for those individuals to develop the relevant skills, knowledge and dispositions through the guidance and instruction of parents, teachers and other educators.

Vygotsky and Bernstein have each, through their different legacies, given us powerful tools for thinking about the role of semiotic mediation in learning and development.

However, it has to be recognized that neither adequately explored the diversity among the individuals who constitute a society or its ethnolinguistically or class-based sub-groups, nor fully recognized the potential of diversity for overcoming the challenges that face our species as a whole. This remains a challenge, both for theory builders and, even more, for those who have the responsibility for the education of each new generation.

References

Bakhtin, M. M. (1986) *Speech Genres and Other Late Essays*, trans. Y. McGee, Austin, TX: University of Texas Press.

Barnes, S., Gutfreund, M., Satterly, D., and Wells, G. (1983) 'Characteristics of Adult Speech which Predict Children's Language Development', *Journal of Child Language*, 10: 65–84.

Bernstein, B. (1971) *Class, Codes and Control*, vol. 1, *Theoretical Studies Towards a Sociology of Language*, London: Routledge & Kegan Paul.

—— (1977) 'Class and Pedagogies: Visible and Invisible', in B. Bernstein (ed.), *Class, Codes and Control*, London: Routledge & Kegan Paul, vol. 3, 116–56.

—— (1981) 'Codes, Modalities and the Process of Cultural Reproduction: A Model', *Language and Society*, 10: 327–63.

—— (1996/2000) *Pedagogy, Symbolic Control and Identity*, 2nd edn, Lanham, MD: Rowman & Littlefield.

Brown, R. (1973) *A First Language: The Early Stages*, London: Allen & Unwin.

Bruner, J. S. (1962) 'Introduction', in L. S. Vygotsky *Thought and language*, trans. E. Haufmann and G. Vakar, Cambridge, MA: MIT Press, v–x.

Chomsky, N. A. (1965) *Aspects of the Theory of Syntax*, Cambridge, MA: MIT Press.

Clay, M. (1972) *The Early Detection of Reading Difficulties: A Diagnostic Survey*, London: Heinemann.

Cole, M. (1996) *Cultural Psychology: A Once and Future Discipline*, Cambridge, MA: Belknap Press.

—— (2006) *The Fifth Dimension: An After-School Program Built on Diversity*, New York: Russell Sage Foundation.

Cross, T. G. (1977) 'Mothers' Speech Adjustments: The Contribution of Selected Child Listener Variables', in C. E. Snow and C. Ferguson (eds.), *Talking to Children: Language Input and Acquisition*, Cambridge: Cambridge University Press.

Donald, M. (1991) *Origins of the Modern Mind: Three Stages in the Evolution of Culture and Cognition*, Cambridge, MA: Harvard University Press.

Engeström, Y. (2007) 'Putting Vygotsky to work: The change laboratory as an application of double stimulation', in H. Daniels, M. Cole, and J. V. Wertsch (eds.), *The Cambridge Companion to Vygotsky*, Cambridge: Cambridge University Press, 363–82.

Gutfreund, M., Harrison, M., and Wells, G. (1989) *The Bristol Language Development Scales*, Windsor: NFER-Nelson.

Halliday, M. A. K. (1975) *Learning How to Mean*, London: Arnold.

—— (1993) 'Towards a Language-Based Theory of Learning', *Linguistics and Education*, 5: 93–116.

Hasan, R. (1986) 'The ontogenesis of ideology: an interpretation of mother child talk', in T. Threadegold, E. A. Grosz, G. Kress, and M. A. K. Halliday (eds.), *Language, Semiotics, Ideology*, Sydney, NSW: Sydney Association for Studies in Society and Culture, 125–46.

—— (2002) 'Semiotic Mediation and Mental Development in Pluralistic Societies: Some Implications for Tomorrow's Schooling', in G. Wells and G. Claxton (eds.), *Learning for Life in the 21st Century: Socio-cultural Perspectives on the Future of Education*, Oxford: Blackwell, 112–16.

Hess, R. and Shipman, V. (1965) 'Early Experience and the Socialization of Cognitive Modes in Children', *Child Development*, 36: 869–86.

Leontiev, A. N. (1981) 'The Problem of Activity in Psychology', in J. V. Wertsch (ed.), *The Concept of Activity in Soviet Psychology*, Armonk, NY: Sharpe, 37–71.

Luria, A. R. (1976) *Cognitive Development: Its Cultural and Social Foundations*, Cambridge, MA: Harvard University Press.

Mahn, H. and John-Steiner, V. (2002) 'The Gift of Confidence: A Vygotskian View of Emotions', in G. Wells and G. Claxton (eds.), *Learning for Life in the 21st Century: Socio-cultural Perspectives on the Future of Education*, Oxford: Blackwell, 46–58.

Newman, F. and Holzman, L. (1993) *Lev Vygotsky: Revolutionary Scientist*, London: Routledge.

Newson, J. (1978) 'Dialogue and Development', in A. Lock (ed.), *Action, Gesture and Symbol: The Emergence of Language*, New York: Academic Press, 31–42.

Rogoff, B. (2003) *The Cultural Nature of Human Development*, New York: Oxford University Press.

Sadovnik, A. R. (1995) 'Basil Bernstein's Theory of Pedagogic Practice', in A. R. Sadovnik (ed.), *Knowledge and Pedagogy: The Sociology of Basil Bernstein*, Norwood, NJ: Ablex, 3–35.

Stetsenko, A. (2010) 'Teaching–Learning and Development as Activist Projects of Historical Becoming: Expanding Vygotsky's Approach to Pedagogy', *Pedagogies: An International Journal*, 5(1): 6–16.

Tomasello, M. (1999) *The Cultural Origins of Human Cognition*, Cambridge, MA: Harvard University Press.

Trevarthen, C. and Hubley, P. (1978) 'Secondary Intersubjectivity: Confidence, Confiding and Acts of Meaning in the First Year', in A. Lock (ed.), *Action, Gesture and Symbol: The Emergence of Language*, New York: Academic Press, 183–230.

Voloshinov, V. N. (1973) *Marxism and the Philosophy of Language*, trans. L. Mtejka and I. R. Titunik, Cambridge, MA: Harvard University Press.

Vygotsky, L. S. (1962) *Thought and Language*, ed. and trans. Eugenia Hanfmann and Gertrude Vakar, Cambridge, MA: MIT Press.

—— (1978) *Mind in Society: The Development of Higher Psychological Processes*, Cambridge, MA: Harvard University Press.

—— (1981) 'The Genesis of Higher Mental Functions', in J. V. Wertsch (ed.), *The Concept of Activity in Soviet Psychology*, Armonk, NY: Sharpe, 144–88.

—— (1987) 'Thinking and Speech', trans. N. Minick, in R. W. Rieber and A. S. Carton (eds.), *The Collected Works of L.S. Vygotsky*, vol. 1, *Problems of General Psychology*, New York: Plenum, 39–285.

Wells, G. (1985) *Language Development in the Preschool Years*, Cambridge: Cambridge University Press.

—— (1986/2009) *The Meaning Makers: Learning to Talk and Talking to Learn*, 2nd edn, Bristol: Multilingual Matters.

—— (1999) *Dialogic Inquiry: Towards a Socio-cultural Practice and Theory of Education*, Cambridge: Cambridge University Press.

Boys, skills and class: educational failure or community survival?

Insights from Vygotsky
and Bernstein

Gabrielle Ivinson

Introduction

The south Wales' valleys had been at the centre of the Industrial Revolution in the 1920s and so at the cutting edge of skilled practices developed in the mining and steel industries. Men came to these remote and typologically impressive places, settled, created communities, brought up families and passed down their skills. The last working mine closed in 2001, following a tremendous battle of resistance in the 1980s from the highly unionised mining community. The boys in these studies were children of the post-industrial era and this chapter investigates their legacies, implications for the current educational focus on skills and their imagined futures.

The chapter starts with a description of the historical dimensions of the places where skills were informally recontextualised within communities. Regeneration policies and the recent aim to upskill young people through education so they can move on and out of these places are discussed. The third section introduces theoretical tools from recent readings of Vygotsky along with developments of Bernstein's code theory to embrace corporeality, imagination and mimesis. The fourth section introduces case studies of Owain, Sam, Dewi and Rhys to illustrate how legacies of skilled practices associated with mining were recontextualised by working class boys and furthermore what light this throws on policy. The concluding section suggests a major shift in thinking away from working class boys' educational failure towards an emphasis on community building, a holistic view of learning and the urgent need for adequate post-16 education.

Time, place and skills

The studies took place in two of the seven ex-mining valleys in south Wales. Towns grew from sparsely populated farming communities to globally important industrial centres in a relative short timespan. Mining communities grew up in a landscape of steep valleys that open from the south and taper to dead ends in the north. The geography ensured that communities remained relatively insulated from each other, cut off by mountains, as there was literally no road out at the ends of valleys to the wilderness beyond. For a brief period from the 1890s to

1920s these towns found themselves at the centre of the industrial revolution, exporting coal all over the world. There were 620 collieries in 1913 employing 233,000 men (Doering *et al.*, 2011). With a rapid rise in prosperity local schools, libraries, cinemas and theatres were built creating dynamic and independent local communities within an area dubbed the American Wales (*ibid.*).

Historically, many boys left school aged 14, and becoming a miner equated with becoming a 'real man'. As well as gaining physical skills they were inducted into the social bonds developed under conditions of danger in which men were dependent on each other for their lives. In stories we heard from ex-miners in the study, men spoke with pride and nostalgia of the strong camaraderie among men who worked underground. Boys were brought up to expect and endure a harsh apprenticeship. Physical strength, bravery and dirty work became highly valued within local mining communities.

Valley communities went into a sharp and persistent decline from the mid-1920s and became increasingly marginalised; they are now imagined to be on the periphery of economic activity, recognised from the outside as abject places. Communities were engulfed by trauma due to the brutality with which the final mine closures were enacted, following Margaret Thatcher's battle with the mining unions led by Arthur Scargill. The highly unionised and historically socialist workers and their families summoned massive, yet eventually fruitless, efforts of resistance. During the miners' strike of 1984–5, people felt that they were literally fighting for their lives. For example, a National Union of Miners (NUM) leaflet declared that, 'Half of all men attempting suicide are unemployed'.[1]

Studies reported below took place in the regions within an area of special concern called the 'Heads of the Valleys' situated at the far ends of valleys where the social and economic problems are most acute. The young people who participated in the studies were aged 14 in 2009 and so were conceived ten years after the mining communities lost their battle for economic survival in 1985.

Regeneration and educational policies

Skills are being lauded as the solution to a ubiquitous moral panic about the UK as a declining industrial nation. Debate centres on what is meant by 'skill' and what is the purpose of education. A recent report by the Work Foundation captures the tension:

> Some have argued that more emphasis is placed on academic success and attaining qualifications rather than the learning of skills required for success in the workplace: 'how to think creatively, how to collaborate, how to empathise'. (Wright *et al.*, 2010: 33)

Policies to regenerate the south Wales' valleys have changed focus over time from employment to education. During the 1920s the political approach was to

1 See: www.llgc.org.uk/ymgyrchu/llafur/1972/BL7205b.htm

abandon the place, encourage outward migration and leave areas derelict (Doering *et al.*, 2011). In the 1930s there was some state-funded redevelopment that established a few small industries such as the Ebbw Vale Steel works and invested in local infrastructure. In 1999 political devolution from the Westminster government saw the introduction of the Welsh Assembly government and National Assembly along with the gradual process of devolution of powers came a new distinctively "Welsh" approach to the Valleys which recognised the area as the location of the post-industrial working class. Even so, the area has suffered a long period of stagnation and most of the jobs that exist are in the public sector (Doering *et al.*, 2011).

Recent regeneration policies no longer include managed, state-aided, transference to post-industrial conditions and instead individual mobility is encouraged within Wales as part of a devolved state and nation-building project (*ibid.*). This is supposed to take place through education rather than industry by equipping young people with 'skills for the knowledge economy located outside of the Valleys in the Coastal Belt of South Wales' (*ibid.*). As Doering *et al.* maintain, there is an, 'overall denial of class effects: redefining the problem of uneven development as a problem of place rather than capitalism's inherent tendency to dispossess the working class'.

In effect, young working-class people are faced with a black hole at the end of compulsory schooling at age 16. In the UK, post-compulsory vocational education and training (VET) provision available to many young people from working-class backgrounds is deeply inadequate for the their needs and those of society (Wolf, 2011). Those not destined for university education for a range of reasons are caught in a trap; either they are forced to undertake job training of such low quality that they become stigmatised with low-level certificates (NVQ level 2) that marks them as educational failures or they enter low-paid 'bad' jobs that allow no possibility for progression (Keep, 2002, 2005). Stuck at the bottom of the training or bad jobs ladder they become caught in a cycle of meaningless and monotonous labour unable to escape. Third-generation unemployed young people who have watched their parents and relatives enter this cycle are responding to their circumstances in a wide range of ways. A popular view is that working-class young people lack the incentives and aspirations to succeed. Findings from our studies refute this and the following sections suggest the need to shift thinking away from working-class educational failure to encompass a broader view of relationships between skills, place and community. The next section analyses the term 'skill' using concepts from Bernstein's sociology of pedagogy and contemporary, Vygotskian inspired socio-cultural or socio-historical approaches to learning. These theories demonstrate that skills are entangled with history, place, class and gender.

Theorising skill: from cognition to becoming

VET education must face up to the issue that skills cannot be divorced from the knower (Bernstein, 1996/2001) nor from the communities, technological advances and historical legacies though which 'skills' developed (Sennett, 2009; Cole and Engeström, 1993; Engeström, 2003). Skilled practices have traditionally been learned through apprenticeship curricula that involve: a joint enterprise, a shared vocabulary, repetition through time, progression and recognition acquired as a result of mastery (Lave, 1988; Lave and Wenger, 1991; Wenger, 1998; Sennett, 2009). Tensions arise when skilled practices developed outside school are taught in formal educational institutions because they divorce practices from the field of production where they were nurtured, anchored and recognized (Bernstein, 1996/2001).

Vygotskian-inspired theories of learning have explained working-class educational failure by examining the way persons appropriate the mediations means afforded by culture. Bernstein's work on working- and middle-class (speech) codes allowed him to describe the ways different groups were oriented to meanings depending on their exposure to, and experience of, specific kinds of social relationships and practices. Inspired by Vygotsky, Luria and Sapir, he developed the concept 'code' to capture the way culture mediates thought and speech. Socio-cultural approaches share with Bernstein's work a concept of 'code'. Minority ethnic, class and gender groups were revealed as disadvantaged because they encountered multiple barriers in gaining access to academic codes referred to as scientific (Vygotsky, 1934/1978) and formal codes (Bernstein, 1974). Bernstein's work sought to characterise the differences between the codes acquired in working-class families and the formal codes of schooling.

Bernstein identified forms of symbolic control, boundary maintenance and orientations to meaning that were characteristics of family types. He identified *positional* and *personal* types in order to define the range of social organisations that children would encounter as they grew up. He was interested in different forms of organic solidarity emerging due to corporate capitalism and so differentiated 'old' middle class as *positional* and a new middle class as *personal*. Code theory is best known for work developed in educational settings which focuses on the alignment or clash between home and school codes to explain working-class underachievement in comparison to middle-class groups. He initially identified two further contexts, interactional and imaginative (Bernstein, 1990: 97). Bernstein's work continues to be used to explain educational difficulties as a clash between home–school codes.

The scientific discourses taught in schools are generally regarded as abstract, decontextualised and higher-order forms of thinking (e.g. Newman *et al.*, 1989; Cole, 1985; Lave, 1988; Wertsch, 1985). Bernstein distinguished meanings that were de-contextualised, abstract or relying on propositional rather than empirical available clues that require immediately present, visual and auditory signs to make sense to another person. In similar ways to Vygotsky and Luria's work in Uzbekistan (Luria, 1976), he identified propositional logics that rely on clues given in previous auditory or literary texts to achieve unambiguous communication accessible to those with some formal education and functional meanings available to illiterate farmers. Yet as the farmers in Uzbekistan insisted, formal logics are so divorced from real situations and their practical priorities that they are functionally useless. Similar issues about the value of these two forms of thinking have re-emerged in the skills debate as the earlier quote from the Work Foundation testifies. The skills debate raises the question about the 'usefulness' of academic knowledge to economic recovery if it does not foster skills such as 'how to think creatively, how to collaborate, how to empathise'.

Similar concerns about the value and status of abstract as opposed to concrete thinking have been raised by socio-cultural scholars. The formulation of higher mental capacities in terms of hierarchical, abstract or 'decontextualised' mediational means (cf. Wertsch, 1985: 33) has been debated and challenged. Re-examining some of Vygotsky and Luria's finding in Uzbekistan, Valsiner (2007: 276–99) has suggested that the highest forms of knowledge refer to expertise and not academic knowledge and thus need to be understood as combinations of abstract *and* vertical elements which he terms abduction (combinations of deduction and induction) or open and closed concepts. Open or ambiguous concepts share features that Wulf (2011) identifies as mimetic process. Accordingly, (scientific) theory should not be viewed as *opposed* to practice, but as dialectically related to it (Chaiklin and Lave, 1996).

The skills debate reflects the growing disillusionment with 'abstract' academic knowledge and a narrow focus on cognition to solve economic and social problems, reflecting a need to shift from pitting codes in opposition to each other, towards recognising practice and theory dialectically intertwined in complex, holistic systems. This way of thinking invites a new approach to working-class codes and the possibility of returning to Bernstein's recognition of the multiplicity of contexts and imaginative worlds that working-class young people have access to. It invites us to revisit the unfortunately named 'restricted codes' that were often associated with working-class groups and to consider the importance of context-dependent or horizontal knowledge in learning. A holistic approach to learning views the learner within processes of becoming, in multiple contexts that involve: affective, corporeal, experiential, subjective as well as socio-cognitive processes.

Western scholars have been paying closer attention to Russian–Spinozian readings of Vygotsky's works (e.g. Kontopodis *et al.*, 2011). At the centre of Vygotsky's work is a tripartite model of cultural development, which Levykh (2008: 84) describes as 'development of personality, cultural emotions, and behavioural mastery' within an 'independent and complex systemic and multirelational process that occurs within a Socio-cultural–historical context'. Vygotsky recognised the dynamic, emergent nature of development in which affect and intellect are inseparable. Levykh points out that in Russia the emotion/ motivational aspect of teaching and learning are central in ways that they have not been in the West. Having a sense of belonging or a way to anchor oneself in the world is a precondition of learning (see Hedegaard and Chaiklin, 2003).

Vygotsky drew on Hegelian dialectical philosophy to imagine development as a struggle that takes place between the organism and the child, and the child and the environment Levykh (2008: 87). Mastery of behaviour represents the highest form of human will power. In self-mastery, newly formed systems mimetically carry forward collective, social forms of behaviour (Wulf, 2005). Cultural forms are captured by the concept of 'tool' which is used to signify the 'sum total of achievements in an industrial, social and intellectual sense' (Levykh, 2008: 95). When young people appropriate the culturally available tools of their locale, they revitalise the whole system of practice through which the tool was developed. While bringing the past forward into the present, they also transform it. Wulf (2005, 2011) has argued that the key to transformation in processes of mimesis is corporeality. In this study, skilled practices were revitalised, recontextualised and reworked when men shared activities with boys. In historically evolving, collective activity systems, motivations are often driven by collective needs that can be difficult to articulate at the individual level (Engeström, 2000: 960).

Everyday rituals: links between individuals and communities

Collective motives can be recognised in the rituals of everyday life (Kontopodis *et al.*, 2011; Metcalf and Game, 2009) such as watching television together, going for a walk or going out for a bike ride together. For example, taking a son or daughter pillion on dad's motorbike is a performative act that binds children to their parents. It is the repetitive aspect of ritual that forges familiar patterns and creates feelings of belonging. The rituals of everyday life come from the available repertoire of performances circulating in communities and reflect historical legacies and ways of 'doing things around here'. The activities of the community in this study had historical legacies in the ritual practices of labour associated with mine and steel industrials and, pre-dating the Industrial Revolution, of farming and land husbandry.

Boys especially, undertook activities such as BMX biking, mountain biking, repairing bikes, working on engines, playing rugby, boxing, going to the gym, building dog kennels, breeding ferrets, hunting, fishing and camping with older boys and men. Mimetic referencing works through corporeality (Wulf, 2011):

> for it is only in movement that a body shows what it is. Thus, the historical study of behaviour is not an auxiliary aspect of theoretical study, but rather forms its very base. (Vygotsky, 1930/1978: 64–5, cited in Kontopodis *et al.*, 2011: 10)

These corporeal practices and movements included features that mimetically resonate with past practices of mining and farming such as being outdoors, being physically active, developing skills and gaining muscle strength. Mimetic referencing points to rituals of the past reactivated in present practices that potentially change and create something new for all participants (Wulf, 2011). The corporeal aspects of mountain biking, dirt biking, rugby and motorbike mechanics provided the creative potential of mimesis (Wulf, 2011). As boys appropriated activities they invented, transformed and recast practices passed down from older generations in ways that included conflict, 'expressed power relations' and which at the same time accepted and questioned a given social order' (*ibid.*: 6). Seen as rituals, the boys' everyday activities transformed and reproduced corporeal practices that carried forward legacies of manual, skilled labour, available due to the place and its geographical typology as well as the social bonds between men that had been essential to the community's survival in dangerous underground conditions of mining. The social bonds of *communitas* and loyalty reflect a social order that is antithetical to neo-liberal, individualistic, competitive, independent, regulative order required to achieve in school contexts particularly in examination and test situations (McDermott, 1996).

Work on the corporeal device (Evans *et al.*, 2008, 2009, 2010) develops Bernstein's code theory using corporeal as well as linguistic elements of practices. Thus, the physical typology and the social bonds forged through time constitute a 'ruler of corporeality'. Rituals make available the repertoire of bodily practices that bestow high status and a sense of belonging on boys and men. They set the limits and possibilities for legitimate masculinity in *this place*. 'Rituals are the cause, the action and the effect of communities' (Kontopodis *et al.*, 2011: 8). Just as Bernstein developed code to capture the way the practices, experiences and rituals of working-class culture structure meanings that are realised as speech forms, so the corporeal device captures the way the rituals of body-practices and patterns of movement structure desire. The pleasure and the pain of hard, physical, outdoor work reaffirmed boys' sense of belonging to the community in this place.

Methodology

Multiple methods were combined to capture different aspects of young people's experiences and perceptions of the place where they were growing up. Case studies presented below came from research carried out as part of a large-scale research programme that aimed to use a wide range of qualitative and qualitative measures to map locales in Wales, Wales Institute of Social & Economic Research, Data and Methods (WISERD). The Young People and Place (YPP) project took place in a location chosen by the wider WISERD project and used a range of ethnographic methods including: observation in schools and in a youth centre, semi-structured interviews, visual and mobile methods and film-making with young people aged between 11 and 18. The case studies are informed by interviews that used specially selected photographs of places in and around the town as stimuli–response material and semi-structured questions with 64 boys and girls aged 13/14 including Sam and Dewi. The following year we returned to the same cohort and invited young people including Owain to take photographs with disposable cameras of places in and around their school. The photos formed the basis of semi-structured interviews about activities and places. In a further phase, the same cohort of young people were invited to participate in an experimental film-making project to work with an independent film-maker over a four-day period to make short films about activities that they valued. Sam, Dewi and Rob worked as a team to create a short film about BMXing.

An earlier study undertaken in 2008–9 investigated young people's social representations of skills in a different valley community. It included a series of teaching experiments with a year nine class of boys (aged 13/14) who were receiving extra support in literacy and numeracy. As part of this, Rhys took photographs of activities he undertook outside school and these formed the basis of in-depth interviews.

Analysis was informed by the Socio-cultural concepts of 'ritual', 'mimetic constellations' 'types of movement' and 'everyday practices' (Kontopodis *et al.*, 2011; Wulf, 2011) and by the concepts of the corporeal device (Evans *et al.*, 2008, 2009, 2010) to encompass the broader emphasis Bernstein placed on codes as practices, interaction and imagination as well as social bonds. The following case studies present pictures of four young people, Owain, Sam, Dewi and Rhys, who were all aged 14 years. Mimetic constellations are examined through their everyday rituals outside school, their social relationships and groups through which they gained a sense of belonging and imagined futures. They were each involved in processes of becoming, in multiple contexts that involved: affective, corporeal, experiential, subjective as well as socio-cognitive processes. The case studies give a flavour of the different ways that they were called into being in their communities while drawing on local resources such as landscapes, others including older men, machines and artefacts while undertaking activities and gaining skills.

Case study 1 Owain: becoming social

Solidarities (1) Leaving street identity at the school gate

Owain had numerous tattoos and body piercings which he spoke about with pride in casual conversation and in interview. He showed us his nipple piercing and where one of his tattoos had gone wrong. He was one of the bigger boys for his age group and regularly worked out in the gym. He had plans for two more tattoos and explained that he had to be careful where to get them done because it was illegal to have tattoos before the age of 16 years. As the bus drew into the schoolyard, Owain said, you unplug the iplayer, take off your hoodie, roll down your sleeves so they can't see the tattoos and put on your tie.

> Owain: This is the entrance of the school. And in the mornings, the buses will drive around and turn around and drop us off about here. And we'll have the teachers standing by the gates.
>
> Owain: As we're getting off the bus, they'll check we're wearing all our uniform and you haven't got earrings in and . . . You have to hide everything before you get off the bus.

The tattoos and body piercing were ways to present himself as older than his actual age and were marks of a working-class identity that he shared with older men. Owain managed the transition from home to school well and was well liked by his peers and teachers. He was in the second to top set in school and was projected to gain a good set of GCSEs. Like many young people his friendship groups were important.

Solidarities (2) groups, friends and 'those we bother with'

Owain used to spend lunchtimes with boys from the top set. However he now spent lunchtime with boys from the set below him who were also some of the boys he met up with after school. Owain was a part of a recognised group who had their own territory which included the hidden smoking area in the schoolyard and a specific table in the dining hall that no one else would use. On a typical day he went home by bus, changed his clothes, had something to eat and left on the 4.20 bus to the next town. He said that he was one of the only young people who made the trip out instead of socialising in the street around their houses; a practice that Owain said set him apart from his peers in school.

He spent his weekends with a group of about twenty-five friends who went into town to do 'Well, stuff that we shouldn't'. Sometime they would 'camp out' all night. Others in his class identified Owain as one of the boys who was part of a large group known for drinking and taking drugs. Although Owain admitted to 'doing things we shouldn't', he was not a follower and gave the impression of someone already older than his peers in school. Omar identified Owain as older than his age when he said, 'He's going to be having babes soon'. Owain made fleeting references to these activities, yet, when we asked him about relationships, he said he did not have a girlfriend. He said, 'No. [I] Find 'em and throw 'em, I do.' He explained that he had seen other boys being hurt when girls they had been going out with rejected them. Owain's view was that, 'it all ends up in arguments and stuff like that. So there's no point.'

Solidarities (3) Extended family networks

Owain lived in one of the housing estates four miles from the town centre. He drew a rectangle to illustrate four streets in his part of the housing estate and marked on it seven houses where most of his extended family lived.

Owain:	Yeah, it's easy, cos if my nan wants to go to my uncles, or go to my aunties, or whatever, you're never locked out really. Cos someone's bound to be in.
Interviewer:	True, true.
Owain:	Cos everyone who lives round here, you've obviously got some of the odd people that ain't my family living in between, like. In between or something, but they're all really close as well. Cos everyone that lives here, lived here for years.
Interviewer:	Oh really? And do you all meet up quite a bit?
Owain:	Yeah, cos in the summer, we'd be like on the steps outside, where everyone lives on the block and everyone's on their steps outside, talking again together.
Interviewer:	Yeah.
Owain:	And you'd have all the little kids, then, playing.

He spoke with warmth of the family parties and rituals such as 'sitting on the steps outside, talking' that created mutual bonds of affection. While the strength drawn from this strong affective base seemed to give him the confidence to strike out and explore further afield, he also spent time babysitting his two-year-old cousin, helping out in the house and being around the men.

Solidarities (4) close family

Owain's dad was working on a construction site in the city approximately 30 miles from the valley town where they lived. He and his dad did carpentry together at home and Owain had aspirations of owning a carpentry business in the future and building his own house. He said he would 'never live in the city' and imagined his future on the housing estate where he lived. His body-practices of going to the gym and staying fit recreated the skilled strong and muscular body that mimetically referenced the man-boy of industrial activities.

Along with a number of young men in our study, brushes with the police were part of their near culture. Owain had been wrongly accused of stealing from a shop, was arrested, interrogated and had his fingerprints taken, before eventually being found innocent. Knowing too much about police cells and procedures normalises these processes as matter-of-fact occurrences. Although vindicated, his details remain on police records. We asked how his parents had reacted:

> Owain: My mum hated it. My mother's always brought us up to, like, pay for stuff. She's always given us money for what we needed. And she just didn't expect it. And she knows the boy who really did it.

He said his father trusted him. 'I think he knew I wouldn't have done something like that.'

> Owain: So after I proved myself, then I rang my father when he was on nights and told him that they found out it wasn't me and stuff like that. And he took me down M***** [to celebrate].

His account demonstrates how important it was that his father trusted him and knew he was innocent. They celebrated together with a night out in the nearest large town.

Owain lived in a family with three siblings. Two were from his mother's previous marriage. Like many families in the study, Owain's father brought up two non-biological children as his own. We asked Owain if he wanted children.

> Owain: Yeah, I wanted one now, but I can't, can I?
> Interviewer: You want one now? Please tell me why.
> Owain: I have to wait about two years. Because one of . . .

He justified his wish to have a child now by referring to his two-year-old nephew.

Owain:	I just like looking after my nephew because I think, I dunno, I want a kid before I get older, I do.
Interviewer:	Yeah.
Owain:	I get used to it, then. But I wouldn't say I treat it bad, because loads of people just say that [inaudible 11: 06]. Like my sister can trust me, if I was looking after him for a couple of hours, because I can feed him, take him out for walks.
Interviewer:	How old is he?
Owain:	Well, he's two, just gone two in May, he was. Last month he turned two.
Interviewer:	And you just find it really satisfying looking after him?
Owain:	Yeah.

His seemed to genuinely embrace the (adult) responsibility of looking after children. He did not associate having a child with having a steady girlfriend or marriage and wished that he did not have to wait until he was 16 to have a child. His next tattoo was going to be his nephew's name.

Owain's family and community provided him with a strong sense of belonging and his ambitions where to stay and literally build his future home in the place where his family had lived for generations. Owain's account epitomised the social bond and solidarities of his community. The link between past and future was perhaps most poignantly signified by his wish to have a child now and his desire to mark his skin with the name of his young nephew, a symbolic reminder of a future life unfolding and a community under threat renewing itself.

Case study 2 Sam: corporeal becomings

Sam has been playing rugby since age five and was a prop for Cwm Dffryn and supported the Blues (rugby team based in the nearby city). His sister's boyfriend was one of the number of people Sam knew who played for the Blues. His ambition was to attend a sports academy and eventually play for a local rugby team. He was also a serious BMXer who enthusiastically described tricks, back flips, barspins and building obstacles for jumps in the street. He explained the need to learn tricks such as back flips before trying them out on concrete, which took him to places such as the skatepark in Oldport where there was a foam bed. Sometimes he was asked to perform tricks in Cwm Dffryn skatepark. He respected the older BMX boys and was friendly with them. He was not influenced by the drinking and drug culture there, and focused instead on learning tricks, having fun and being outside and independent.

He had owned a motorbike but had sold it the previous year. Before getting a motorbike he had scouted the landscape to find the mountain trails created by generations of men and boys who had ridden there before him. He said that people phoned the police to complain about the noise and he had been chased a number of times. He blamed his bike for letting him down because it broke down just when he was making a dash for it. The police gave him a warning that time. He was hoping to get a new motorbike when he was 16 years old. He said two years ago lots of people protested about a police ambush aimed at stopping boys riding motorbikes in the mountains and since then the police did not chase them so much.

His enjoyment of physical movement led him far and wide as he sought out places to learn new tricks. He camped out near the reservoir with friends who amused themselves with midnight swims, fishing and lighting fires which he particularly enjoyed. He had bought a fishing licence the previous year and caught small trout. His desire for new challenges took him across the countryside, down B roads, and across the moors, to rivers and cliffs. He learned where to go through independent exploration and through his extensive networks of peers and adults.

Sam lived to increase his skill in physical activities. Corporeality afforded him pleasure, independence, purpose and ambition. His family appeared to exert less surveillance over him than Owain's and this may well have encouraged Sam to retain a wide range of social networks while being aligned with none in particular. He had become resourceful and seemed to embrace his freedom. He was a warm, empathetic and mature 14-year-old to talk to. While his practices appeared to be entrepreneurial, there was a sense that his future was precarious, for he was unlikely to find a sport academy to attend when he left school.

Case study 3 Dewi: history in becoming

Dewi was a mountain bike enthusiast. His dad was also a keen mountain biker and they went off together at weekends. They had a garage up in his house in Waun with 'loads of bikes in it' and spent time there messing about and fixing them. He said he was good at fixing bikes because he had been doing it with his dad for a while. He loved living in Waun, which was outside Cwm Dyffryn, because 'there were few people around that you do not know, it's quiet' and there were community officers whom he knew well. He said that the local community liked to see the community officers around. Living in Waun made Dewi feel very secure.

Dewi went to the skatepark in Cym Dyffryn because of the jumps. His mum sometimes dropped off money for him and he always felt safe because there was a community guard in the adjoining sports centre who patrolled the skatepark each day. His mum knew the guard. He left the skatepark at 8.45 p.m. and the community guard went home at 7.30 p.m. Dewi said he felt closer to his family than his friends; he did not say much about having best friends, and instead explained that:

> Dewi: I sometimes just stay in sometime then
> . . . and have a break . . .

But when asked about where he encountered friends he spoke of the skatepark and having a feeling of never being alone.

Dewi:	The skatepark
Interviewer:	So quite a sociable, quite a big social place?
Dewi:	Yes, a lot of people there, loads of friends down there too so
Interviewer:	So you don't go anywhere you like to be on your own or anything, you like to
Dewi:	I'm never on my own
Interviewer:	You're never on your own?
Dewi:	No, I am never on my own when I go out on my bike
Interviewer:	Is that cos you don't want to be on your own or
Dewi:	My . . . I never go on my own really when I go on my bike, cos what it is I fall off and hurt myself nobody to call the ambulance then so, that's why I go with friends mostly.

Dewi exuded a ubiquitous sense of being connected to, cared for and served by numerous social networks within the community. He wanted to do well at school as well as pursing his interest in bikes. His mum was a manager at a local supermarket and his dad was a kitchen fitter. He said that his dad had promised that he could work with him for five years once he left school. Although Dewi was already good at carpentry and fixing things, his main interest was in 'things with two wheels, but mainly bikes'. He was strongly motivated to becoming a skilled mountain biker and constantly pushed the boundaries of his physical skill. He found going fast down a mountain trail extremely exhilarating. During an extensive interview in 2009, he constructed a strong social identity as a biker. However, two years later when Dewi joined a group to make a film about BMX biking, another identity emerged.

While driving on a back road over a desolate moor, en route to a mountain bike park we spotted a group of wild horses and stopped to test out the camera gear. Rob, a new boy to the school, was part of the group. His dad owned a farm and stables and as he trained the camera on one of the horses, he offered to catch one for me to ride. It turned out that Rob had been working with horses all his life and was an accomplished rider and had won medals showing his horses at a number of events. Recently Sam and Dewi had started working with Rob on his dad's farm at weekends. The following day, while filming in a skatepark, we conducted a group interview in which Sam, Dewi and Rob were supposed to talk about their BMX activities. However, within minutes of turning the camera on, they animatedly told stories about working with horses, hunting with their fathers, learning to use guns, breeding ferrets, handling dogs and working on the farm. They had tacked up horses, groomed them and helped to prepare them for the hunt. They explained in detail how the hunt no longer involved foxes and instead used decoys. The boys had bonded over these joint activities and seemed unable to talk about BMX biking until they had told these stories. Three days later, while finishing the film, we found out that Dewi's grandfather had been a gamekeeper and had passed down many skills to his son who in turn was teaching them to Dewi.

Dewi's becomings can be seen to recreate continuity with past practices anchored in his grandfather's job. Throughout our studies, farming was described as an undesirable job by young people in valley communities. Dewi's skills of hunting, working with horses, breeding ferrets and showing dogs had remained hidden until the chance sighting of the wild horses sparked a line of flight (Deleuze and Guattari, 2004), which prompted Rob's animated offer to catch a horse for me to ride. The boys had become connected through joint interests and the opportunities to earn money on Rob's dad's farm. All three boys said they had helped to prepare horses and dogs for the hunt. Although being a gamekeeper was a traditional working-class job, it usually involved working for a landlord. Could it be that activities such as farming, working on the land and with animals made mimetic reference to a class-based division of labour reaching back to a time before the Industrial Revolution? Boys did not talk about these skills at school and when they emerged in interviews they were often hidden behind 'modern' skills such as BMX or mountain biking that endowed boys with high status within peer interactions. Farming and working with animals can be viewed as ancient skills that were possibly tinged with working-class shame (see Abreu, 1995) that reached back to a time before the Industrial Revolution and the pride associated with machines and mechanics.

Case study 4 Rhys: becoming nature

Rhys came to school with his arms covered in mud. During a teaching experiment with a small group, Rhys recounted a story about having seen a dog being run over by a car at the weekend. The other boys laughed, enjoying descriptions of blood and gore. Rhys reprimanded them saying, 'How would you like it if your dog had been run over?' Rhys had reared dozens of ferrets and was able to talk at length about how to hunt rabbits with them. He described the precise legal position on hunting deer and using a shotgun. He had learned these skills from his dad and uncles, who were long-term unemployed. He had a knowledgeable, caring and respectful relationship with animals and had bought and sold at least six dogs, demonstrating entrepreneurial skills. He had learned to build kennels for his dogs in the backyard with his dad, and explained why some dogs must sleep outside. He had hand-reared a pup that had been abandoned by its mother, which involved feeding it every four hours for the first few weeks, getting up in the middle of the night and racing home from school to catch feeding time. He had enlisted his mum to take over when he could not make a feed. He had given his pup to the lady whose dog had been run over at the weekend. Rhys had had a difficult life, yet had enormous empathy with animals and with people. We came to realise that the mud on his arms was worn as a badge of honour, a mark of his relationship with the land.

Rhys was in a class with a group of seven boys who were taken out of lessons to receive extra help with literacy and numeracy. The teacher had been wary of letting me work with the boys and warned me not to expect them to do any writing. These boys lived on the margins of school life; for many reasons, they found it difficult to cope with the rituals of schooling. Although his teacher knew that Rhys had nurtured a pup, none of his skills were recognised or given credit within the school. As with Dewi and his friends, these skills remained relatively hidden and could not be used as cultural capital within peer groups. His skills working with animals were doubly invisible and if anything stigmatised him as a marginal participant in school life. Rhys was excluded from school before the study came to an end. Like many boys in his class, he found it difficult to conform to the behaviour, including being physically passive, required in lessons. During one interview he told me that his father's friend had just bought his daughter a BMW. He said that everyone in his network outside school was unemployed, yet still managed to get all the things they wanted. For Rhys there was no point being in school and nothing to be gained from education. In being expelled, Rhys slipped out of the only remaining institution that connected him to the public realm, leaving him to slide into the hidden cultures of ex-mining valley life.

Discussion

Skills are intricately linked to time and place. Appropriating and revitalising cultural tools involves mimetic references to earlier times, communities and practices in which they were developed. In this study, skilled practices were revitalised, recontextualised and reworked when men shared activities with boys. When they shared trail biking, mountain biking and motorbiking they made potential mimetic connections with corporeal practices developed in the industrial past through the ordinary everyday rituals of physical, outdoor activities with machines. Participating in these activities engendered feelings of excitement, adventure and danger. Sporting activities such as rugby union and going to the gym recontextualised hard labour. By participating in these skilled practices, boys experienced the pleasure and pain of physical work that mimetically referenced the miner's body. For a short period the Industrial Revolution demonstrated that there could be such a thing as working-class prosperity, and hence pride. Other activities such as those associated with the land and animals mimetically referenced labour before industrialisation and seemed to evoke less straightforward feelings such as pride within families; yet in school and most peer groups such skills remained hidden. BMXing and skateboarding are modern skills that mimetically reference wider global youth subcultures reinforced via online websites.

In self-mastery, newly formed systems mimetically carry forward collective, social forms of behaviour (Wulf, 2005). Spinozian readings of Vygotsky recognise the person as a representative of society as a whole. When young people appropriate the culturally available tools of their locale, they revitalise the whole system of practice through which the tool was developed. In their acts of becoming through skilled practices, boys could be said to bring the community forward. Each of the boys in the case studies achieved this in different ways.

Owain's rituals and everyday practice focused on belonging to a range of different groups such as peers, large groups, near and extended family. Each afforded him different ways of becoming, through the kinds of solidarity they offered. Owain's role models were older men and he marked his solidarity with them through tattoos, body piercing and his ambitions to become a self-employed carpenter and build a house that would stand among those of his extended family. His activities mimetically referenced the physical fitness and sociality of the man-boy of the industrial era recontextualised through available sporting and body aesthetic practices. His father's generation retained links to the productive era when working-class men worked hard, had pride in their muscle power and built things for themselves and their families. In his imaginative trajectory Owain was set to continue this line and so epitomised the potential for community survival.

Sam was strongly motivated to develop physical skills. Through mimesis the body copies movement from others and at the same time changes them. Sam epitomised Wulf's contention that mimesis works through corporeality. As Sam turned tricks, rode far and wide across the landscape, mountains and valley terrains and worked hard physically he revitalised the importance of the typology of place that first drew people to live there. Mimetic learning involves confronting negative influences as well as becoming similar to others (Wulf, 2011: 90). Sam was able to confront and resist the drinking and smoking culture of the skatepark while copying skills performed by the older skateboarders. His activities created 'difference, particularity and creativity' (*ibid.*). Through corporeal movements, Sam revitalised the potential of the physical and geographic resources of the place.

Dewi's acts of becoming created family continuity across time. Although he initially presented himself as a mountain and BMX biker, his hidden connection with the land and nature emerged to reveal a wealth of skills around animal husbandry. The boys who were in the know were able to share and enjoy this expertise, despite a ubiquitous threat of being exposed as having a shameful working-class identity that resonates with the image of the 'country bumpkin' (see Jamieson, 2000). During the film-making process Rob fell out with his father, pointing to presence of conflict and power relations within forms of becoming. Rob was struggling to be accepted in a new school and seemed to have adopted the BMXer identity in place of this framing identity in order to fit in. Dewi had been in the school longer and had better coping strategies. He may have felt a need to hide his skills with animals to protect a cultural inheritance valued within his family, that was not publicly valued within peer groups in school or in the skatepark. Dewi had ways to retreat into his family away from peer group networks taking, as he put it, 'time out'. While Dewi's becomings can be seen to create continuity with ancestors, there was a threat that he might be exposed.

Unlike Dewi, Rhys only had one strategy and one identity to present to the world. His skills of hunting, shooting, rearing and trading animals took place in the hidden social networks of unemployed men. Teachers were very far removed from the social networks that provided Rhys with the resources, skills and social bonds for his becoming and he was marginalised within the school. The gulf between his everyday and night rituals was not being breached and like many boys in his class he was simply known for his 'bad behaviour' (see McDermott, 1996). However, bad behaviour was often a manifestation of boys' inability to get their bodies to sit, stand and move to the rhythms of the institution. Rhys's skills with animals displayed empathy, creativity and unfortunately a difference so great that the school misrecognised them and him as 'other'. Characterising Rhys as 'becoming nature' captures both the positive and negative aspects of what was becoming his fate. He was heading on a trajectory into nature and a world that was not publicly valued within public institutions.

Conclusions

In their recent report entitled *Poorer Children's Educational Attainment: How Important Are Attitudes and Behaviour*, Goodman and Gregg (2010) identified: aspirations, attitudes and behaviour of parents as primary factors contributing to educational attainment and cycles of intergenerational poverty. They identified the transfer of cognitive abilities from one generation to the next as an important element, suggesting that working-class families did not pass on the right kinds of aspirations to their children. Our findings suggest that 'abstract' cognitive skills are only a small part of the process of learning. Second, that parents in communities marked by poverty often pass on rich resources to their children equipping them with a range of skills such as empathy, creativity and entrepreneurship as well as specific skills with engines, bikes, building materials, animals and the land. There was no lack of aspiration, imagination or ambition in the 14-year-old boys in our studies. However, the severe lack of adequate post-16 education that could recognise and build on these skills (Keep, 2005; Wolf, 2011) leads young working-class boys into a cul-de-sac. Surely it should be possible to provide the kind of training that would equip Owain with the technical skills to bring his ambitions to fruition? Sam needed access to a sports academy and there were none in the vicinity. Dewi may end up working with his father if he does not find a suitable education involving bikes, while Rhy's atunement with animals and the land had already excluded him from formal education.

The skills learned outside school in the community could be recognised as residues of technical knowledge (mechanics, carpentry, animal husbandry, farming) recontextualised as sports and leisure activities. The value attached to the skilled, strong and dirty body mimetically referenced labour from the industrial era and before that farming. Mining and farming had provided jobs for men and women in this place. The rupture caused by the loss of industry in the area has created a gulf between school and adult employment for young people in this place. Young people have to find ways to imaginatively fill this gap if they are to retain any sense of hope and a future trajectory. Boys in this study had many creative ways to fill this gulf through their involvement in networks outside school. They threw themselves practically, imaginatively and creatively into a range of activities. Hope was extended to boys via the care, enthusiasm and shared expertise of older men (and women) motivated we suspect by a community spirit to survive (see Walkerdine, 2010). Older men shared skills, know-how and resources with boys in any ways they could. However, young people's future imaginaries are precarious and vulnerable unless bridges can be constructed between hope and fulfilment. Education in post-industrial places cannot be confined to formal schooling; it needs to take account of time, place and community.

The term *skill* has already emerged as a leitmotiv to capture what is wrong with the kind of knowledge taught in schools and academies along with a tantalising suggestion that an alternative kind of knowledge, called skill, can solve current economic problems (Keep 2002, 2005). To break out of a cycle that traps young people into low-paid jobs and useless qualifications, the UK needs a credible and meaningful skills education.

Present neo-liberal educational policies dispossess working-class communities laying the foundations for further 'black spots' where people are driven to extreme measures, including entering black economies to survive (see Steinberg, 2011). Education does not only take place in schools. Learning skills are acts of becoming that relate to collective motivations within communities threatened with economic death.

Owain, Sam, Dewi and Rhys were each taking their community forward though acts of becoming in their ordinary everyday activities. In doing so, not only were they developing skills, they were revitalising community bonds, and so life in a specific kind of landscape forged in farming and industrial pasts. They were the shoots of post-industrial community survival. Appropriate post-compulsory education could provide the bridge that would allow these shoots to grow.

We need to return to Bernstein's concerns with the social shaping of consciousness and broaden debates about learning yet further by engaging anew with praxis and power by recognising how corporeality mimetically transforms acts of becoming. The role of desire, affect and pleasure are important, yet still underdeveloped areas in theories of learning (e.g. Hedegaard and Chaiklin, 2005).

'Not only does Vygotsky conceive child development and schooling as cultural-historical phenomena, he also poses the question of how human history can lead to a new type of society and a new type of human being' (Vygotsky, 1934/1994, cited in Kontopodis *et al.*, 2011: 10). As Chaiklin maintains, when performance becomes a mirror for performability it entails the possibility for disruption (2011: 224). Through performances of skilled practices, boys recontextualised working-class masculinities which act as 'troubling mirrors' to challenge some of the pathologising discourses of today's 'youth culture' and create locations for a 'politics of possibility' (*ibid.*).

Acknowledgements

Although I have written the chapter as a single author, I gratefully acknowledge the collective work and thinking of the research team. When I have used the term 'we' I am invoking the full YPP research team: Emma Renold, Bella Dicks, Kate Moles, Mariann Märtsin and others without whom I could not have written this paper and who I thank for their intellectual generosity.

This publication is based on research supported by the Wales Institute of Social and Economic Research, Data and Methods (WISERD), which is funded by the UK Economic and Social Research Council (Grant number: RES-576-25-0021) and the Higher Education Funding Council for Wales.

References

Abreu, G. (1995) 'Understanding How Children Experience the Relationship Between Home and School Mathematics', *Mind, Culture and Activity*, 2(2): 119–42.

Bernstein, B. (1974) *Class, Codes and Control 1: Theoretical Studies Towards Sociology of Language*, 2nd, rev. edn, London: Routledge.

—— (1990) *The Structuring of Pedagogic Discourse*, London and New York: Routledge.

—— (1996/2001) *Pedagogy, Symbolic Control and Identity: Theory, Research, Critique*, London: Taylor & Francis.

Chaiklin, S. (2011) 'The Role of Practice in Cultural-Historical Science', in M. Kontopodis, C. Wulf, and B. Fichtner (eds.), *Children, Development and Education: Cultural, Historical and Anthropological Perspectives*, New York: Springer, 227–46.

Chaiklin, S. and Lave, J. (1996) *Understanding Practice: Perspectives on Activity in Context*, Cambridge: Cambridge University Press.

Cole, M. (1985) The Zone of Proximal Development: Where Cultural and Cognition Create Each Other, in J. V. Wertsch (ed.), *Culture, Communication and Cognition*, Cambridge: Cambridge University Press.

Cole, M. and Engeström, Y. (1993) 'A Cultural-Historical Approach to Distributed Cognition', in G. Deleuze and F. Guattari (2004) *A Thousand Plateaus: Capitalism and Schizophrenia*, trans. Robert Hurley, Mark Seem and Helen R. Lane, London: Athlone Press.

Deleuze, G. and Guattari, F. (2004) *A Thousand Plateaus: Capitalism and Schizophrenia*, trans. Robert Hurley, Mark Seem and Helen R. Lane, London: Athlone Press.

Doering, H., Moles, K. and Dicks, B. (2011) 'Semiotics of space: class(ify)ing identities', paper presented at BSA Annual Conference, London, 6–8 April.

Engeström, Y. (2000) 'Activity Theory as a Framework for Analyzing and Redesigning Work', *Ergonomics*, 43(7): 960–74.

Evans, J., Rich, E., Davies, B. and Allwood, R. (2008) *Education, Disordered Eating and Obesity Discourse: Fat Fabrications*, London: Routledge.

Evans, J. Rich, E and Davies, B. (2009) *The Body Made Flesh: Embodied Learning and the Corporeal Device*, British Journal of Sociology of Education, 30(4): 389–91.

Evans, J., Davies, B. and Rich, E. (2010) 'Bernstein, Body Pedagogies and the Corporeal Device' in G. Ivinson, B. Davies and B. Fitz (eds.), *Knowledge and Identity: Concepts and Applications in Bernstein's Sociology*, London: Routledge.

Goodman, A. and Gregg, P. (2010) *Poorer Children's Educational Attainment: How Important Are Attitudes and Behaviour*, York: Joseph Rowntree Foundation.

Hedegaard, M. and Chaiklin, S. (2005) *Radical–Local Teaching and Learning*, Aarhus, Denmark: Aarhus University Press.

Jamieson, L. (2000) 'Migration, Place and Class: Youth in a Rural Area', *Editorial Board of the Sociological Review*, 203–23.

Keep, U. (2002) 'The English Vocational Education and Training Policy Debate – Fragile "Technologies" or Opening the "Black Box": Two Competing Visions of Where We Go Next', *Journal of Education and Work*, 15(4): 457–79.

—— (2005) 'Too Good to Be True? – Three Scenarios of the English VET system in 2015', SKOPE, University of Warwick.

Kontopodis, M., Wulf, C. and Fichtner, B. (eds.) (2011) *Children, Development and Education: Cultural, Historical and Anthropological Perspectives*, New York: Springer.

Lave, J. (1988) *Cognition in Practice: Mind, Mathematics and Culture in Everyday Life*, Cambridge: Cambridge University Press.

Lave, J. and Wenger, E. (1991) *Situated Learning*, Cambridge: Cambridge University Press.

Levykh, M. G. (2008) 'The Affective Establishment and Maintenance of Vygotsky's Zone of Proximal Development', *Education Theory*, 58(1): 83–101.

Luria, A. R. (1976) *Cognitive Development: Its Cultural and Social Functions*, Cambridge, MA: Harvard University Press.

McDermott, R. P. (1996) 'The Acquisition of a Child by a Learning Disability', in S. Chaiklin and J. Lave (eds.), *Understanding Practice – Perspectives on Activity and Context*, Cambridge, Cambridge University Press.

Metcalf, A. and Game, A. (2010) 'Creative Practice: The Time of Grace', *Time and Society*, 19(2): 165–79.

Newman, D., Griffin, P. and Cole, M. (1989) *The Construction Zone: Working for Cognitive Change in Schools*, Cambridge: Cambridge University Press.

Sennett, R. (2009) *The Craftsman*, London: Penguin Books.

Steinberg, S. (2011) *Boston Review* (available online at www.bostonreview.net.1/steinberg. php; last accessed 29 March 2011).

Valsiner, J. (2007) *Culture in Minds and Societies: Foundations of Cultural Psychology*, London: Sage.

Vygotsky, L. S. (1934/1987) 'Thinking and Speech', trans. N. Minick, in R. Rieber (ed.), *The Collected Works of Vygotsky*, vol. 1, *Problems of General Psychology*, New York and London: Plenum, 39–288.

—— (1981) 'The Genesis of Higher Mental Functions', in J. V. Wertsch, ed. and trans., *The Concept of Activity in Soviet Psychology*, Armonk, NY: Sharpe.

Walkerdine, V. (2010) 'Communal Beingness and Affect: An Exploration of Trauma in an Ex-Industrial Community', *Body and Society*, 16(1): 91–116.

Wenger, E. (1998) *Communities of Practice: Learning, Meaning, and Identity*, Cambridge: Cambridge University Press.

Wertsch, J. V. (1985) *Vygotsky and the Social Formation of Mind*, Cambridge, MA: Harvard University Press.

—— (1991) *Voices of the Mind: A Socio-cultural Approach to Mediated Activity*, Cambridge, MA: Harvard University Press.

Wolf, A. (2011) *Review of Vocational Education* (Wolf Report), Department for Education, UK.

Wright, J., Brinkley, I. and Clayton, N. (2010) *Employment and Skills in the UK: Redefining the Debates*, London: Work Foundation.

Wulf, C. (2005) *Zur Genese des Sozialen. Mimesis, Performativtät*, Ritual. Bielefeld: transcript.

—— (2011) 'Mimesis in Early Childhood: Enculturation, Practical Knowledge and Performability', in M. Kontopodis, C. Wulf and B. Fichtner (eds.), *Children, Development and Education: Cultural, Historical and Anthropological Perspectives*, New York: Springer, 89–102.

10 'Identity' as a unit of analysis in researching and teaching mathematics

Stephen Lerman

Introduction

In two recent London art exhibitions the notion of identity has come to the fore: in one case in the choice of presentation by the curator Belinda Thomson; and in the second by the artist/photographer himself. The first was a retrospective of Gauguin at the Tate Modern between 30 September 2010 and 16 January 2011, in which the curator chose to organise the works in themes:[1]

> Rather than following a strictly chronological sequence, *Gauguin: Maker of Myth* is organised according to thematic sections that emphasise the parallels between different stages in his career. Bringing together works made in Paris, Martinique, Brittany, Tahiti and the Marquesas, it traces motifs and ideas as they are revisited and deepened in objects and images that he produced years and many thousands of miles apart.

In the first room she collected self-portraits from across almost forty years, claiming that:

> Gauguin's self-portraits were a vital tool for the fashioning and refashioning of his identity. From bourgeois banker and family man to bohemian martyr and the notorious 'savage' of his later years, his shifting persona was a source of puzzlement and speculation for his contemporaries. These diverse guises can be seen as the careful crafting of a public image, but also they reflect a multiplicity of attempts to see and understand himself.

Looking at these paintings through the eyes/words of the curator one could indeed imagine an intention across those times and places by Gauguin to present himself as he wanted to be seen, an outward manifestation of his inner sense(s) of self, but I was certainly convinced of this as a successful story told by Ms Thomson and not necessarily anything based on information about the self-portraits from the artist.

1 The quotes from the two exhibitions are taken from the handbooks distributed at the galleries.

The second exhibition, held at Tate Britain from 8 September 2010 to 6 January 2011 was of the revolutionary photographer Eadward Muybridge 'whose pioneering contributions to art and technology transformed late 19th-century American and European culture'. He was born Edward James Muggeridge in 1830. He arrived in America in the early 1850s and seems to have used both Muggeridge and Muygridge as surnames. From 1865 he changed that to Muybridge, though it was sometimes mistaken for Maybridge. He often published under the name Helios. In 1875 he adopted the name Eduardo Santiago Muybridge but in 1881 changed his first name to Eadweard. On his memorial stone the name Eadweard Muybridge is recorded. It seems that these changes were all about self-marketing, choosing names as representing the self that he thought most saleable at particular times in his life.

I have chosen these examples, one in which the observer creates an account of identity of the observed, the other in which the person constructs their own identities, to set the scene for this chapter in which I examine how the notion of identity, as a construction of the self, is being seen by researchers in education as a way of conceiving of the engagement, or the lack of engagement, with the educational enterprise by pupils, but from quite a wide range of theoretical perspectives.

There has been a convergence of literature in the social sciences in general[2] and education in particular in recent years that places notions of identity at the heart of analysing how children become who they become and how learning is described and perceived. At the same time, just as it was the 'convergence, within the field of the production of intellectual discourse, on the concept of competence by the disciplines of the social and psychological sciences' (Bernstein, 2000: 44) that led to the competence model of pedagogy, we may be seeing the emergence of a new model of pedagogy at this time, signalled perhaps in Bernstein (1993). In this chapter I propose to bring together these two trends and I will suggest that identity, constructed appropriately, can provide a particularly productive unit of analysis for research in the field of education, and specifically in the sub-field of mathematics education, at this time of a general recognition of the role of context and of culture in the learning experiences in our multilingual, multiethnic classrooms.

Among sociologists of education, Bernstein has perhaps developed the most useful grammar for addressing the connections between the macro forces in society and the micro nature of pedagogic interactions. He developed a strong grammar, that is, with a conceptual syntax capable of generating unambiguous empirical descriptions, and while this language presents great challenges to research students who want to understand and work with his theories it is precisely its strength that makes it so powerful and applicable. Furthermore, as Bernstein himself explains (1993), his theory and Vygotsky's

---

2 In 1996 Stuart Hall said, 'There has been a veritable explosion in recent years around the concept of "identity"' (p. 1), to which Zygmunt Bauman (2001) added, 'The explosion has triggered an avalanche.'

have the same origins and inspiration: that of Marx. Worked together, I and many others have found that these sociological and cultural-historical theories respectively provide insights into how children learn in a way that enables one both to understand how and why children fail and to be able to propose and research strategies to do something to change that. In the mathematics education research community we have built up a substantial body of work based on ethnomathematics (d'Ambrosio, 2010) and also on critical approaches that have nevertheless, I suggest, not provided us with appropriate tools to achieve those changes. We need the sociological insights and the cultural-historical analysis offered by these two great thinkers.

The notion of identity in educational thinking

Perhaps the key impetus for this focus on identity in education can be attributed to Jean Lave who wrote:

> We have argued that, from the perspective we have developed here, learning and a sense of identity are inseparable: They are the same phenomenon. (Lave and Wenger, 1991: 115)

While her perspective has been taken up in most areas of education (Kirshner and Whitson, 1997) it has had particular impact in mathematics education because of the associated influence of her work on situated cognition which developed from Lave's studies of mathematical activity in apprenticeship situations (Watson and Winbourne, 2007). Furthermore, the idea, at the heart of the mathematics school curriculum all over the world, that mathematical knowledge learned in the abstract in school can be applied by students outside school in everyday problems, the notion of transfer, is comprehensively challenged by the idea that knowledge is situated, not carried in decontextualized concepts in the mind. Differences between within school and out-of-school competences were also challenged by Nunes *et al.* (1993).

At the same time, the association of 'being good at mathematics' with being a geek or nerd, or at least as being unusual and different, as experienced by so many of us when mentioning our mathematical proclivities at parties, raises questions of what it is like to be a mathematician, or how one comes to be one, when so many people have such negative experiences of learning mathematics at school. Hence here too the notion of identity seems an obvious place to examine learning. It matters enormously in mathematics of course, since it is unreasonably significant for students' future life possibilities. In the UK, for example, one cannot gain a place in university for the one-year postgraduate teacher education course, even if one is to teach art at secondary school, without certification in mathematics. In France the highest level of mathematics needs to be taken in the *baccalauréat* if one is to gain a place at the top universities, once again even if mathematics scarcely figures in the course. Mathematics is seen, unjustifiably I suggest, as a general measure of intelligence and capacity.

Bernstein's last book (2000) was entitled *Pedagogy, Symbolic Control and Identity*, emphasising the importance of the notion for him. For Bernstein, the identity of the teacher and the student are consequences of the pedagogic device and its realisation in particular forms of classification and framing.

> The form and modality of pedagogic identity are an outcome of the classificatory relations (relations between categories) *and* the form of the realisation of the classificatory relations, that is the strength of the framing (relations within). In other words the code modality is the outcome of 'relations between' and 'relations within'. (pp. 204/205)

Bernstein shows how identity is differentially produced for different social groups in pedagogic forms, focusing on the performance model and the competence model. In a paper for the first meeting of the international group Mathematics Education and Society, we (Lerman and Tsatsaroni, 1998) examined Bernstein's description of these models and their modes and recontextualised them into the sub-field of mathematics education.

We argued that the liberal–progressive mode is represented by the various models of 'reform', as they are labelled across the world, and are versions, more or less radical, of constructivist learning theory and pedagogies (Goldin, 1990; von Glasersfeld, 1990). The populist mode is seen in the substantial international work under the umbrella of Ethnomathematics (D'Ambrosio, 2010), and the radical mode manifests as critical mathematics (Skovsmose, 1994). As is signalled in Singh's diagram, the Performance model appears in mathematics education as a singular, atomistic in emphasis, with the vertical absolutely privileged.

More importantly, for this chapter, we conjectured the emergence of a new model, a competence model but with a new reading, located in a Wittgensteinian emphasis on use (Lerman, 2006):

Competence Model	Liberal–progressive	Populist	Radical
	Child-centred primary curricula	Separatist curricula (e.g., feminine or culturally specific content and methods)	Critical pedagogies
Performance model	Singular	Regional	Generic
	History Physics Mathematics	Studies in Society and Environment Cultural Studies	Competency-based education

Figure 10.1 Bernstein's typology of types of pedagogy

(Singh, 1996: 12)

For a *large* class of cases – though not for all – in which we employ the word 'meaning' it can be defined thus: the meaning of a word is its use in the language. (Wittgenstein, 1967, para. 43)

but also Vygotskian theories based on the materialism of Marx (e.g. Lerman, 2001), and poststructuralist work, in particular recontextualising the work of Foucault (e.g. Evans, Morgan and Tsatsaroni, 2006), expressed in terms of subjectivity and discursive practices.

Specifically in mathematics education we suggested the emergence of two directions in research approaches: studies drawing on Vygotskian psychology; and studies we termed discursive practices. We can therefore modify and extend Singh's diagram as follows:

Competence model	Liberal–progressive	Populist	Radical
	Reform, constructivist learning theory and pedagogy	Ethnomathematics	Critical mathematics
Performance model	**Singular** Mathematics		
New competence model	**Discursive approaches** Discourse analysis Foucauldian studies	**Vygotskian studies**	

Figure 10.2 Extended typology of types of pedagogy

Subsequently we designed and carried out a research project, entitled 'The Production of Theories of Teaching and Learning: The Case of Mathematics'[3] in part to examine empirically our conjecture, although there were many other elements in our study. The aim of our research project in general was to analyse the processes whereby mathematics educational 'theories' are produced and the circumstances whereby they become current in the mathematics education research field, how they are recontextualised, and are acquired by teachers and teacher educators. We constructed a representation of the field of mathematics education research through which we explored the reproduction of identities, as positions, of researchers and teacher educators in the field, the recontextualisation of pedagogic knowledge and the reproduction of identities of mathematics teachers. We intended to explore, as sub-questions, who produces theories in mathematics education, with what methodologies and to what consequences for

---

3 Project supported by the Economic and Social Research Council in the UK, No. R000 22 3610.

research and for school practice. Through examining the structure of the knowledge-discourse in its field of production we aimed to explore the conditions and factors that affect the movements of the positions within the discourse, thereby exploring questions such as the following: who are managed, whose identities are produced and who are the managers of these identities (e.g. the funding agents, journal publishers, etc.). We aimed to talk about identities of academics, and changes in those identities over time and place.

Our method of working to create this picture was to look at specialised texts of the research field, namely a representative sample of the papers in the proceedings of the leading international research group in the field and the two leading international journals. We developed a special analytical tool to carry out the analysis of the sample. We discussed our programme with Bernstein some months before he died. He offered us some suggestions for the construction of the tool and its application to the analysis of the data.

In relation to our conjecture, we indeed found that an increasing number of papers in all three types of text draw on Vygotskian theory, and that the papers drawing on sociological and socio-cultural theories were also on the increase, as well as the use of linguistics, social linguistics and semiotics in all three types of text, though the number of papers drawing on these was still small in the timeframe we examined, from 1990 to 2001.[4]

I want to examine here two aspects of our proposal of a new competence model: where this shift might have come from; and what effect it might have on teachers and students.

Relations in the pedagogic field of recontextualisation

In a paper on evaluation we (Morgan *et al.*, 2002) produced the following diagram and its rationale, drawing on Morgan (1998) and Bernstein (1996):

> The official discourse of evaluation is produced by agents operating in the *Official Pedagogic Recontextualising Field* (OPRF) (Bernstein, 1996), for example, the examination boards, government departments and agencies. To produce this discourse, official agents have drawn on a set of discourses and practices, available within the sub-field of recontextualisation, and have subsumed them under their own aims and purposes. Among such discourses are those produced in the field of production of knowledge by the activities and practices of the mathematics education research community and circulated within the *Unofficial Pedagogic Recontextualising Field* (UPRF) (Bernstein, 1996) such as teacher training courses. Elements of these are appropriated by official agents, often constituting central elements of the official discourse. Elements of discourses produced by other educational communities and circulated within the UPRF, such as discourses on school

---

4 For a full report of the findings of the project, see Tsatsaroni *et al.* (2003).

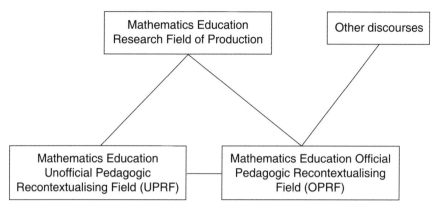

Figure 10.3 Recontextualising fields of mathematics classrooms

management, school effectiveness, etc., might also become elements of the official discourse. Therefore the official discourse of evaluation consists of a variety of elements from heterogeneous discourses, including those of mathematics and other education research, inspection reports, productions of other government agents, parents, and wider social discourses. However, discourses produced by the mathematics education research and other communities might remain outside the official pedagogic discourse, forming *unofficial, oppositional educational discourses* on evaluation. (pp. 448/9)

Using the same model, we can conjecture that appearance of language common in the research field and in professional teacher journals in national curriculum documents might provide evidence of some openness by the OPRF to the UPRF and/or to the research field of production. In fact we find the language of scaffolding appearing in such documents as a recommended teaching strategy[5] and a strong emphasis on raising teachers' awareness of the need for culturally sensitive pedagogy as possible indicators. One can certainly find a substantial shift in the literature to which student teachers are introduced during their pre-service education towards Vygotskian studies, to sociological perspectives on schools and classrooms, and focuses on how power operates in discourses at play in the educational setting.

Identity effects of a new performance model

As in the specification Bernstein provides for the traditional performance model, we can expect stronger framing in the new performance model, as the role of the

---

5 The new UK government has removed non-statutory documents from the official website while they review the National Curriculum. It is not therefore possible to demonstrate the use of 'scaffolding', though see Myhill and Warren (2005) as an indication.

teacher is seen as more fundamental than in the competence model: 'where instruction is foregrounded, where cultural formations are privileged as tools rather than systems or structures internal to the individual, pedagogic practice is necessarily foregrounded' (Bernstein, 1993: xv). In the competence model the idea of the 'guide on the side' took over from the 'sage on the stage', bringing with it an invisible pedagogy. In the new performance model the teacher sees herself as having the responsibility for apprenticing students into both mathematical language and mathematical ways of thinking, as the role of the intersubjective in Vygotskyian thought indicates or as in the subjectification of power/knowledge analyses of discursive practices. Activity in the zone of proximal development calls for the teacher to gradually withdraw support as the student takes over the problem-solving capacity and we can see this as an initially visible pedagogy moving gradually to becoming more invisible as students acquire the recognition and realisation rules of the practice.

Drawing these two trends together, I will suggest that identity as a unit of analysis is appropriate particularly at this time of the emergence of a new performance pedagogic model and I will illustrate this with some current research in the next section.

Unit of analysis

In educational research we have a much harder task than in many fields in order to identify our object of research. If one looks at students' learning one has to take into account, in some way, whether teaching, researching or both: their prior learning; their home life; their relationships with other students and the teacher; their goals in life and at the moment we are observing them; and also of course what the teacher is trying to teach them, what resources are used, and how their knowledge might develop. If we look at the teacher, then we find a similar difficulty of what to look at and what to put aside.

I turn briefly to the issue of how we might observe, as researchers, what we might claim to see, or what we might say about our observing that is useful for education, that is, issues of methodology. Vygotsky pushes us here directly into a post-positivist turn ontologically, in that while the existence of the world is not in doubt, or not worth doubting, what anything is or means is always mediated through language, which differs across cultures and times. Furthermore, we work at a time of the impossibility of representation (Lather, 2007) whereby people represent themselves to the researcher, the researcher then writes her/his account, a double layer of interpretation.

To add another word about the children we teach in the 'rich' parts of the world (developed and developing, or Western and non-Western are not really adequate categorizations given that there is wealth and poverty in every country), they are growing up at a time of a kind of connectedness, access, and communication that differs hugely from that of people even ten years older. They are multitasking: on their mobile phones; their tablets/laptops; watching television; eating; and more. I find myself quite exhausted just watching them. They expect instant gratification from whatever they are interacting with. They are concerned with how something might be good for them; they are willing to be seduced and excited but are, at the same time, quickly and easily bored.

Furthermore one cannot but be aware of the manifestations of identity in all aspects of children's lives, whether it be in the clothing they wear, to conform, to identify with a sports team or sports star, or with a media star, or in the music they listen to, through which, in their choices, they express conformity to one group or another, or resistance to conformity. There are racial and cultural styles of dress, speech and gestures which students may adopt, sometimes independent of whether they 'belong' to that social group or not. 'Belonging' is perhaps best judged by the person, not by an observer. In the outward expression of religion, through dress, we are again strongly aware of identity and identification.

The late Jim Kaput suggested that identity would be the major research and development issue in mathematics education (Roth, 2007: 40) and indeed we can see a proliferation of research with identity as the focus in our field.

In her 1997 book (revised as Boaler 2002a) Boaler demonstrates very powerfully how different forms of pedagogy have the effect of producing different mathematical identities in the two schools in her study. In a later study Boaler and Greeno (2000), drawing on Holland *et al.* (1998), interviewed students in advanced placement calculus classes. They characterised the schools as discussion-based and didactic. In the latter the 'students presented their worlds as structured, individualized and ritualized, the other group as relational, communicative and connected' (p. 178). Their study showed how, in more traditional classrooms, the image of a mathematical identity was not one that female students in particular would choose; it differed so greatly from how they described their own identities. 'They talked not about their inability to do the mathematics, but about the kinds of person they wanted to be – creative, verbal, and humane.' They saw the identity of a mathematician, in their perception, as one with which they did not identify, indeed from which they felt alienated. They saw themselves as imaginative and creative, in stark contrast to how they perceived a successful mathematician.

Boaler (2002b) proposed a triangle of knowledge, identity and practice to represent the learning process, and she argued that some learners advance through the 'dance of agency' (Pickering, 1995), the interchange between human and disciplinary agency, others through a more passive relationship.

Sfard and Prusack (2005) write of 'actual identities' and 'designated identities' in their search for a way of using narratives around identity as a research tool. They preface their argument in their abstract by signalling that, 'In this article, the authors make an attempt to operationalize the notion of *identity* to justify the claim about its potential as an analytic tool for investigating learning' (p. 14).

I am arguing that 'identity' is an appropriate unit of analysis for research, given the emergence of a new form of performance model, but what theory of identity? In so many studies the term is used unproblematically but I consider it vital to set out the sense in which 'identity' is being used; without such an account issues of methodology are ungrounded and interpretation is unjustified.

Roth (2007) suggests that the notion is a derivative one:

> In the context of cultural-historical activity theory, identity is a derivative construct in the sense that it presupposes the existence of the subject who, regulated by emotions, engages with an object of motive-directed activity, and who becomes aware of itself as self. Identity presupposes the presence of memory and consciousness (Ricoeur, 2004). The construct of identity pertains to who someone is. However, we do not know *who* a person is independent of the actions of that person. (p. 56)

Of course Roth's argument captures Vygotsky's vision of *Mind in Society*, or Wertsch's formulation of 'individual(s)-acting with mediational means' (1991: 12). Vygotsky had already called for the integration of affect and cognition: 'the influence of thought on affect and volition' as an integral aspect of activity becomes evident only when intellect and affect are theorized and analyzed as complementary expressions of the same unit. (1986: 10). In a chapter written in 2000 I argued for a unit of analysis that takes Vygotsky's concept and incorporates the regulative features of discursive practices and the multiple motives, goals and practices that emerge in the classroom. While Roth wishes to return to the notion of self, I consider that a notion of identity that incorporates the complexity I have described can be productive in accounting for persons and their actions.

In the final section, I present an extract of some current work that attempts to satisfy these conditions. I draw on Holland and Lachicotte (2007) for this study.

Case study

Bernstein (2000) shows that disadvantage, in relation to children from working class backgrounds, has its origins in the home, in restricted as compared to elaborated language, and is reproduced at an early stage of primary schooling. Thus the option to choose to study mathematics at the upper levels of schooling appears to have been taken away from working-class students at a very early age. However, students can and do find ways to resist and make choices that may appear surprising to teachers and researchers, and indeed the students' families.

In this chapter I will present the story of Jane,[6] not quite a school drop-out but certainly distracted at school, partly by social class but also by circumstance, who found her way to becoming a teacher of mathematics and, most recently, a head of faculty of science and mathematics in a secondary school.

Retrospective accounts such as this story, and the others I am collecting, clearly do not enable the listener/reader/observer to have anything to say about the formation of the person's trajectory. But in not enabling those insights it does enable other possibilities; in providing her view of her life story the narrator

6 A pseudonym.

presents herself as she chooses. She makes her selection from the twists and turns in her life path, giving her considerable control in an interview situation in which she might otherwise feel vulnerable. The narrative emerges somehow whole but, potentially, subject to the researchers' motives and interpretations, revealing of other identities along the way. The researcher's account, therefore, will be a narrative of its own and calls for reflexivity and openness by the writer and multiple elements to be presented by the researcher (Lather, 2007; Scheurich, 1997).

In this respect, then, I must note that I was one of Jane's tutors when she took a master's degree; I am male; and she knows that I was a former secondary school mathematics teacher myself and a former head of mathematics.

Perhaps you can start by telling me what you did after school, what your teacher training was, what courses you did?

I actually went to college to do A[7] levels and my actual focus was really on a secretarial course and I only did 2 A levels which were computer science and accountancy, and I absolutely loved accountancy, it was a real buzz and I wanted to go to University to study accountancy but I didn't get the grades.

I didn't get the grades I needed to study accountancy and I got in through clearing to G_ University to do computer science, 'cos that was my other A level. But that was . . . I couldn't even work out my timetable, it was *so completely* [her emphasis] out of my league . . . academically completely out of my depth . . .

I got a job to train as an accountant with the local authority . . . While I was auditing, part of my role was to audit financial management controls in schools in G_ . . . I was going round to primary and secondary schools auditing stuff within the school but every time I went into the school the ethos, the feel of the place, the kids, everything I just loved it, I absolutely loved it. Ummm, so I was at the back of my mind thinking no this is something I didn't want to do from school I wasn't confident enough to be a teacher, at 18 I was a real kid I didn't know what I wanted to do. I just wanted to go out and have a good time basically but I'd always at the back of my mind thought I'd like to teach but I'm not ready yet.

So going to schools made me start thinking about it again and then one of my jobs I had to audit student grants . . . I realised in my position, I was on my own with a couple of kids and a mortgage I could get quite a substantial student grant perhaps I could go back to University and train to teach, so I did. I had reached a point where . . . there was no kind of passion for it (accountancy) . . . The situation in my life had changed where it was just me and the kids . . . I knew I was going to have to be doing a job that I felt quite passionate about rather than something that I went to every day . . . so I made the move from accountancy and went back to University for 4 years, at the age of 30 . . . and I had decided to do primary . . . so I studied primary with a specialism in maths, so all my teaching

7 English National pre-University high-stakes assessment.

practices were at primary but maths was the thing, all throughout that I absolutely adored, my dissertation was maths, that was my subject specialism, I loved it and I worked really hard and I got my first . . . I absolutely loved every minute of my studies . . . I got the top grade, and it did kind of make me think – you're not so stupid after all . . .

Then I started teaching, I was only in primary . . . I got on really really quickly in school, I think by the end of my NQT year I was a mentor, I was lecturing at (ITE institution) in primary maths, I was a leading maths teacher, I was a maths coordinator . . . A job came up . . . and they advertised as someone who had experience in the numeracy strategy in primary to help us introduce the key stage 3 strategy in secondary . . . So I got the job . . . I had no training, there was no transition period, I was just straight in teaching secondary school maths and fortunately it wasn't academically challenging because it was only up to year 11 and . . . I think my grounding in primary maths helped me to be a good teacher because I knew what I had to teach, I knew all the preceding steps . . . I really enjoyed it, and again in secondary I took on responsibility for the key stage 3 strategy. I was happy to embrace some of these changes whereas other secondary school teachers weren't . . . I was there for three years and again had gone about as far as I could . . . they said we'd like you to be an Advanced Skills Teachers, so I went through the accreditation . . . So then I thought right well I've got to be a Head of Department . . . so here I'm Head of Maths and Science . . . There's 4 Heads of Faculty and I'm one of them . . . So I'm still able to concentrate on the maths and things I want to do within maths but I've got more leadership clout . . .

What was maths like for you at school?
I was brilliant at maths . . . I was top of my class and they put me in the top set that was doing their O[8] level a year early so suddenly from being absolutely loving it I was suddenly right down the bottom of the class, and I took it a year early and got a C and that was a bad experience because I was enjoying it, it really, loved the learning, suddenly I was struggling.

Then I studied additional maths for a year but by then my confidence was shot to pieces and I surprised myself, I got a D, which was just a fail.

Were you always good at maths? What about primary?
Yes, I think I was always very numerate . . . I was very fond of my maths teachers during secondary, but at primary . . . they said I was careless, a bit sloppy, didn't work as hard as I could have done but I was always able to see numbers quickly.

Was that a family thing? What about your parents, were they encouraging you in maths?
They didn't go further at school than their O levels or whatever they were called then. They are both very numerate . . . I was encouraged at school . . . my Dad

8 English National high-stakes assessment at age 16.

was very much off the scene, my Dad was a senior policeman so was away a lot, my Mum worked in school she was an ancillary. I don't remember being nagged or I mean I did very little work, that's why I got the grades I got at O level, I think there was the expectation, I feel they expected me to do well.

Do you recall any difficulties being good at maths and a girl?
No, I just remember my experiences in my class before I moved just loving it, absolutely loving it, I think I only can remember me and the teacher to be honest, that's how much I enjoyed it, and it was a male teacher, I remember he was a Canadian, and he gave me so much praise, I absolutely felt like a star as soon as I walked in that room . . .

. . . and I wanted to please him I wanted to do well and I think this was why they moved me up, I think I was far and above the other people in the class, so they didn't really figure, but I don't remember there being any gender issues at all.

I don't know if that's the kind of person I am the kind of personality I've got but I don't remember feeling intimidated or not able to do things because I was a girl.

Holland and Lachicotte (2007) contrast Erikson's and Mead's notions of self/identity. They describe Erikson's interpretation (he is credited by Gleason (1983) as having put the term into common use in the 1950s), drawing on Penuel and Wertsch (1995), as 'a sense, felt by individuals within themselves, and as an experience of continuity, oriented toward a self-chosen and positively anticipated future' (p. 83). On the other hand Mead took identity to be a sense of oneself as a participant in the social roles and positions defined by a specific, historically constituted set of social activities – multiple, perhaps even contradictory, and performative. Holland and Lachicotte suggest that there is a strong complementarity with Vygotsky's elaboration of the sociogenetic formation of self, as 'ways in which social interaction, mediated by symbolic forms, provide crucial resources . . . for self-making' (p. 105). They add: 'In Vygotskian terminology, an *identity* is a higher-order psychological function that organises sentiments, understandings, and embodied knowledge relevant to a culturally imagined, personally valued social position.' (113; emphasis in original)

Drawing on Burke and Reitzes's (1991) Meadian account, they suggest that:

'Identities are simultaneously (1) *social products*, that is, collectively developed and imagined social categories; (2) *self-meanings*, developed through a sociogenetic process that entails active internalization; (3) *symbolic*, when performed they call up the same responses in one person as they do in others; (4) *reflexive*, providing a vantage point from which persons can assess the "implications of their own behavior as well as of other people's behaviors" (1991: 242); and (5) *a source of motivation for action*, particularly actions that result in the social confirmation of the identity' (Holland and Lachicotte: 109; emphasis in original).

I will draw these elements into the narrative I will construct of the story as an analytical framework.

Turning then to Jane, what was striking was the sense of a trajectory, a coherence of life path, leading to who she is today, a gradual unfolding of who she could be. To an extent this progressive narrative will have been a product of the interview situation, having been invited to look back and tell her story to me to account for how she arrived at her current situation from a background that could be seen to threaten a dead end. She was both eager to tell her story and needed very little prompting from me.

At first reading/listening, Jane's story is Eriksonian, a continuity, oriented toward a self-chosen and positively anticipated future, though with a series of circumstances that provided opportunities which she grabbed. She was always good at mathematics though her potential development towards the goal was interrupted by circumstance. Nevertheless, the retrospective account shows her current sense of her own achievement and strong identity as having emerged almost inevitably through the stages of her life.

Jane's story can also be read as Meadian. By her account, Jane was a dutiful daughter (*social product*) but strong-willed (*self-meaning*); disadvantaged by school pressure and expectations but lack of support (*social product*); not ready for university, overwhelmed and out of place (*social product*), though this is partly attributed to being too much a party girl (*self-meaning*). Jane became a wife and mother and then a single mother needing to provide for herself and her children (*social product* and *motivation for action*). Jane was successful at accountancy and loved it, providing her with experience of achievement (*symbolic*). The accountancy led her into schools where she loved the atmosphere and activity and this led her back to college to study to become a teacher. Her early perception of herself as 'I was brilliant at maths . . . I was top of my class' now could re-emerge (*reflexive*). The subsequent steps from primary school teaching specialising in mathematics, to advisory teacher, into middle school and then secondary school mathematics, combined with the confidence gained through managing the single parent situation and doing well with accountancy gave her what was required for head of faculty (*social product*, *self-meaning* and *motivation for action*).

Concluding remarks

Although it might appear that Erikson's and Mead's (also Vygotsky's) notions of identity are dichotomous paths for the reader's analysis of Jane's account, it seems to me that both provide theories of identity that are revealing in the story. In retrospective accounts at least, people have a need to present themselves externally and perhaps internally too, as a coherent identity/self, constructed possibly from pushes and pulls in different directions through our lives, but purposefully, in pursuit of the person we wish to be. At the same time we reveal elements of that construction that would have been produced, and have been produced, from a range of different situations and hence identities, some in which one feels powerful and others in which one feels powerless (Walkerdine, 1989). Both notions contribute elements, in writing an account of a person's retrospective story.

Jane's story indicates that teachers might be significant others for students, offering them visions of themselves, possible identities that can be empowering for those students. What a teacher might do, consciously, about that well-known information is rather more problematic! Second, I would argue that teachers, as well as students, need to be offered a range of alternative ways of being teachers or students. From these accounts, and so much other research too, it is clear that there is no single way of being a student (or teacher) that will or will not lead to a rich life. Being offered a range of alternative images of how to become can be supportive of alternative identities/selves. Third, Arnot and Reay (2004) warn of the danger of being unable to use ever more fragmented accounts in ways that might be helpful to learners of mathematics. What Jane's story confirms is that although structures of social class and others represent still present trends in society, no individual's potential can be reduced to those trends, and teachers (also parents and others) need to beware of the damage that can be done by the self-fulfilling effects of expectations of students' abilities and potential.

Returning to my discussion above, the search for a productive notion of identity arose in mathematics education out of a recognition that the psychological perspectives that had dominated in the field were inadequate to account for the strong association between student failure and social class. The social turn (Lerman, 2000) draws its perspectives from sociology and socio-cultural theory, the confluence of which has been the main focus of this chapter. The strengthening of initially explicit instruction, followed by the gradual withdrawal of the teacher to the position of providing support as the rules for recognition and realisation are internalised by the learner, shared by Vygotsky and Bernstein in their different terms are poorly captured by the term 'scaffolding', but nevertheless have become part of the lexicon of teachers in many parts of the world. Much work needs to be done for these ideas to permeate teacher education programmes in a deep way, and much remains to be done to found notions of 'identity' on useful and informative bases.

References

d'Ambrosio, U. (2010) 'Plenary Lecture: From Ea, through Pythagoras, to Avatar: Different settings for Mathematics', in M. F. Pinto and T. F. Kawasaki (eds.), *Proceeding of the 34th Conference of the International Group for the Psychology of Mathematics Education (PME)*, Brazil: Belo Horizonte, vol. 1, 1–20.

Arnot, M. and Reay, D. (2004) 'Voice research, learner identities and pedagogic encounters', paper presented at Basil Bernstein Conference, Cambridge.

Bauman, Z. (2001) *The Individualized Society*, Cambridge: Polity.

Bernstein, B. (1993) 'Foreword', in H. Daniels (ed.), *Charting the Agenda: Educational Activity after Vygotsky*, London: Routledge, xiii–xxiii.

—— (1996) *Pedagogy, Symbolic Control and Identity: Theory, Research, Critique*, London: Taylor & Francis.

—— (2000) *Pedagogy, Symbolic Control and Identity: Theory, Research, Critique* (rev. edn), New York: Rowman & Littlefield.

Boaler, J. (1997) *Experiencing School Mathematics: Teaching Styles, Sex and Setting* Buckingham, UK: Open University Press.

—— (2002a) *Experiencing School Mathematics: Traditional and Reform Approaches to Teaching and Their Effects on Student Learning*, Mahwah, NJ: Lawrence Erlbaum.

—— (2002b) 'The Development of Disciplinary Relationships: Knowledge, Practice and Identity in Mathematics Classrooms', *For the Learning of Mathematics*, 22(1): 42–7.

Boaler, J. and Greeno, J. G. (2000) 'Identity, Agency and Knowing in Mathematical Worlds', in J. Boaler (ed.), *Multiple Perspectives on Mathematics Teaching and Learning*, Westport, CT: Ablex, 171–200.

Burke, P. and Reitzes, D. (1991) 'An Identity Theory Approach to Commitment', *Social Psychology Quarterly*, 54: 239–51.

Evans, J., Morgan, C. and Tsatsaroni, A. (2006) 'Discursive Positioning and Emotion in School Mathematics Practices', *Educational Studies in Mathematics, Affect in Mathematics Education: Exploring Theoretical Frameworks*, a PME special issue (guest editors: Jeff Evans, Markku S. Hannula, Rosetta Zan and Laurinda C. Brown), 63(2), 209–26.

Glasersfeld, E. von (1990) 'An Exposition of Constructivism: Why Some Like It radical', in R. B. Davis, C. A. Maher and N. Noddings (eds.), *Constructivist Views on the Teaching and Learning of Mathematics, Journal for Research in Mathematics Education*, 4: 19–29.

Gleason, P. (1983) 'Identifying Identity: A Semantic History', *Journal of American History*, 69(4): 910–31.

Goldin, J. (1990) 'Epistemology, Constructivism and Discovery Learning in Mathematics', in R. B. Davis, C. A. Maher and N. Noddings (eds.), *Constructivist Views on the Teaching and Learning of Mathematics, Journal for Research in Mathematics Education*, 4: 31–47.

Hall, S. (1996) 'Introduction: Who Needs "'Identity'"?', in S. Hall and P. du Gay (eds.), *Questions of Cultural Identity*, London: Sage, 1–17.

Holland, D. and Lachicotte, W. (2007) 'Vygotsky, Mead, and the New Socio-cultural Studies of Identity', in H. Daniels, M. Cole and J. V. Wertsch (eds.) *The Cambridge Companion to Vygotsky*, New York: Cambridge University Press, 101–35.

Holland, D., Lachicotte, W., Skinner, D. and Cain, C. (1998) *Identity and Agency in Cultural Worlds*, Cambridge, MA: Harvard University Press.

Kirshner, D. and Whitson, J. A. (1997) *Situated Cognition: Social, Semiotic and Psychological Perspectives*, Mahwah, NJ: Lawrence Erlbaum.

Lather, P. (2007) *Getting Lost: Feminist Efforts Towards a Double(d) Science*, Albany, NY: SUNY.

Lave, J. and Wenger, E. (1991) *Situated Learning: Legitimate Peripheral Participation*, New York: Cambridge University Press.

Lerman, S. (2000) 'The Social Turn in Mathematics Education Research', in J. Boaler (ed.), *Multiple Perspectives on Mathematics Teaching and Learning*, Westport, CT: Ablex, 19–44.

—— (2001) 'Accounting for Accounts of Learning Mathematics: Reading the ZPD in Videos and Transcripts', in D. Clarke (ed.), *Perspectives on Practice and Meaning in Mathematics and Science Classrooms*, Dordrecht: Kluwer, 53–74.

—— (2006) 'Cultural Psychology, Anthropology and Sociology: The Developing "Strong" Social Turn', in J. Maaß and W. Schlöglmann (eds.) *New Mathematics Education Research and Practice*, Rotterdam: Sense, 171–88.

Lerman, S. and Tsatsaroni, A. (1998) 'Why Children Fail and What Mathematics Education Studies Can Do about It: The Role of Sociology', in P. Gates (ed.), *Proceedings of the First International Conference on Mathematics, Education and Society (MEAS1)*, Centre for the Study of Mathematics Education, University of Nottingham, 26–33.

Morgan, C. (1998) *Writing Mathematically: The Discourse of Investigation*, London: Falmer.

Morgan, C., Tsatsaroni, A. and Lerman, S. (2002) 'Mathematics Teachers' Positions and Practices in Discourses of Assessment', *British Journal of Sociology of Education*, 23(3): 445–61.

Myhill, D. and Warren, P. (2005) 'Scaffolds or Straitjackets? Critical Moments in Classroom Discourse', *Educational Review*, 57(1): 55–69.

Nunes, T., Schliemann, A. D. and Carraher, D. W. (1993) *Street Mathematics and School Mathematics*, Cambridge: Cambridge University Press.

Penuel, W. R. and Wertsch, J. V. (1995) 'Dynamics of Negation in the Identity Politics of Cultural Other and Cultural Self: The Rhetorical Image of the Person in Developmental Psychology', *Culture and Psychology*, 1(3): 343–59.

Pickering, A. (1995) *The Mangle of Practice: Time, Agency, and Science*, Chicago: University of Chicago Press.

Roth, W.-M. (2007) 'Emotion at Work: A Contribution to Third-Generation Cultural-Historical Activity Theory', *Mind, Culture and Activity*, 14(1–2): 40–63.

Scheurich, J. J. (1997) *Research Method in the Postmodern*, London: RoutledgeFalmer.

Sfard, A. and Prusack, A. (2005) 'Telling Identities: In Search of an Analytic Tool for Investigating Learning as a Culturally Shaped Activity', *Educational Researcher*, 34(4): 14–22.

Singh, P. (1997) Review Essay: Basil Bernstein (1996) *Pedagogy, Symbolic Control and Identity*, London: Taylor & Francis (and in *British Journal of Sociology of Education*, 8(1): 119–24).

Skovsmose, O. (1994) *Towards a Philosophy of Critical Mathematics Education*, Dordrecht: Kluwer.

Tsatsaroni, A., Lerman, S. and Xu, G. (2003) 'A Sociological Description of Changes in the Intellectual Field of Mathematics Education Research: Implications for the Identities of Academics', ERIC# ED482512.

Vygotsky, L. S. (1986) *Thought and Language*, Cambridge, MA: MIT Press.

Walkerdine, V. (1989) *Counting Girls Out*, London: Routledge.

Watson, A. and Winbourne, P. (eds.) (2007) *New Directions for Situated Cognition in Mathematics Education*, New York: Springer.

Wertsch, J. V. (1991) *Voices of the Mind: A Socio-cultural Approach to Mediated Action*, Cambridge, MA: Harvard University Press.

Wittgenstein, L. (1967). *Philosophical Investigations*, 3rd edn, trans. G. E. M. Anscombe, Oxford: Blackwell.

11 Schooling the social classes

Triadic zones of proximal development, communicative capital, and relational distance in the perpetuation of advantage

Carolyn P. Panofsky and
Jennifer A. Vadeboncoeur

We "must not overlook the constitutive practices that are the foundation of inequality, which . . . operate in two important contexts: the interaction between educators and students and the interaction between the home and school. From the practices implemented in both settings, aspects of students' lives are generated."

(Mehan, 1992: 16)

Introduction

Poverty, social inequality, and educational disadvantage have recently resurfaced as newsworthy topics (e.g., Censky, 2011; Steinberg, 2011), although understanding the relationship between them has always been a research-worthy endeavor (e.g., Liebow, 1967; Steinberg, 1989). Apart from the vagaries of public attention, Vygotsky (1997) noted, in lectures given in the early 1920s, that "education has, at all times and in all places, borne a class-based character, whether or not its adherents or apostles were aware of it" (p. 56). Social class differences play out in the relationships between students, teachers, and parents, as well as in home and school relations, with effects on learning and development for children and youth. Although most work, including our own, has focused on the disadvantages for those positioned lower in the class hierarchy, here we join a growing number of scholars focused on the class-based character of advantage and how it works through public schooling.

The class-based character of schooling was also a given for the influential theorist (Bourdieu 1986; Bourdieu and Passeron, 1990). Indeed, educational theorists from various backgrounds generally agree that the potential for schooling to afford equal opportunities to all learners and play a transformative role in improving the status of students with less privilege is severely limited (see Labaree, 2010).[1] A number of reasons are noted in the literature, including the role of

---

1 Labaree (2010) noted that "the school system has let us have it both ways, providing access *and* advantage, promoting equality *and* inequality" (p. 3; emphasis in original).

schools in the development of relationships to the mode of production (Anyon., 1980), the ideology and impact of the pedagogy of 'the Right' and the official curriculum (Apple, 1979, 2001), the policy and practice of tracking and ability grouping in schools (Kelly and Price, 2011; Oakes, 2005), and educators' expectations of learners (e.g., Rist, 1970/2000) as mediating students' opportunities for learning.

Nevertheless, in recent debates, some have claimed that social class is no longer relevant as a category of social analysis (Kingston, 2000; Pakulski and Waters, 1996). However, others have argued the opposite: that social class is a "salient causal structure with important ramifications" (Wright, 1996/2008: 33) and one that intersects with gender and race analyses among others. Despite what the former may say, there is a growing disparity between social classes and persisting social inequality and educational disadvantage (Duncan and Murnane, 2011). For example, Gamoran (2008) documented the persistence of social class inequalities in twenty-first-century schooling. In their examination of socio-economic status (SES), Tozer *et al.* (2002) found that "[t]aking all ethnic groups and genders [into account], low-SES students drop out *six times as often* as high SES students and almost three times as often as middle-SES students" (p. 154; emphasis in original). We suggest that persistent social class inequality is reason enough for class analysis.

In our work, conducted from a Vygotskian perspective, we have begun to address the effects of social class differences in relation to educational experiences and outcomes. One discussion examined the ways that relationships between students and teachers are differentiated by social class and emphasized the social and semiotic mediation of what children learn in school (Panofsky, 2003). Another discussion noted social class differences in interactions between children and parents, arguing that the question of "why" these differences exist must be foregrounded (Portes and Vadeboncoeur, 2003). The literature on social class in schooling that we draw on takes a critical perspective on the dominant cultural assumption that schooling functions on a meritocratic basis. In this work, individual achievement in schooling is not viewed as reflecting individual "merit," or lack thereof. Instead, a critical perspective exposes how individual outcomes are largely socially structured, rather than simply the result of individual effort and ability (see Panofsky, 2003, for discussion). In this chapter, we take up the question of "how" these differences are structured.

Our interest in this chapter is to extend the work of Vygotsky (1978, 1997) and Bourdieu (1986) to look more closely at how social class difference is structured through schooling. Elaborating Mehan's (1992) idea, quoted at the opening of this chapter, we examine relationships between students, parents, and teachers and the social relations between home and school as constituted in social practices. First, we begin with the role of parents in negotiating zones of proximal development (ZPD) between their children and teachers. We introduce the notion of a triadic ZPD (TZPD) to emphasize, from a Vygotskian perspective, the insertion and outcomes of a parent's proleptic view on the relational ZPD between a student and a teacher as one way social class advantage is perpetuated. Second, as confirmatory evidence, we highlight the cultural and social capital that parents exploit in parent/teacher relationships. Here, we include literature that documents social class differences in experiences between middle- and low-income students and parents and introduce the notion of *communicative capital* to illustrate the ways both cultural and social capital intersect to enable recognition and reduce *relational distance*. Finally, we note tentative conclusions and implications.

The mediation of parental prolepsis as a Triadic ZPD

Research shows that both middle-class and low-income parents advocate on behalf of their children by negotiating with school personnel, including teachers and administrators (e.g., Brantlinger, 1985a, 2003b; Lareau, 2000, 2003; Useem, 1992). However, the research also shows that middle-class parents advocate more frequently and they tend to be far more successful at doing so: they negotiate by drawing on semiotic practices that are recognizable to educators, and these practices also reflect social membership in privileged groups. Fluent in the semiotic practices that are valued, middle-class parents work in a concerted way to cultivate their children's growth, rather than assuming that growth occurs naturally (Lareau, 2003). As a result, middle-class and upper-middle-class parents are able to provide a customized set of experiences for their children at home, as well as to shape the experiences their children have in schools.

How might we understand what is taking place as parents intervene on behalf of their children? One way of looking at this situation is through Vygotsky's (1978) notion of the zone of proximal development (ZPD): the learning/teaching space constructed in relationship between child and adult, or more experienced other, that supports learning and development. However, we extend Vygotsky's dyadic conception of the ZPD constructed between child and adult to a triadic version of the ZPD constructed between child, teacher, and parent. Integral to this construction is that middle-class parents insert a proleptic vision for their children's future into the zone of proximal development. In this way, parents purposefully mediate the student–teacher relationship. The ZPD becomes triadic, enabling the teacher to have a rich understanding of the child as a child, rather than simply as a particular kind of student. This assists the teacher to see the child differently, it identifies and establishes a resource base for the child's educational experiences, and leads ultimately to the perpetuation of advantage, or educational profits, from one generation to the next. In the following, we define and extend prolepsis, the triadic ZPD, and the possibilities constructed for middle-class children whose parents engage in these practices.

From a cultural-historical perspective, *prolepsis* is typically defined as the attribution of meaning, or intention, to an infant's movements or to a less experienced individual's actions in a manner that projects an intended future on the infant or child (Cole, 1996; Vygotsky, 1978). Prolepsis both anticipates and constructs an educational future of who a child may become. It is one way the cultural and social world of a child contributes to the child's development (Cole, 1996). For example, when an infant is born, caregivers, in particular parents, attribute intent and meaning to the early movements of the infant. The attribution of intention behind a baby's waving hand, or the interpretation of meaning behind a baby's first sounds, are based on cultural understandings that are socially shared between the small group of family and friends that gather around a new baby. Vygotsky's (1978) now famous example, used to illustrate internalization, is the baby who makes a grasping movement that is ultimately interpreted as "the act of pointing" by her mother (p. 56). Reaching for something is shaped through the mother's perspective as a gesture toward or for an object. Her response is to act on this interpretation and this engages the infant in acting *as if* the interpretation of the meaning of the gesture were correct.

In this way, the mother represents "a future in the present" (Cole, 1996: 184); she expects her baby to use gesture to indicate and communicate and acts as if this is so. The mother begins acting with this future in mind before the future exists. From the first moments of an infant's life, her actions are interpreted and have meaning through a "system of social behavior" (Vygotsky, 1978: 30). A parent or caregiver creates a method for making sense of movement; "the path from object to child and from child to object passes through another person" (Vygotsky, 1978: 30). The cultural understandings that exist between members of families and extended families are based on the norms, expectations, hopes, and worries embedded in social relations and mediated by semiotic practices located in social, historical, and ideological contexts.

Later, during formal schooling, parents also contribute to their child's education when they insert their vision of their child's future into the ZPD created in the relationship between their child as a "student" and "the teacher." This vision is most often a "best picture" of their child that includes attributions of the child's abilities, her learning potential, and, in effect, an imaginary but prospective educational future. This vision is made more real to the teacher given its basis in the intimacy of family life. While the child's abilities, and possibly her challenges, are foregrounded, additional information is shared including stories that illustrate what she is capable of and how hard she will work, that she is motivated and desires to learn, that she has a purpose for education, and that her family has an educated future in mind. These stories may also help to explain why an assignment was late ("home renovations") or why a test score could have been higher ("she's concerned about her Nana in hospital").

By sharing stories of their children, parents mediate a process that transforms "a student" into "their particular child," with a particular history, and embedded in a set of relationships. Key to this process is the identification of the parents as a resource base for the child. Parents are keen to help the child with homework, to ensure the motivation is there for schoolwork generally, and to support the child's teachers' requests for task and goal-oriented behavior. All of this activity is part of the "concerted cultivation" that Lareau (2003) identified as the child-rearing approach of middle-class parenting. The stories parents share with the teacher enrich the relational context of the ZPD. As a result, the teacher may better understand the child, have higher expectations, have a positive sense of the capability, effort, motivation and desire of the child. The teacher is equipped with "insider" knowledge and equipped with additional tools, including knowledge that enables her to better care for and guide the child. The initial relational distance between teacher and student has been significantly reduced and with this perspective, with the construction of this triadic ZPD, the teacher is more likely to give a child "the benefit of a doubt," a view that is typically reserved for parents who maintain that their children are able to do all sorts of things, even in the face of evidence to the contrary.

Cole (1996) argued that "the parents' (purely *ideal*) recall of their past and imagination of their child's future become a fundamental *materialized constraint* on the child's life experiences in the present" (p. 184; emphasis in original). We add to this that middle-class parents, with a past of successful experiences in schools and knowledge of ways to navigate the educational system (their *cultural capital*), use their lived experiences, as well as their idealized recollections, to fashion educational futures for their children. Just as the parents' views of the child both afford and constrain the material forms of interaction in which parents and child engage, the triadic ZPD also begins to guide the interaction between the child and teacher in ways that define the range of material forms of interaction, for example, in relation to expectations of ability and achievement. The relational distance between student and teacher is likely much greater for children whose parents have not negotiated a TZPD. Without a home–school relationship that provides enabling conditions for the child, without a joint proleptic view, many low-income children experience material constraints that establish barriers, rather than pathways for success in schooling.

The insertion of parents' proleptic vision is not simply a matter of imposition, of parents imposing their imagined futures for their children on beleaguered teachers. This work is a negotiation that entails recognition by teachers that middle-class parents can negotiate knowledge, status, and power to both make these demands *and* support the development of this particular educational vision. In short, this work establishes such parents as teachers' ally, as well as potential adversary. Some research found that when middle-class and well-connected African-American parents volunteered in schools – for example, in classrooms and on school committees – and established a presence in the school, teachers experienced a feeling of surveillance: teachers noted that their classroom practices were being scrutinized (Hassrick and Schneider, 2009).

In studying families of three income levels, Lareau (2008) related findings about middle-class parents' role in shaping children's experiences in schooling and other settings. She identified a set of "generic class resources" that parents, both white and black, draw on and she highlighted three aspects of middle-class perceptions:

> first, parents presume that they are entitled to have the institution ac-commodate to their child's individualized needs; second, they feel comfortable voicing their concerns with people in positions of authority; and third, they are willing and able to climb the hierarchy of authority to pursue their interests. (p. 131)

In contrast, the low-income parents studied by both Brantlinger (1985a, b, c; 2003b) and Lareau (2000, 2003) repeatedly mentioned their frustration in trying to talk to teachers or administrators, with parents sometimes revealing that they felt powerless in their use of language. In the next section, we take a closer look at what parents say about their interactions with school personnel, at the kinds of semiotic practices middle-class and low-income parents use, and at the results of parents' work advocating for their children.

Communicative capital: signs of recognition and relational distance between students, parents, and teachers

In this section, we look at how parents use cultural and social capital to "do relationships" with teachers, including the communicative resources of speech genres, social languages, and discourses, as well as how they approach and engage with teachers, and the strategies they use to negotiate relationships. We highlight two forms of capital, *cultural* and *social capital*, and, extending Bourdieu (1986, 1990), note the way cultural and social capital combine in the form of *communicative capital* to be utilized by individuals and recognized by others as signs of class-based social relations.[2] Parents use their communicative capital to reduce the *relational distance* between their children and the teachers of their children through triadic zones of proximal development.

Both cultural and social capital have a "multiplier effect" on the economic capital that parents possess (Bourdieu, 1986). Cultural capital is the knowledge of and from the educational system: the experience of education, the resulting credentials, and the values learned through the process (Bourdieu, 1986). Of particular interest to us is linguistic capital, an embodied form of cultural capital, which includes language practices and relation to language (Bourdieu and Passeron, 1990). Cultural capital is shared between parents and children over time through family activities, including dinner table talk, telling stories, sharing responsibility for chores, and playing together. Social capital includes both the actual and the potential resources that are accessible by members who participate in and are recognized through a network of social connections – relationships and mutual acquaintances. In addition, social capital arises from an "endless effort at institution . . . to produce and reproduce lasting, useful relationships that can secure material or symbolic profits" (Bourdieu, 1986: 249). Cultural and social capital can be converted in exchanges from one form to the other and are potentially difficult to distinguish: for example, when language practices are used to establish and build relationships that are then used to access resources, such as information about how to navigate school waiting lists and advice about which teacher is most experienced.

We introduce the concept of *communicative capital* to highlight the intersection between cultural and social capital, in particular, when parents advocate in schools

2 Vygotsky's ideas have been supported and/or extended through the work of Bourdieu by several authors, including Wertsch (1991), Lave and Wenger (1991), Holland and Cole (1995), Gutiérrez and Stone (2000), and Holland and Lachicotte (2007).

in ways that reduce the relational distance between their children and teachers, as well as to highlight the advantage that adheres in being recognized implicitly as a member of the middle-class. Consistent with cultural-historical theory, *recognition* of class membership occurs, in part, as individuals engage in social relations through social practices that are comprised of speech genres, social languages, and discourses. These semiotic resources afford communicative exchanges that transform the forms of communication into "signs of recognition": mutual recognition constitutes both the group and the limits of the group (Bourdieu, 1986: 250).

Schooling creates *relational distance* through the expectations that individuals have for each other on the basis of institutional position, such as "teachers" or "students," and group membership, including ethnic group, social class, gender identity, language differences. Relational distance impedes the development of trust, care, and respect in relationships when: (1) teachers see students, rather than children, and students see teachers, rather than caring adults, and (2) much of what teachers see is socially constructed difference and students perceive this. The relationship between children and parents, between parents and their children's teachers, and the relationships between parents and their social networks are contexts through which to revisit ethnographic research that compares the experiences of parents across social classes. These relationships contrast sharply in terms of parents' class location.

Semiotic practice I: the speech genre(s) of advocacy and deference

We take the concept of speech genres from Bakhtin (1986) to refer to the many ways that speech is used to accomplish specific purposes in specific contexts: "each sphere in which language is used develops its own *relatively stable types* of . . . utterances" (p. 60; emphasis in original). Speech genres include both the language in use and the accompanying positions that obtain from using language in specific ways. In the research literature, there are many examples of parents using speech genre(s) of advocacy to intervene on behalf of their children in school. When parents use a speech genre of advocacy and are able to engage teachers as interlocutors in the process of negotiation, they are positioning themselves in a particular way in relation to educators and schools – and in a way that needs to be recognizable by teachers as legitimate. Not all parents use a speech genre that is recognized as advocacy. Indeed, when narrating their attempts to advocate for their children many low-income parents reveal a speech genre that is distinctly deferential. Throughout this part, we use italic emphases to highlight features of speech genres we observe in the narratives of parents.

Lareau (2000) presented one particularly interesting example of successful advocacy in which a parent used writing to renegotiate his daughter's planned retention in second grade because of her slow progress in reading. Following a summer of extensive work with professional tutors and much reading, the father explained:

I sent a letter saying *these were our thoughts. We had great confidence in* [the teacher who recommended retention] . . . *but it appeared* that some things *may have changed over the summer.* That was the *additional information* we were *putting in the formula. Based on that*, we wanted *to talk again about Emily being retained.* (p. 131; our emphases)

Lareau reported that the principal, after conferring with the reading specialist and classroom teacher, "agreed to this change; [the father] also said the principal thanked him for the 'professional way' in which he and his wife had handled the matter" (p. 131). In this interaction, successful use of this speech genre included: explicit display of respect for professionals' expertise and depersonalization of the situation; an explanation of why an earlier decision warranted reconsideration; and tentative, respectful, and firm, rather than combative, language used throughout.

In a study of middle school mathematics placements, Useem (1992) interviewed parents about their children's experiences. Some upper-middle-class parents were effective in negotiating their children's placements:

My son . . . who was one of the top math students in his class . . . at first had some concern [about being placed in accelerated math] because the school said it was very selective . . . and that scared my son, so he considered it for a week. *I called the sixth-grade teacher . . . and said to her "Can you help me with this?"* . . . Academically there was no question . . . If he had refused accelerated math, I would have said he *should* do it and would have made a deal with him to try it for one month . . . I felt it was a psychological issue. (p. 274; our emphases)

This parent knew how to talk with the teacher about a placement issue in a way that was recognized by the teacher, advocating for her son by enlisting the teacher's aid. Another example shows parents' confident use of advocacy and negotiation:

Toward the end of fifth grade, we realized our son was not in the top math group, but we felt he could handle it. *We talked to the teacher, and he put our son in the top group* [where he did well] . . . *They listened to us and responded . . . If you are aware of what's going on.* (p. 273; our emphases)

Middle and upper-middle-class parents used speech genre(s) of advocacy when they interacted with teachers and other school personnel, especially when their children were struggling in school or when the parents wanted their children to receive different placements or resources.

In the studies reviewed, parents of children in working-class and poor communities were less likely to question the teacher's and school's authority (Horvat *et al.*, 2003), and advocated less for their children because, typically on the basis of past experience, they thought they would be ignored or that their actions would not succeed (Brantlinger, 1985a). Indeed, Useem (1992) found that less-privileged parents, who typically had not gone to college, deferred to the authority of school personnel. One parent said with regard to deciding her son's math placement:

> School personnel did it all . . . *I left it up to them and what they thought was best . . . I have no idea* [what courses he will take in junior high] . . . *They know him and know what he needs and doesn't need.* So far I've had no problems. (p. 273; our emphases)

Other parents made similar comments. For example, one noted "*I choose [courses] very little. I rely heavily on the school's recommendation.* My job as a parent is to pick the *best* public school . . . and move to that neighborhood. That was my strategy . . . to take advantage of what they offer" (p. 274). Another noted, "[My daughter's math placement] was most influenced by the school's teachers and counselors. *Whatever they agreed on . . . They must know. They have her more than I do*" (p. 274).

Low-income parents typically respected the authority of the teacher and/or school in making decisions for their children. This deferential speech genre included features such as passive voice, teachers as grammatical agents, and parents as agents only in support of teachers' recommendations. When low-income parents did advocate for their children, they often did so in ineffective ways, or ways that were not recognized by educators as demanding a response. For example, Horvat *et al.* (2003) noted that if working-class or poor parents did challenge a teacher action, they did so individually, drawing on the resources of their family ties, and registering their dislike of the action taken. When a bus driver pushed her daughter, a mother noted:

> I was off that day. And I took her up and spoke to one of the counselors and she said the principal wasn't in yet, so I said OK and I let her go to class and I came home. *I went back up when the principal came in and I sat down and talked to the principal. She seemed like a real nice person. She said she'll see what's going on. He is supposed to fill out slips and not touch students. So ever since then, she hasn't come home and said anything about the bus driver touching her.* (Horvat *et al.*, 2003: 333; our emphases)

As in this example, working-class and poor parents tended not to demand a response, an apology, or an action against school personnel from the administration. They typically did not feel they had the right to intervene, unlike the middle- and upper-middle-class parents who readily demanded specific responses or actions.

Semiotic practice II: the social language of education professionals

Social language is Bakhtin's (1981) concept for "a discourse peculiar to a specific stratum of society [professional, age group, etc.] within a given social system at a given time" (p. 430). We use *social language* to highlight the jargon and technical terminology used by education professionals, and the way access to this social language provides middle-class parents with a method for claiming an understanding of what is said by educators, as well as a rationale for being heard. Throughout this part, we use italic emphases to highlight the parent's specific use of the social language of education professionals.

In the studies reviewed here, privileged parents were able to successfully participate in the use of this social language, as several examples show. Lareau (2000) offered the following example of a parent who was discussing his son's disappointing performance in school, which both parents had been questioning all year long. The teacher, who lived in the same neighborhood, shared some information that finally addressed the parents' concerns. The father explained:

> [The teacher] did not tell us until the end of the year . . . The conference had ended; she said to us, "OK, I am going to tell you something as neighbors. You ought to have Jake *tested for OT* [occupational therapy]. He might need OT." *There was no "might" about it. Jacob desperately needed OT.* And we would have sat here, fat, dumb, and happy today if she had not had the courage to *override* the school authorities and the school rule and take us aside. (p. 117; emphases added)

In this excerpt, the parents used the term "OT" after it had been introduced by the teacher. However, in many cases, parents introduced the terms themselves. As Lareau (2000) described, at the upper-middle-class school, "parents of low-achievers knew the formal terms to describe their children's problems" (p. 77). As another example, one mother described her seven-year-old child's reading problem:

> Some of the reading is *developmental*. Emily has good language strengths. She has the *language strengths of a nine-year-old*. Yet she has the *auditory perception of a five-year-old*. Somewhere we have to get these two more in line. (Lareau, 2000: 77; emphases added)

Another upper-middle-class parent provided a detailed assessment of the academic problems her son was having. She noted:

> His *attention span* is poor. He has *auditory reception problems*, which I guess means what he is hearing he didn't quite understand sometimes. He needs real *specific directions*. I noticed a lot of times in class when I was there and the teacher would give the children instructions he would be confused because he couldn't seem *to remember a list of things to do*. I thought that was a big problem. (Lareau, 2000: 77; emphases added)

For the middle-class parents in Useem's study (1992), the situation was similar. This example shows a parent who had already internalized the social language of educators:

> The sixth-grade teacher really didn't know who our son was and said our son was *borderline* [between accelerated and regular math]. But [our son's] *standardized test scores were very high.* The teacher tried to talk me out of *placing him in accelerated math,* but I was insistent . . . It is pretty hard to move up if you don't start high. You can always move down . . . I've been advised by mothers of older children that *you have to watch where they're placed.* (p. 273; emphases added)

In such cases, parents incorporated the precise technical terms used by educators, such as "placed" rather than "put," or "accelerated" rather than "high," in order to negotiate on behalf of their children. The social language used by this particular parent, who appeared to have been coached by another parent, illustrates one of the ways that cultural and social resources combine as "communicative capital": this parent strategically drew on the resources within her social network, both as knowledge and connections. She used cultural capital, including the social language of educational professionals, and her social capital obtained through advice from other mothers, to successfully negotiate her child's placement.

In contrast, many people, especially if they are not college educated, find the language of educators incomprehensible and intimidating, as in this example, typical at the working-class school studied by Lareau (2000):

> It all depends on the person and how they treat you. *If they start using big words, you think, "Oh God what does that mean."* You know, it is just like going to the doctor's. And *it makes you feel a little insuperior to them.* Because *I don't have the education they do. You know, I just* **don't**. (p. 108; emphasis added; bold in original)

In particular, this parent referred to the "big words" that are central to the social language of any profession, in this case education, as well as the feelings that result when access to this vocabulary is not available.

Semiotic practice III: the discourses of parent involvement and scientific testing

Another reason that middle-class parents are successful is that they are able to position themselves as recognizable within the normative view produced by dominant educational discourses, including the discourses of parent involvement and scientific testing. In referring to "discourses," we use the conception offered by Fairclough (2003): "discourses are different ways of representing aspects of the world" (p. 215). Through the concept of discourse, language is a social practice that reifies, transforms, and/or challenges the social structure and the asymmetrical power relations that constitute it (Fairclough, 1995). Ideologies shape the use of language and are naturalized and seen as commonsense, that is, as "based in the nature of things or people, rather than in the interests of classes or other groupings" (Fairclough, 1995: 35). Dominant ways of making sense of student participation and performance in schooling, for example, incorporate specific understandings of parent involvement and scientific testing. Throughout this part, we use italic emphases to highlight parents' application of these discourses of schooling.

The *discourse of parent involvement* presents a particular worldview on parent involvement and naturalizes that view as the only legitimate way for parents to be involved in their child's education (Nakagawa, 2000; see also Panofsky, 2000). Through definitions and understandings of parent involvement, this discourse structures a "common sense" for relations between parents and educators that exists prior to any family–school interactions and includes expectations for the roles that educators and parents should play. These roles differ according to the social class and ethnic background of parents, and in relation to general and special education contexts (Lai and Vadeboncoeur, in press). The "prevailing discourse says that the good, involved parent is one who visits the school site and participates in sanctioned school activities" (Nakagawa, 2000: 466). Helping in class, going on field trips, attending parents' night, and fund raising – in effect, methods of involvement that are controlled by the school – structure the time and space of parental involvement. Parents who are involved in their child's education in other ways, or in ways that are not observable by school personnel, are not recognized as parents who care, parents who are involved, parents who expect or have the "right to expect quality education for their children" (Nakagawa, 2000: 466). As a result, privileged parents were frequently reified as "good parents" when their form of involvement reflected the worldview of the dominant discourses. Working-class parents, and parents from different ethnic backgrounds, were commonly positioned by these discourses as inappropriately involved in the ways involvement was deemed legitimate by the school: either under-involved, for example, not present in classrooms and on committees, or over-involved, for example, asking questions about disciplinary practices.

Another discourse pertinent here – we call it the *discourse of scientific testing* – draws upon scientific discourse to link testing with assumptions about a child's or student's innate ability. Through this discourse, the role of the teacher is imbued with authority, as the assessor, and expertise, as the interpreter of the test. The worldview presented here positions teachers as knowing what students' educational abilities and needs are, and how to develop or remedy them, as a function of objective and valid testing and measurement. Parents, without access to tests and an educator's expertise, do not and cannot diagnose and treat the educational needs of their child. Linked with medical discourse as well, this discourse is also historically grounded in the discourse of IQ testing and hereditarian notions of "intelligence" as fixed, inheritable, and immutable (see Gould, 1993; Mirza, 1998). We did not find any discussion of how middle-class and low-income parents respond when a test benefits a child, as in the case when a child is assessed at a high level. Perhaps this is not surprising. Knowing how important perceptions of a child's innate abilities can be, it is likely that few parents would argue with a scientific test that identified their child as "smart," even if they did not believe in the science behind the test or its validity.

In response to less favorable scores, however, middle-class parents *are* likely to either challenge this discourse, as a method for creating an alternative perspective about their child, or to marshal resources to overcome a poor assessment, as noted by this parent who responded to a note from her son's teacher, saying "'Writing numbers is difficult for Sam,'" as follows:

> I met with his teacher, *approved a special needs assessment, set up a summer tutor, provided developmentally appropriate activities at home,* and *impressed upon the school the importance of a first grade teacher who would respect Sam's developmental pace while actively supporting his growth.* I could do this because I am a white, middle class professional who knows the institution of school and my child was read as a future member of that very same group. (Graue *et al.*, 2001: 468; emphases added)

Consistent with this position, the middle- and upper-middle-class parents in Lareau's (2000) research "did not express self-doubts" (p. 112). One parent described his feelings about talking to teachers in a way that displayed his sense of unconstrained privilege and awareness of a shared professional status:

> So *if I have a problem I will talk to them. I have a sense of decorum. I wouldn't go busting into a classroom and say something. Obviously, for they are professional people. But there aren't any barriers in that sense.* They are not working for me, but they also aren't doing something that I couldn't do. It is more a question of a division of labor. (pp. 112–13; emphases added)

As middle-class professionals themselves, these parents sometimes took up the discourse of scientific testing and used it to challenge placements that were generated as a result of test scores. In the next example, a parent uses features of this discourse when explaining how he got his son's placement changed:

> The sixth-grade teacher didn't see our son as *highly motivated,* and he didn't do quite well enough on the *standardized test* [to be recommended for accelerated math]. But we saw that the lack of peer-group support and poor teaching *accounted for his low motivation,* and we thought he should *try* [the accelerated class for seventh grade] ... He is *competitive* ... We asked the principal's opinion, and she said, "If he wants to be *challenged,* then *override.*" (Useem, 1992: 273; emphases added)

Lareau (2000, 2003) described many upper-middle-class parents who felt their children were not being adequately challenged or believed that their children's abilities were not being appreciated. These parents knew about the existence of special programs, often because they were able to access information from the parents of their children's friends. They knew the names of the programs, the social language, and they knew how to get their children into the programs (e.g., "gifted," "resources," "enrichment," "speech therapy"). Middle-class parents' knowledge of the discourses of parent involvement and scientific testing were used to successfully contest grades, placements, and assessments, either on the basis of their own knowledge or by consulting experts outside the school setting through their social ties.

In contrast, in Lareau's (2000) research, a mother at a working-class school told this story of the placement conference when her daughter was being placed in special education:

> She [a staff person] put that paper in front of me with all of this stuff, and you know, *half of it I didn't understand. But everyone wanted to get up and go. The psychologist couldn't wait to leave, and I thought, "Why sit here and ask all these questions?* I am going to talk to the one next year there when Jill goes to school. I will get all of the information from her that I need to know. *There is no sense in my asking it all now so that I can forget it all or have to repeat the thing next year.* Better just to go in there fresh next year with a new teacher." (pp. 108–9; emphases added)

Typical of the experiences of many working-class parents in the literature, this parent deferred to educators' professional expertise and the scientific assessment of her child. Against the discourse of scientific testing, this parent had no recourse. In addition to her assuming the assessment to be objective and valid, the result reifies a categorization of her child's innate abilities: there is no claim to social construction here, this child *has* innate special educational needs. Rather than demand a full accounting about her daughter's placement, the parent, doubting her standing, intimidated by lack of knowledge, simply acquiesced.

Each of the three semiotic practices exemplifies the communicative capital that middle- and upper-middle-class parents employ to construct a triadic ZPD for their children. Since the space for development is "relational," rather than "in the child," it *must* be constructed: it relies on the parents' proleptic vision to bring it into being. In the absence of communicative capital, low-income parents are ineffective at offering or inserting their vision of their child because they do not have the requisite language or way of being to be *recognized* as credible authors of their child's future. The stories they tell, the semiotic practices they use, are not *recognized* by education professionals. Parents who do not engage in these practices perceive themselves to be at a significant disadvantage in advocating for their children and their children to be either actively disfavored by educators, or at least not among those students more favored (Brantlinger, 1985a, b, c; 2003b). In this way, the notion of the triadic ZPD makes visible the reproduction of advantage through parents' use of communicative capital to reduce relational distance in support of their children's futures.

Without this recognition and the legitimacy it conveys, low-income parents are far less able to reduce the relational distance that characterizes the typical high student to teacher ratio found in any public school setting. In the absence of parental communicative capital that the examples of middle- and upper-middle-class parents illustrate, a student's opportunities are likely to be far less extensive. In a study of students' views of teachers, Brantlinger (1994, 2003a) found that high-income students took it for granted that teachers liked them, whereas low-income youth believed that teachers were preferential and biased toward students from affluent families; low-income students "liked teachers who were helpful and did not humiliate them" (Brantlinger, 1994: 195). In addition, low-income adolescents "saw teachers as members of a social class that was different from their own" (p. 194); they had "hunches about how affluent people felt about members of their class – themselves included" (p. 194) and; they were well aware of and bothered by their teachers' attitudes toward them. While the differences noted here highlight the importance of overcoming relational distance in terms of individual children, this concept also foregrounds the work that must be done to overcome the relational distance constructed continuously through stereotypes and prejudices about members of different social classes.

Conclusions and implications

We began this discussion by quoting Vygotsky's (1997) largely ignored comment that "education has, at all times and in all places, borne a class-based character, whether or not its adherents or apostles were aware of it" (p. 56). In this discussion, we have tried to explicate one of ways that the class-based character of education works and to connect that explication in a meaningful way with an important concept from Vygotsky's theoretical framework, the zone of proximal development. A triadic ZPD results when parents insert their proleptic vision of their children's educational abilities, learning potential, and an imaginary but prospective educational future into the relational space between students and teachers. This vision includes intimate information about the child that reduces the relational distance between child and teacher, as well as information regarding parents' resources, including cultural and social capital. The triadic ZPD relies on parents' use of communicative capital – semiotic practices, including the speech genre(s) of advocacy, the social language of educational professionals, and the discourses of parent involvement and scientific testing – to mediate, or negotiate, the relationship between children and their teachers.

Our discussion is not meant as a critique of parents who use their communicative capital, nor are we suggesting that parents be prevented from doing so. Parents are simply doing what parents do – though less-privileged parents experience a distinctly "unlevel playing field," a problem that certainly needs to be redressed. We see this discussion as presenting yet another rationale for ending the structuring of privilege at the institutional level through the practices of ability grouping and tracking, and promoting practices that are most likely to mitigate relational distance between students and teachers and to foster greater social connections and connectedness. Practices like looping, in which a teacher works with students over a multi-year period, and mixed grades and other heterogeneous groupings have the potential to provide students with access to different perspectives and social networks as they work together within their ZPDs.

Changing classroom and school practices, however, is not enough. In addition, the critical project that we understand Vygotsky to have been undertaking and the critical reflexive project of Bourdieu must be linked with a goal of pursuing cultural-historical research for equity and social justice. Such a project must be committed to uncovering the way power and inequity are structured through schooled practices and, in particular, must focus on the role of social class, as well as the intersections between class, ethnicity, and gender, in the process of schooling. To escape the charge of "bias" in such a project, Bourdieu argued that "it is *only* through a reflexive practice of social inquiry that one can hope to achieve a desirable degree of objectivity on the social world" (Swartz, 1997: 11). As privileged members of the middle-class, especially of an academic elite, we must necessarily recognize the class-based position of academics in the research on the practices we have examined. It is essential that academics and researchers not ignore our own positionality in such work.

Nor can we afford to affect the traditional "outside stance" of positivist social science, as if one could avoid having an *interest* in the analysis. We view such a position as artificial, one that inevitably leads to a romanticized vision, and one that is bound to fail in its goal. Locating ourselves, however, by taking – in Harding's (1992) words – a position of "strong objectivity", may enable us to move forward ethically. Cultural-historical researchers need to think more deeply about ways of applying Vygotsky's ideas to achieve the potential ends of a more just and equitable society. In this way, our project includes extending our understanding as researchers of Vygotsky and developing a perspective as a community of scholars that takes the class-based character of education seriously.

References

Anyon, J. (1980) 'Social Class and the Hidden Curriculum of Work', *Journal of Education*, 162: 67–92.

Apple, M. (1979) *Ideology and Curriculum*, Boston, MA: Routledge & Kegan Paul.

—— (2001) *Educating the 'Right' Way: Markets, Standards, God, and Inequality*, New York: RoutledgeFalmer.

Bakhtin, M. M. (1981) *The Dialogic Imagination: Four Essays*, ed. M. Holquist, trans. C. Emerson and M. Holquist, Austin, TX: University of Texas Press.

—— (1986) *Speech Genres and Other Late Essays*, ed. C. Emerson and M. Holquist, trans. V. W. McGee, Austin, TX: University of Texas Press.

Bourdieu, P. (1986) 'The Forms of Capital', in J. Richardson (ed.), *The Handbook of Theory and Research for the Sociology of Education*, New York, NY: Greenwood, 241–58.

Bourdieu, P. and Passeron, J.-C. (1990) *Reproduction in Education, Society, and Culture*, 2nd edn, Thousand Oaks, CA: Sage.

Brantlinger, E. (1985a) 'Low-Income Parents' Perceptions of Favoritism in the Schools', *Urban Education*, 20(1): 82–102.

—— (1985b) 'What Low-Income Parents Want from Schools: A Different View of Aspirations', *Interchange*, 16(4): 14–28.

—— (1985c) 'Low-Income Parents' Opinions about the Social Class Composition of School', *American Journal of Education*, 93(3): 389–408.

—— (1994) The Social Class Embeddedness of Middle School Students Thinking about Teachers', *Theory Into Practice*, 33(3): 191–8.

—— (2003a) 'Who Wins and Who Loses? Social Class and Student Identities', in M. Sadowski (ed.), *Adolescents at School: Perspectives on Youth, Identity, and Education* Cambridge, MA: Harvard Education Press, 107–21.

—— (2003b) *Dividing Classes: How the Middle Class Negotiates and Rationalizes School Advantage*, New York: Routledge Falmer.

Censky, A. (2011) 'Income Inequality in America: How the Middle Class Became the Underclass', at CNNMoney.com. (available online at http://money.cnn.com/2011 /02/16/news/economy/middle_class; last accessed 16 March 2011).

Cole, M. (1996) *Cultural Psychology: A Once and Future Discipline*, Cambridge, MA: Belknap Press.

Duncan, G. and Murnane, R. M. (eds.) (2011) *Social Inequalities and Educational Disadvantage*, New York: Russell Sage Foundation.

Fairclough, N. (1995) *Critical Discourse Analysis: The Critical Study of Language*, New York: Longman.

—— (2003) *Analysing Discourse: Textual Analysis for Social Research*, New York: Routledge.

Gamoran, A. (2008) 'Persisting Social Class Inequality in US Education', in L. Weis (ed.), *The Way Class Works: Readings on School, Family, and Economy*, New York: Routledge, 169–79.

Gould, S. J. (1993) *The Mismeasure of Man*, New York: W. W. Norton.

Graue, M. E., Kroeger, J., and Prager, D. (2001) 'A Bakhtinian Analysis of Particular Home–School Relations', *American Educational Research Journal*, 38(3): 467–98.

Gutiérrez, K. D. and Stone, L. D. (2000) 'Synchronic and diachronic dimensions of social practice: An Emerging Methodology for Cultural-Historical Perspectives in Literacy Learning', in C. D. Lee and P. Smagorinsky (eds.), *Vygotskian Perspectives on Literacy Research: Constructing Meaning through Collaborative Inquiry*, New York: Cambridge University Press, 150–64.

Harding, S. (1992). 'After the neutrality ideal: Science, politics, and "strong objectivity"'. *Social Research*, 59(3), 567–87.

Hassrick, E. M. and Schneider, B. (2009) 'Parent Surveillance in Schools: A Question of Social Class', *American Journal of Education*,115(2): 195–225.

Holland, D. and Cole, M. (1995) 'Between Discourse and Schema: Reformulating a Cultural-Historical Approach to Culture and Mind', *Anthropology and Education Quarterly*, 26(4): 475–90.

Holland, D. and Lachicotte, Jr., W. (2007) 'Vygotsky, Mead, and the New Socio-cultural Studies of Identity', in H. Daniels, M. Cole., and J. V. Wertsch (eds.), *The Cambridge Companion to Vygotsky*, New York: Cambridge University Press, 101–35.

Horvat, E., Weininger and Lareau, A. (2003) 'From Social Ties to Social Capital: Class Differences in the Relations between Schools and Parent Networks', *American Educational Research Journal*, 40(2): 319–51.

Kelly, S. and Price, H. (2011) 'The Correlates of Tracking Policy: Opportunity Hoarding, Status Competition, or a Technical–Functional Explanation?', *American Educational Research Journal*, 48(3): 560–85.

Kingston, P. (2000) *The Classless Society*, Stanford, CA: Stanford University Press.

Labaree, D. F. (2010) *Someone Has to Fail: The Zero-Sum Game of Public Schooling*, Cambridge, MA: Harvard University Press.

Lai, Y. and Vadeboncoeur, J. A. (in press) 'The discourse of parent involvement in special education: A critical analysis linking policy documents to the experiences of mothers', *Educational Policy*.

Lareau, A. (2000) *Home Advantage: Social Class and Parental Intervention in Elementary Education*, Lanham, MD: Rowman & Littlefield.

Lareau, A. (2003) *Unequal Childhoods: Class, Race, and Family Life*, Berkeley, CA: University of California Press.

—— (2008) Watching, Waiting, and Deciding When to Intervene: Race, Class, and the Transmission of Advantage', in L. Weis (ed.), *The Way Class Works: Readings On School, Family, and the Economy*, New York: Routledge, 117–31.

Lave, J. and Wenger, E. (1991) *Situated Learning: Legitimate Peripheral Participation*, New York: Cambridge University Press.

Liebow, E. (1967) *Tally's Corner: A Study of Negro Streetcorner Men*, Boston, MA: Little Brown.

Mehan, H. (1992) 'Understanding Inequality in Schools: The Contribution of Interpretive Studies', *Sociology of Education*, 65(1): 1–20.

Mirza, H. S. (1998) 'Race, Gender, and IQ: The Social Consequence of a Pseudo-Scientific Discourse', *Race, Ethnicity and Education*, 1(1): 109–26.

Nakagawa, K. (2000) 'Unthreading the Ties that Bind: Questioning the Discourse of Parent Involvement', *Educational Policy*, 14(4): 443–72.

Oakes, J. (2005) *Keeping Track: How Schools Structure Inequality*, 2nd edn, New Haven, CT: Yale University Press.

Pakulski, J. and Waters, M. (1996) *The Death of Class*, Thousand Oaks, CA: Sage.

Panofsky, C. P. (2000) 'Examining the Research Narrative in Early Literacy: The Case of Parent–Child Book Reading Activity', in M. A. Gallego and S. Hollingsworth (eds.), *What Counts as Literacy: Challenging the School Standard*, New York: Teachers College Press, 190–212.

—— (2003) 'The Relations of Learning and Student Social Class: Toward Re- "socializing" Socio-cultural Learning Theory', in A. Kozulin, B. Gindis, V. S. Ageyev, and S. M. Miller (eds.), *Vygotsky's Educational Theory in Cultural Context*, New York: Cambridge University Press, 411–31.

Portes, P. R. and Vadeboncoeur, J. A. (2003) 'Mediation in cognitive socialization: The influence of socio-economic status', in A. Kozulin, B. Gindis, V. S. Ageyev, and S. M. Miller (eds.), *Vygotsky's Educational Theory in Cultural Context*, New York: Cambridge University Press, 371–92.

Rist, R. (1970/2000) 'Student Social Class and Teacher Expectations: The Self-fulfilling Prophecy in Ghetto Education', *Harvard Educational Review*, 70(3): 257–301.

Steinberg, S. (1989) *The Ethnic Myth: Race, Ethnicity, and Class in America*, Boston, MA: Beacon Press.

Steinberg, S. (2011) 'Poor Reason', *Boston Review* (available online at www.bostonreview. net/BR36.1/steinberg.php; last accessed 29 March 2011).

Swartz, D. (1997) *Culture and Power: The Sociology of Pierre Bourdieu*, Chicago: University of Chicago Press.

Tozer, S., Violas, P., and Senese, G. (2002) *School and Society: Historical and Contemporary Perspectives*, 4th edn, Boston, MA: McGraw-Hill.

Useem, E. L. (1992) 'Middle Schools and Math Groups: Parents' Involvement in Children's Placement', *Sociology of Education*, 65(4): 263–79.

Vygotsky, L. S. (1978) *Mind in Society: The Development of Higher Psychological Processes*, ed. M. Cole, V. John-Steiner, S. Scribner, and E. Souberman, Cambridge, MA: Harvard University Press.

—— (1997) *Educational Psychology*, ed. V. V. Davidov, trans. R. H. Silverman, Boca Raton, FL: St Lucie Press.

Wertsch, J. V. (1991) *Voices of the Mind: A Socio-cultural Approach to Mediated Action*, Cambridge, MA: Harvard University Press.

Wright, E. O. (1996/2008) 'The Continuing Importance of Class Analysis', in L. Weis (ed.), *The Way Class Works: Readings on School, Family, and Economy*, New York: Routledge, 25–43.

12 The pedagogies of second language acquisition

Combining cultural-historical and sociological traditions

Arturo Escandón

The theoretical base of the study is grounded in both the cultural-historical tradition and Bernstein's code theory (CT). The intention is to recontextualise the second language acquisition (SLA) notion of communicative language teaching (CLT) pedagogy by providing a language of description that takes into account Vygotsky's sociogenetic notion of development as well as Bernstein's ideas on orientation to meaning with the purpose of understanding how subjects take and co-configure these pedagogies according to their social position.

CLT represents an interesting case of SLA pedagogy because it seems to reproduce Vygotsky's framework of sociogenetic development. Explaining CLT's principles, Ellis (2003) asserts that communication involves two general functions: the interactional and the transactional. Development will vary as a consequence of how language is used in socio-communicative and representational functions. Furthermore, Ellis (2003) and Holliday (1994) coincide in distinguishing between a 'weak' and 'strong' version of CLT. The former assumes that the components of communicative competence can be recognised and systematically taught, involving explicit instruction. The latter claims that language is acquired through communication, and involves tacit instruction. I argue that the combined use of cultural-historical activity theory (CHAT) and Bernstein's CT may shed light on these forms of instruction, which in fact are more intertwined within any L2 pedagogy than previously thought.

As is the case with Vygotsky's (1978, 1987) unit of a 'complex mediated act' or 'word meaning', the point of departure of Bernstein's CT is semiotic mediation. Codes, according to Bernstein (1990), are culturally determined positioning devices. The position subjects take with respect to dominant and dominated forms of communication is class regulated. Ideology is established through and in such positioning. In a very general sense, codes are the result of the transformation of language or discursive possibilities by the social structure. Thus codes elicit, constrain and reinforce the social relationships necessary for the reproduction of the social structure. In other words, social relationships act selectively on the speech possibilities of the individual, constraining behaviour.

Unlike other forms of structuralism, in CT, the transmission/acquisition process or semiosis is open to change and divergence. Bernstein's accent on performance, rather than on competence, ensures that synchronic and diachronic change are taken into account, placing CT somewhere closer to Vygotskian and Bakhtian theories of verbal communication than to other contemporaneous forms of structuralism. Thus, the creative aspects of linguistic production as a case of social interaction (message) generate the eventual change of the social structure (voice).

The difficulty lies, as Halliday (1995) points out, in determining the exact midpoint location the observer needs to position in within the synchronic–diachronic scale. I believe this is overcome by (a) applying a Hegelian–Marxian unit of analysis not unlike the one advanced by Vygotsky (b) incorporating A. N. Leont'ev's (1977, 1981) structure of activity into the analysis and (c) positioning the observer between microgeny and ontogeny. This can only be done by paying attention to pedagogical developmental goals, an issue that, although touched by systemic functional linguistics, has remained largely undertheorised in CT as such.

I argue that CT presents, nonetheless, various complementary advantages over cultural-historical approaches. Assessing the subject's position by means of analysing (a) the subject's recognition of discursive practices or discursive production (realisation) informed by (b) the social division of labour through an empirical account of the distribution of power (classification) and the interrelations within through the examination of the principles of control (framing) opens a way to dealing with the nonspecific reference to culture in the dialogic tradition. Thus, the advantage of drawing on CT is that it offers a theoretical explanation and ways of empirically analysing the close link between the configuration of the social structure, especially through the analysis of the division of labour and the legitimation of its boundaries – the principles and rules that regulate social interaction and the subject's selection and integration of relevant meanings and forms of realisation, including speech forms (Bernstein, 1971, 1990).

Pedagogic communication and development

Bernstein (1990, 2000) distinguishes two systems of rules regulated by interaction (framing). These are the rules of the discursive order (instructional discourse) and of the social order (regulative discourse). Bernstein maintains that the instructional discourse is embedded in the regulative one. This relationship, however, is a very complex one and a full analysis of its implications is beyond the purpose of this chapter. Suffice it to point out, though, that its complexity depends upon (a) the given knowledge structure of a subject matter (b) the particular (historical) form sanctioned as correct transmission and (c) the relation between the form of transmission and the development of psychological functions.

In his later work, Bernstein goes beyond Vygotsky's ideas about the interdependence of everyday and scientific/theoretical concepts and representational and communicative functions by proposing a language of description of knowledge transmission. Bernstein (1999) uses the notions of horizontal and vertical discourses to refer to 'everyday common-sense knowledge' and 'school, knowledge' (p. 158). The first refers to forms of knowledge that are context dependent, multilayered, usually orally and tacitly transmitted, and contradictory across contexts but not within. The second refers to context-independent forms of knowledge that could be structured either hierarchically (e.g. the sciences) or as a series of specialised languages (e.g. the social sciences). Transmission is carried out explicitly, usually resourcing to the written text or other graphic tools such as schemes or diagrams. Furthermore, within horizontal knowledge structures, Bernstein introduces the notions of 'weak' and 'strong' grammar (p. 164). The latter refers to those horizontal knowledge structures whose languages have an explicit conceptual syntax, capable of somewhat accurate empirical descriptions or capable of generating formal modelling of empirical relations, for example linguistics, logic and mathematics. The former refers to those languages where such capabilities are weaker, such as sociology, social anthropology and cultural studies. It is important to notice that Bernstein makes a distinction between the acquisition of weak and strong grammar knowledge structures. In the case of hierarchical knowledge structures, acquirers easily know if they have acquired the discourse or not. The strong grammar clearly indicates if this is the case. The problem arises in the case of weak grammar. Acquisition is measured by gaining a particular 'gaze', that is, a particular form of recognition and realisation of what counts as authentic discourse (p. 165). Hence, acquirers have more difficulty in recognising if they have mastered discursive forms or not.

Although these characterisations afford a more complex description of transmission, in fact any form of transmission intertwines horizontal and vertical knowledge. The question here is how model-based instruction, with its tacit knowledge structure, can be characterised in the end as a form of vertical discourse. Gamble (2010) conjectures that tacit regulative discourse may give learners access to meaning orientations that are not context dependent but abstract. I believe this conjecture is crucial to understanding forms of transmission that heavily rely on imitation or modelling, which is the case of L1 and L2 transmission.

The aforementioned paradox amounts, at a sociological level, to the contradiction pointed out by Vygotsky (1987) between thinking and word when he advanced the unit of analysis 'word meaning', at the intersection of two vectors of development: thought becomes verbal and speech rational, allowing abstract, conceptual build-up. Wertsch discusses this dialectical relation, referring to two kinds of semiotic mediation found in Vygotskian theory: explicit and implicit. The former is 'intentionally and overtly introduced into problem solving activity, often by an outside party', especially by means of a material tool, whereas the latter is 'informal in that it typically involves spoken language, whose materiality is transitory and seemingly ephemeral' (p. 191), that is, it involves the use of a psychological tool: speech. The distinction is also contained in language's representational and socio-communicative function: some words address the object of the activity and some are used in sustaining the social bonds needed to accomplish it. In fact, Wertsch's depiction is an extension of Vygotsky's method of 'dual stimulation'.

By the same token, Hasan (2005), drawing on Bernstein, understands 'visible' semiotic mediation as 'the conscious discourse aimed at mediating a specific category of reasoning'. In contrast, 'invisible' semiotic mediation is understood as 'how the unself-conscious everyday discourse mediates mental dispositions . . . how it puts in place beliefs about the world one lives in' (p. 152).

I argue that CT and CHAT represent complementary theoretical frameworks and methodologies. On the one hand, the recourse to activity in CHAT helps identify the interrelation between the form of the pedagogical communication – such as the one used in setting, organising and carrying out pedagogical tasks – and the ideal object of a given social formation, from which an assessment of the vectors of development can be done. In other words, the projected vectors of development are a function of the relation between the pedagogical task (microgeny) and the intended object of activity (ontogeny). This permits a move away from CT's implicit naturalistic conception of instructional time, which is due to its lack of a unit of analysis of pedagogical interaction (a unity capable of accounting at once for the internal and the external and recognising pedagogical joints and breaks).

CT offers a way to identify those vectors of development in terms of restricted or elaborated coding and subsequently assess how the subject takes position (orientations to meaning). This allows assessment of the subject's recognition and accomplishment of pedagogical tasks framed under the developmental requirements set within particular co-configured social formations. It represents an empirical approach towards assessing subjects' ability to figure out the object of activity and therefore become co-subjects in true joint activity (see Davydov and Markova, 1983). More specifically, Bernstein (2000), notices that differences in distribution of power (classification) and principles of control (framing) give rise to two sets of 'recognition' and 'realisation' rules that regulate text production. Subjects must be able to recognise the context (recognition rules) and produce a text adequate to that context (realisation rules). This is called 'coding orientation'. Failure to produce a text adequate to a context may indicate lack of recognition or realisation rules or both. Consequently, 'passive realisation' is defined by the possession of recognition rules but the lack of realisation rules, whereas, 'active realisation' is defined by the possession of both.

Socially situating semiosis

Drawing on Davydov and Markova (1983), D. A. Leont'ev (1992) and Bernstein (2000), I argue that independent discovering and acceptance of tasks is closely linked to subjects' recognition and degree of acceptance of forms of mediation and the position they take toward the objects of mediation (e.g. the object of mediation or the mediation form itself may be supported or resisted in many ways or turned into something else, redefining the intended object of activity). A shared operational structure is predicated on the recognition of explicit mediation (e.g. the recognition of the object of a task, what the problem is all about). Moreover, a shared motivational-sense structure is fundamentally a function of the recognition and acceptance of implicit mediation (e.g. recognition of appropriate ways of approaching and organising the task).

Thus, the combined used of the cultural-historical tradition and CT allows establishment of a correspondence between development and forms of communication, weakening the view that the form of pedagogic communication is independent from particular forms of development. In other words, the setting of certain development targets narrows the repertoire of pedagogic communication or forms of instruction; the choice of particular forms of pedagogic communication implies, in turn, setting a particular vector of development. Finally, combined use of CHAT and CT allows more accurate comparisons of pedagogies across organisations or pedagogical contexts.

Subject position in different organisational and pedagogic contexts

The empirical focus of the study is on determining subjects' position by analysing the relation between acquirer's trajectories, coding orientation (recognition of instructional discourses) and their realisation.

Two organisations were chosen to conduct case studies (BU and CU below). Each case study comprised one introductory grammar and communication course, with their respective instructors and students. While CU acquirer participants (13 students) majored in Spanish, their counterparts in BU (19 students) did not. Data on acquirer participants from BU were collected over a 15-week semester, during autumn 2007. Data on acquirer participants from CU were collected over two 14-week semesters starting in autumn 2008 and ending in winter 2009. Data on and from transmitter participants were collected, respectively, over a similar time span but lasted four weeks longer. Apart from communication courses, the curricula at both organisations comprised several courses in Spanish grammar for first-year students.

The structure of activity and speech activity

Based on A. N. Leont'ev's activity theory (see A. N. Leont'ev, 1977, 1981), A. A. Leont'ev (1981) advances an ideal sequence of speech-related activities paying attention to acquirers' development of psychological functions. That sequence, together with Gal'perin's (1969, 1992) insights into internalisation and Bakhtin and Holquist's (1981) views on verbal communication, was used for the description and analysis of classroom interaction.

Motive-action (or *educational task*) was the unit of analysis used in codification of classroom interaction, which was respectively framed within the four types of motive-activity advanced by A. A. Leont'ev (foundation, structural, functional and rhetorical), including one more (management) referring to activities aimed at managing the course. The unit was based on the distinction between collective activity and individual action based on the principle of division of labour. What makes activities different from one another is their object or 'motive'. Nonetheless, it is only when that motive is shared by subjects who are part of the activity system and a concrete plan of action (operational structure) emerges spontaneously or is explicitly formulated that the activity can be called a 'joint activity'. D. A. Leont'ev (1992) maintains that in joint activity not only the operation structure but also the motivational-sense structure of this activity is shared by its co-subjects. The unit of analysis or germ-cell containing the possibility of joint activity of classroom interaction is the motive-action or educational task as a way to achieve the larger object of motive-activity. Thus, an accurate distinction of courses is based upon variance of framing values for each motive-activity across organisational and pedagogical settings. Courses were also compared in terms of time spent on performing each of the aforementioned motive-activities.

Trajectories

These categories were based on participants' perceived educational trajectory in terms of a dominant activity in which they partook throughout their schooling (see Wertsch, 1998; Griffin and Cole, 1984). Dominant or leading activities were extracted from A. A. Leont'ev (1981) (italics below), whereas the trajectories were as follows: Trajectory 1 comprised acquirers who did not express their involvement in any particular L2 activity. Their only experience derived from their participation in the education system in Japan, especially in activities recognisable as *speech activity*. Trajectory 2 included acquirers who expressed their involvement either in *speech acts* as part of *non-verbal activity* (e.g. 'I could give directions to a foreigner so that he could reach the place he/she was looking for') *or communication activity* in Japan. Trajectory 3 comprised acquirers who responded that the activities helping them learn a language the most, or were more satisfactory or enjoyable, were associated with having been abroad, either for a short high-school trip, as part of a home-stay programme, or because they were living abroad. These activities are associated with speech acts that are part of *non-verbal activity* and *communication activity*. However, because the experience of communicating while being abroad was presumably more demanding and varied, these activities were considered of a different nature to those included in Trajectory 2. One key aspect of activities in this trajectory is that they might have included what Gal'perin (1969) calls 'model-determined acts', where the learner did not have an indication of how the act should be carried out (the kind of instruction one is exposed to when learning a language in the country where it is spoken, without formal schooling or training).

Acquirer participants filled out a questionnaire administered by their respective instructors during the third week of study. All questions were open and sought to find out instances that marked their learning trajectories. In CU's case, interviews were held with acquirer participants over a period of two weeks, and after the third week of classes had started during the first semester.

Regulative and instructional discourses

Indicators and their framing descriptions, validated elsewhere (Escandón, 2008), were used to determine framing levels within motive-action units. Resulting figures were given in mean form instead of median because of repeated counts within the unit. A 1–4 scale was used. Especial attention was paid to the roles within the zone of proximal development (ZPD), especially when evaluating textual production. Differences between evaluation serving the purpose of assessing text production (instructional discourse) and evaluation that serves the purpose of reasserting hierarchy in the transmitter–acquirer relation or asserting a model of conduct (regulative discourse) were acknowledged.

In discourse studies IREF patterns are recognised as the most essential of teaching exchanges, consisting of a triadic dialogue. Each exchange incorporates an initiation move (I), usually a question asked by the transmitter, a response move (R), a reply made by an acquirer, and an evaluation move (E) made by the transmitter towards the acquirer's response, also known as the follow-up move (F). Veel (1999) asserts that evaluation moves in IREF exchanges are symptoms of hierarchical systems whereby the transmitter assumes the role of primary knower.

Recognition

A questionnaire was administered to acquirer participants by their communication instructor at the end of the course. The questionnaire listed 37 sample items of transmitters' instructional discourse. The items were coded, representing different framing values of instructional and regulative discourse. Participants had to determine if the sample came either from a grammar or a communication course using a 9-point response format, from 'grammar' (point 4) to 'both' (point 0) to 'communication' (point 4).

Realisation

Data were collected from communication instructors to establish the mastery level (active realisation) of individual acquirers in communication courses. Mastery could not be considered plain linguistic 'competence' since the aim of the course and the assessment method includes acquisition of social rules. Instructors were asked to hand students' grades and to place individual photographs of acquirers on a chart across the axis where they perceived acquirers as having 'achieved the objectives of the course' or 'does not achieve the objectives of the course'. Instructors were then asked what distinguished one acquirer from another, or one group of acquirers from another group, so as to configure a network of positions – how they built the relational space of their own students. Further data on realisation is reported in the next section.

Organisational, pedagogical contexts and CLT

The classroom interaction for each course (one 90-minute session each) was divided into motive-actions with their correspondent classroom time and framing values and those motive-actions classified according to motive-activity structural levels. Motive-activities were then contrasted across organisations and learning settings in terms of framing values. This allowed comparing framing values within the same motive-activity structural level across organisations and learning settings.

The first set of results included in Figures 12.1–12.4 presents BU's and CU's courses' motive-activity structure as a function of time spent on those activities.

CU's communication course presented a very different motive-activity structure than the rest of the courses, as can be seen in the figures below. Tasks (motive-action) had a functional purpose. This difference was linked to lifting of

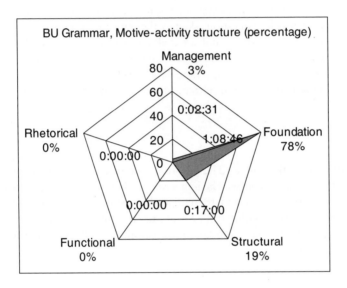

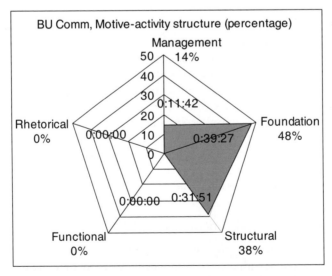

Figures 12.1 and 12.2 BU grammar and communication, motive-activity structure as a function of time spent (percentage)

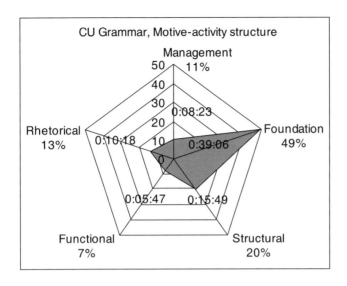

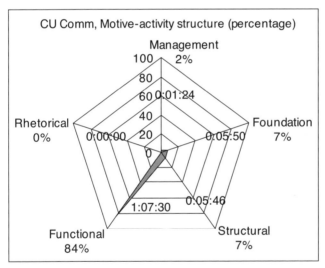

Figures 12.3 and 12.4 CU grammar and communication, motive-activity structure as a function of time spent (percentage)

controls over the dialogic effects of discourse (e.g. weak framing of contents, instructional sequence and pace). A functional motive-activity structure is aligned with a strong version of CLT.

BU's communication course was more similar to BU's and CU's grammar courses. In fact, it looked much closer to CU's grammar course than to CU's communication course. BU's communication course's accent on structural speech activity was more aligned with a weak version of CLT.

CU's communication course framing values

The course presented weak framing values in key areas related to CLT, especially in functional motive-actions (see Figures 12.5–12.8). The instructional practice presented weaker framing in selection of contents, selection of classroom jobs and instructional sequence. Acquirers were *to a certain extent* allowed to choose contents, to bring their own experiences or knowledge to instructional practices, to have a say about whom they worked with during instructional tasks and to alter the instructional sequences of those tasks to find their most suitable sequence.

Weak framing of selection of contents was accompanied by a surge of concept translation at this stage in functional motive-activities (see Figure 12.8). Acquirers

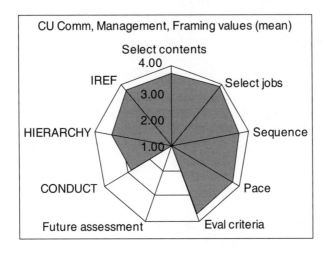

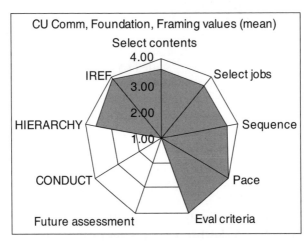

Figures 12.5 and 12.6 CU's communication course, management and foundation motive-activity framing values (mean)

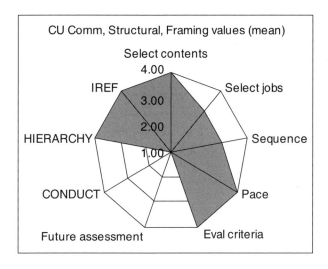

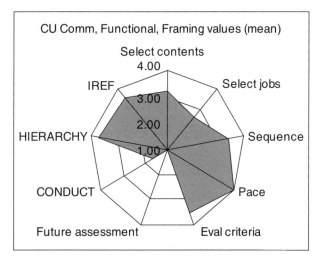

Figures 12.7 and 12.8 CU's communication course, structural and functional
motive-activity framing values (mean)

might have felt compelled to 'use' the transmitter as a 'living dictionary', especially
if communication unfolded more spontaneously (i.e. not leaving enough time for
the acquirer to use the dictionary to find a word). Weakening of framing in
selection of contents and consequent surge in conceptual translation (see Figure
12.8) might have also been linked to strengthening of hierarchy in functional
motive-activities.

In contrast, at foundation motive-activity level (see Figure 12.6), questioning
was followed by a relative weakening of hierarchy. There were more instances in

which the transmitter resorted to not answering questions directly but facilitating answers in such a way that she had acquirers answering the very same questions they had made by guiding them through.

The values for each framing indicator suggested that, in general, acquirers engaged in experiential socio-communicative functions. Nonetheless, regulative practice was still strongly framed, with the exception of conduct regulation. Conduct regulation appeared constant because most motive-actions were framed within a functional motive-activity, that is, the purpose of regulating acquirers' conduct was linked to the need of *requesting spontaneity* from them.

The transmitter exerted a tight control through questioning (IREF) individual acquirers or groups of acquirers and asserted her position as primary knower. The transmitter's evaluation criteria were strongly framed as well. This meant that the transmitter assumed the role of primary evaluator and was involved directly in correction of textual production.

Framing of selection of classroom jobs varied depending on motive-activity structure, experiencing a weakening of framing values the higher in the motive-activity structure the discourse belonged to, as Figures 12.5–12.8 indicate.

The analysis of classroom interaction suggested that the transmitter did not rely on pair-work at management, foundation and structural levels. The transmitter addressed the class as a whole – a selection of classroom jobs linked to traditional pedagogies – at those levels. At the structural level, though, the transmitter weakened the framing of classroom jobs by asking questions to the whole class but allowing volunteers to answer them.

Framing of evaluation criteria seemed to weaken at the functional level as well, although there were minimal differences at management, foundation and structural levels. Again, the search for automaticity might have overwritten the need for grammatical correction in certain instructional tasks.

BU's communication course framing values

The course had a strong component of foundation and structural motive-activities where the Spanish language was analysed and reflected upon. It presented strong framing values in key instructional practices such as selection of contents and instructional sequence. Acquirers were not allowed to bring in their own experiences or find their most suitable instructional sequence since the sequence was provided to them and enforced by the transmitter. Contents were constrained as well. The areas of weaker framing were ones related to hierarchy and evaluation criteria.

Framing of selection of classroom jobs seemed to weaken the higher the discourse belonged to the motive-activity structure, as is shown in Figures 12.9–12.11. Thus, at management level, selection of classroom jobs was strongly framed (the transmitter addressed acquirers as a whole), but less so at foundation and structural level.

The analysis of classroom interaction suggested that transmitter and acquirers resourced more to concept translation the higher their interaction belonged to motive-activity structure.

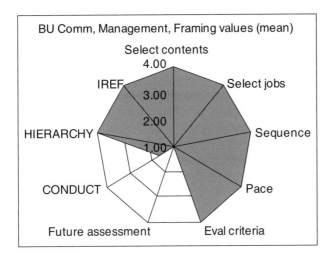

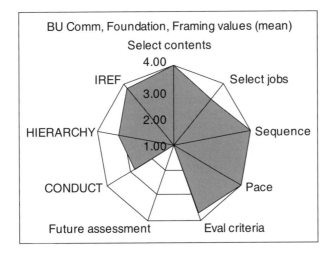

Figures 12.9 and 12.10 BU's communication course, management and foundation motive-activity framing values (mean)

Strong framing of conduct at structural motive-activity level also was partly associated with the fact that the transmitter commanded acquirers to ask him questions (see Figure 12.11). This produced a surge in forced questioning from acquirers that was framed explicitly under the instructional input of the transmitter (strong framing). However, it did resemble CU's communication foundational motive-activity. BU's communication transmitter was encouraging acquirers at all times to ask him questions in Spanish.

Moreover, strong framing values at the structural level were associated with a tighter control of acquirers who did not comply with the transmitter's instructions

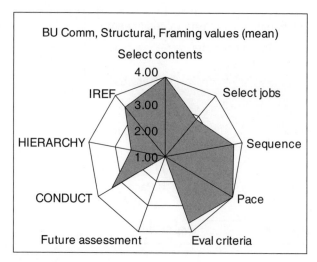

Figure 12.11 BU's communication course, structural motive-activity framing values
(mean)

(e.g. to be quiet, or to form pairs), including deviance from the instructional
sequence. Conduct regulation at this level seemed linked to solving problems
arising from instructional practice rather than making general statements about
appropriate conduct.

CLT contexts

Analysis of instructional and regulative discourse in the two communication
pedagogical contexts was done from codification of framing according to each
motive-activity. These are the main findings:

BU's communication course was informed by a weak CLT version for the
following reasons:

1   The course structure privileged structural motive-activity, that is, speech acts
    were closely monitored to comply with grammatical norms or grammatical
    structures or objectives set in tasks.
2   Contents selection was strongly framed. Acquirers could not bring their own
    personal information or experiences into the learning process. The personal
    information they provided was reduced to a quasi-binary system: 'I know' or
    'I don't know' answers to questions.
3   The transmitter tightly controlled the instructional sequence enforcing ac-
    quirers' compliance. The transmitter ensured acquirers used the targeted struc-
    ture (strongly framed instructional sequence), focusing thus on language form.
4   The transmitter's approach to instructional tasks contained in the textbook
    was to focus on repetition of language patterns as a means of transforming
    speech acts into operations.

CU's communication course was informed by a strong CLT version for the following reasons.

1   The course structure privileged functional motive-activity.
2   The selection of contents was strongly framed but framing values were the weakest of the four courses. Instructional contents were provided but some personal information or experience was elicited from acquirers.
3   The instructional sequence was strongly framed but, again, framing values were the weakest of all four courses. Even though acquirers were not encouraged to find their most suitable instructional sequence, the transmitter left enough room for acquirers to modify instructional sequences. Creativity was encouraged within certain limits.
4   The transmitter's approach to task-based instructional tasks contained in the textbook was to alter them by means of sustaining a personal dialogue with acquirers on a one-to-one, pair or group basis while they were carrying out the instructional task. Thus, the instructor brought the objectives of the instructional task to the personal realm of acquirers, making the few instructional tasks that did not include sharing acquirers' personal information an experiential learning opportunity.

Discussion 1

CLT's weak version was characterised by a top-down move within the ZPD and strong framing in selection of contents and instructional sequence. Acquirers lacked control over instructional tasks because top-down movements required them to work on conceptual systems – unlike the development of conceptual systems in their L1 – without being able to resort to everyday knowledge, simply because they had not acquired 'spontaneous' concepts in the L2, nor they could access a repertoire of internalised culture-specific activity predicated on what Luria (1987) called 'immediate, individual, and concrete experience' (p. 366). Furthermore, acquisition of L2 concepts seemed to depend, to an extent greater than expected, upon the mediation of the semantic system of the L1, at least in formal language education contexts. This is not to say that direct non-conscious and non-voluntary acquisition of concepts in an L2 is impossible, but rather it is restricted until the newly acquired L2 mediates the acquisition of L2 scientific/theoretical concepts.

The most prominent characteristic of CLT's strong version is the bottom-up move within the ZPD and the weakening of framing in selection of contents and instructional sequence. Nonetheless, even within this pedagogic context, the apparent 'horizontality' of CLT's strong version gives way to a 'vertical' aggregation of pragmatic/functional 'competences'. In CLT's weak version, the formal system (grammar or pragmatics) is the point of departure, whereas in CLT's strong version, it is the point of arrival.

Analysis of class interaction linked to motive-activity structure revealed that instructional and regulative framing values were as much a function of targeted vectors of development as a function of the idiosyncratic characteristics of a learning setting. Thus, in a strong CLT context, strengthening of regulative discourse (conduct, hierarchy, IREF) was accompanied by weakening of instructional discourse because the transmitter was required to regulate the unexpected unfolding of textual production or even stress the importance of engaging in 'real' communication (e.g. requesting spontaneity), with its own deviation quota and room for unexpected turns. On the contrary, strengthening of regulative discourse in a weak CLT context was associated with keeping the instructional sequence in place, avoiding deviation, and commanding students to ask questions in the L2.

Acquirers' trajectories and coding orientations

Using a correlational research design supported by the partial least square (PLS) path modelling statistical technique (see Chin, 1999; Haenlen, 2004), a multivariate statistical model was constructed to measure the variance in the participants' realisation in terms of recognition (of grammar, communication and weakly framed communication instruction sample items) and test the effect of moderators (trajectory, organisation). A baseline model that used data from both courses (N = 32) was used as a benchmark. Following Hair's (2010) protocol for testing moderators, additional models were constructed for participants in trajectory 1 (Model I); participants in trajectory 2 (Model II); participants in trajectory 3 (Model III); participants at BU (Model IV); and participants at CU (Model V). Three types of parameters were computed: (a) factor loadings between indicator variables and latent variables, using principle components factor analysis, with loadings measuring the correlation ranging from –1 to +1. Loadings > 0.5 were interpreted as 'strong', 'high' or 'heavy' while loadings < 0.5 were interpreted as 'weak', 'low' or 'light'; (b) path coefficients (standardised, ranging from –1 to 1; interpreted in the same way as the standardised regression or β weighted coefficients in a multiple regression model) between the latent variables and (c) the effect sizes (R^2 values > .15 were assumed to be large enough to imply practical and theoretical importance).

The variance in active realisation (instructor's grade) explained in terms of recognition tended to be high when the participants were characterised by a relatively strong ability to recognise grammar instructional discourse. The proportion (R^2) ranged very widely from a minimum of 19.2 per cent (Model III), associated with low grammar recognition, to a maximum of 56.9 per cent (Model V), associated with high recognition of grammar instructional discourse.

The variance in active realisation explained in terms of recognition was higher among trajectory-1 participants, who had a preference for strongly framed learning (a *traditional* language learning pedagogy), characterised by a relative strong ability to recognise grammar instruction (Model I); and lower among the members of trajectories 2 and 3, who have a preference for weakly framed learning, characterised by a relatively weak ability to recognise grammar instructional discourse (Models II and III).

The variance in active realisation explained in terms of recognition was higher among acquirers at CU, specialising in foreign language education, characterised by a relatively strong ability to recognise grammar instructional discourse (Model I). The variance in realisation explained in terms of recognition was lower among the students at BU not specialising in foreign language education (Model IV). The variance in realisation explained in terms of recognition was lower among the students at BU not specialising in the teaching of L2 (Model IV). The students at CU (Model V) were characterised by a stronger ability to recognise grammar instructional discourse than the students at BU. The evidence for this difference was that grammar was a stronger predictor of recognition at CU (path coefficient = .739) than at BU (path coefficient = .494). Nevertheless, at both BU and CU, recognition of grammar was important. Recognition of communication discourse was not so important at CU, indicated by the negative correlation (path coefficient = –.182) between recognition and communication compared to that at BU (path coefficient = .495). This confirmed the view that the curriculum of CU's communication course was, paradoxically, more hierarchically sequenced than BU's one. Nonetheless, even at BU, recognition of grammar instructional discourse was a stronger predictor of realisation than recognition of communication instruction.

The findings supported the view that trajectory and organisational differences act as moderators of recognition and ultimately of active realisation. In conclusion, evidence was provided to indicate that the recognition of grammar instruction (an elaborated coding orientation) is crucial in attaining higher levels of language mastery.

Taking into account how recognition of grammar, communication and weakly framed communication instructional practices behaved as predictors of realisation, Figure 12.12 plots eight orientations to meaning, which are indicated by the

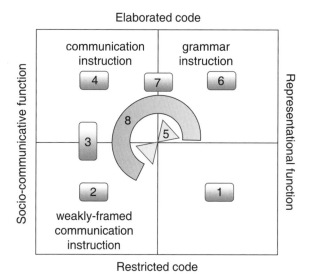

Figure 12.12 Orientations as recognition of grammar, communication and weakly-framed instructional discourses, expressed as modes of self-regulation in elaborated and restricted codes

numbers inside the different grey shapes. These orientations are modulated by two opposite vectors of development, the representational and socio-communicative functions, expressed as modes of self-regulation in elaborated and restricted codes. Orientation 1 represents a confounded recognition.

Evidence was provided to indicate that acquirers who possessed an elaborated coding orientation (recognition of elaborated-code instructional discourse, especially grammar instructional discourse), that is, orientations 4, 5, 6, 7 and 8, attained higher levels of language mastery (realisation) in learning settings either informed by CLT's weak or strong version.

Discussion 2

What communication transmitters required simultaneously from acquirers was the possession of a complex set of instructional rules and social order rules that can be rendered as recognition of vertical instructional mediation, realisation of reflective trial approaches to communicative instructional tasks and realisation of simulated horizontal intersubjective relations. Orientation-1, -2 and -3 acquirers might have confused the requirement of simulated horizontal intersubjective relations as a call to engage in model-determined approaches to learning as they could not switch coding orientation (from a restricted to an elaborated coding orientation) because they did not possess recognition rules for grammar instruction. Furthermore, it is not unlikely that they might have successfully applied model-determined approaches, which fundamentally rely on trial and error, in previous learning experiences. However, in formal communication pedagogic contexts as the ones analysed, the assumption that an informal approach is valuable seemed a deceptive one since transmitters demanded that acquirers engage in communication tasks in a reflective trial fashion (a learning method more reflective than the trial-and-error method), that is, taking calculated risks and paying attention to the correct organisation and sequence of tasks, including ways to interact with peers in team work regardless if the course is informed by weak or strong versions of CLT. In consequence, horizontal relations, such as the ones that take part in spontaneous learning, were part of a simulacrum. In fact, they were not horizontal at all.

In light of the findings, it is suggested that in the long run lack of recognition of grammar instructional practices is heavily penalised. Students who do not possess recognition rules for grammar instruction do not report good levels of realisation, while those who possess them do acquire fair levels of realisation rules even in a context shaped by a strong version of CLT. The situation is contradictory since the context shaped by a strong version of CLT (CU's communication course) presents weaker framing values than the context shaped by the weak version (BU's communication course). One could presume that in a pedagogic context shaped by a strong version of CLT the socio-communicative function would prevail, but that is not the case. Even in BU's communication course, recognition of weakly framed communication instruction alone did not present an advantage for acquirers if it was not accompanied by the recognition of grammar instruction. The socio-communicative function seemed not horizontally sequenced, nor seemed the evaluation criteria, which sought vertical integration of skills, that is, one communicative skill was built upon another. In other words, in a pedagogic context informed by a strong version of CLT, acquirers cannot sit back and disregard the use of learning skills or strategies used in tasks that aim at developing representational functions, even if the course's subject is 'communication' and it is weakly framed. Since CU's communication course presented weaker levels of classification and framing, there were fewer (explicit) calls for conduct regulation than in BU's communication course, especially for conduct-on-action or past performance, which could be interpreted by informal and communicative orientation acquirers as a general neglect of future assessment. As CT suggests, weakly framed instruction operates under tacit rules. However, lack of assessment criteria might in the long run be detrimental to informal and communicative orientation acquirers.

General discussion

Weak and strong versions of CLT and the code–communication dilemma (explicit and implicit instruction) reflect the dialectical contradiction between top-down and bottom-up moves within the ZPD. This contradiction can be said to be between meaning and sense or between scientific/theoretical and everyday concepts. A general assessment of the status of SLA reveals that SLA scholars and practitioners alike have treated these opposite moves as if they were exclusive. In the dialogical tradition, the opposite directions within the ZDP are rather seen as complementary. In fact, development depends upon this contradiction and therefore instruction should be based on a double move (Hedegaard, 2002; Hedegaard and Chaiklin, 2005), which Davydov (1998) understands as the essential aspect of formal learning or education activity. L2 education does not constitute an exception.

The difference between L1 and L2 acquisition is that, in the former, the contradiction stems from the dialectic relation between pseudoconcepts and everyday or empirical concepts (at pre-schooling level) first, and between pseudo and everyday concepts and scientific/theoretical concepts (at schooling level) later. In the latter, the contradiction stems from the dialectical relation between L1 and L2 concepts. In other words, in L1 acquisition, the contradiction is between the subjective and objective (social) organisation of the world; whereas in L2 acquisition, the contradiction is primarily between the subjective and the objective organisation of linguistic means. The instruction of grammar and of contrasting linguistic consciousness in the native and target languages is not opposed to the instruction of communication/pragmatics (i.e. functional grammar). In fact, the deployment of methods of instruction of grammar and linguistic consciousness represent a bridge between the meaningless abstraction of grammar systems and meaning in a concrete cultural system, which demands particular forms of explicit instruction. Put another way, every form of explicit instruction does not necessarily equate with the proper transmission of scientific/

theoretical systems that can operate as links between the abstract and the particular. Nonetheless, instruction cannot completely depend upon the transmission of conceptual systems (i.e. verbalism), since eventually the emergence of true concepts is a consequence of actual solving of practical tasks, i.e. tasks informed by CLT's strong version, in this case. This is an unavoidable call to rethink and recontextualise 'grammar' instruction, especially the grammar–communication divide so omnipresent in the teaching of L2 education in Japan.

However, although it may not necessarily follow the verticality of grammar, the evidence that stems from this investigation supports Bernstein's conjecture that every study programme cannot *but* be instructionally staged and hierarchically sequenced. This seems to be the case in this study with communication courses across organisations, whether they represented a weak or strong version of CLT or whether they belonged to a programme in a university specialising in L2 education or not. This seems in agreement with Bourne's (2008) and Gamble's (2010) views that express that even though model-based instruction seems to resemble the horizontal discourses of everyday life, pedagogic discourse is always vertical. It is important that study programmes acknowledge this fact and communication transmitters stage instruction accordingly, setting explicit evaluation criteria and adequately informing acquirers of them. The apparent horizontality of instruction plays against those acquirers who do not have a grammar orientation to instructional discourse. In cases of less elaborated coding instruction, acquirers may believe that communicating in the target language is enough, whereas in actual fact they are being evaluated by their capacity to build operation upon operation in a hierarchical way, that is, they require a representational 'gaze'. Explicit regulative discourse was dominated by two paradoxes: (a) in CLT's weak version there was a *demand to ask questions*, while (b) in CLT's strong version there was a *demand for spontaneity*. Tacit regulation was dominated by the need to approach the tasks in which those demands were made in a reflective trial fashion.

The methodological instruments helped determine eight orientations as functions of passive realisation in three areas that until now have been unknown or confounded: weakly framed communication, communication and grammar pedagogical discourses. These orientations enabled, in turn, examination of the problem of mastery in terms of asymmetric access to cultural resources and a conclusion that those acquirers who only possess a restricted coding orientation attain either mediocre or lower levels of mastery.

The interface between activity theory and Bernstein's CT proved helpful in determining pedagogical contexts across organisations, enabling the comparison of particular forms of semiotic mediation and improving the generalisation of the study's findings. The adoption of A. A. Leont'ev's views on language development as psychological functions whose motive-activity varies according to the general type of activity permitted a more accurate analysis of semiosis, such as determining particular messages (framing) according to the structural level of activity being focused on. Moreover, setting motive-action/educational task as the unit of analysis permitted the adoption of a non-naturalistic framework to study classroom interaction or any other pedagogical relation in its social dominion (as the possibility of joint activity). This supersedes the naturalistic view of (interaction) time (e.g. framing categories as a percentage of *natural* time) and allows a more accurate analysis of interaction according to functions. At the same time, this unit – being at the intersection between activity and action/operation – comprises the complexities of both ontogenesis and microgenesis.

The use of Bernstein's CT in combination with CHAT's notions on the structure of activity helped develop strong internal and external languages of description, paying attention to all the merits of the theoretical bodies that were chosen, but giving voice to the views that stem from the participants themselves, constituting a truly dialectical approach to research on pedagogy.

References

Bakhtin, M. M. and Holquist, M. E. (1981) *The Dialogic Imagination: Four Essays*, Austin, TX: University of Texas Press.

Baron, R. M. and Kenny, D. A. (1986) 'The Moderator–Mediator Variable Distinction in Social Psychological Research: Conceptual, Strategic, and Statistical Considerations', *Journal of Personality and Social Psychology*, 51: 1173–82.

Bernstein, B. (1971) *Class, Codes and Control*, vol. 1, *Theoretical Studies: Towards a Sociology of Language*, London: Routledge & Kegan Paul.

—— (1990) *Class, Codes and Control*, vol. 4: *The Structuring of Pedagogic Discourse*, London: Routledge.

—— (1999) 'Vertical and Horizontal Discourse: An Essay', *British Journal of Sociology of Education*, 20 (2),157–73.

—— (2000) *Pedagogy, Symbolic Control and Identity: Theory Research Critique*, rev. edn, Oxford: Rowman & Littlefield.

Bourne, J. (2008) 'Official Pedagogic Discourses and the Construction of Learners' Identities', in N. H. Hornberger (ed.), *Encyclopaedia of Language Education*, New York: Springer, vol. 3, 41–52.

Chin, W. (1999) 'The Partial Least Squares Approach for Structural Equation Modeling', in G. A. Marcoulides (ed.), *Modern Methods for Business Research*, Hillsdale, NJ: Lawrence Erlbaum, 47–50.

Davydov, V. V. (1998) 'The Concept of Developmental Teaching', *Journal of Russian and East European Psychology*, 36(4), 11–36.

Davydov, V. V. and Markova, A. A. (1983) 'A Concept of Educational Activity for Children', *Soviet Psychology*, 2(2): 50–76.

Ellis, R. (2003) *Task-based Language Learning and Teaching*, Oxford: Oxford University Press.

Escandón, A. (2008) 'Bernstein's pedagogic codes and the issue of control in communicative approaches to second language acquistion (SLA)', paper presented to the 5th International Basil Bernstein Symposium, Cardiff (UK), 3 July.

Gal'perin, P. I. (1969) 'Stages in the Development of Mental Acts', in M. Cole and I. Maltzman (eds.), *A handbook of contemporary Soviet psychology*, New York: Basic Books.

—— (1992) 'Stage-by-Stage Formation as a Method of Psychological Investigation, *Journal of Russian and East European Psychology*, 30(4): 37–80.

Gamble, J. (2010) 'Exploring the Transmission of Moral Order as Invisible Semiotic Mediator of Tacit Knowledge', in P. Singh, A. R. Sadovnik and S. F. Semel (eds.), *Toolkits, Translation Devices and Conceptual Accounts: Essays on Basil Bernstein's Sociology of Knowledge*, New York: Peter Lang.

Griffin, P. and Cole, M. (1984) 'Current Activity for the Future: The Zo-ped', in B. Rogoff and J. V. Wertsch (eds.), *Children's Learning in the Zone of Proximal Development: New Directions for Child Development*, San Francisco, CA: Josey-Bass, 45–63.

Haenlen, M. and Kaplan, A. (2004) 'A Beginner's Guide to Partial Least Square Analysis', *Understanding Statistics*, 3: 283–97.

Hair, J. J., Anderson, R. E., Babin, B. J., Tatman, R. L. and Black, W. C. (2010) *Multivariate Data Analysis*, 7th edn, New Jersey: Prentice Hall.

Halliday, M. A. K. (1995) 'Language and the Theory of Codes', in A. R. Sadovnik (ed.), *Knowledge and Pedagogy*, Westport, CT: Ablex.

Hasan, R. (2005) *Language, Society and Consciousness*, vol. 1: *The Collected Works of Ruqaiya Hasan*, London: Equinox.

Hedegaard, M. (2002) *Learning and Child Development: A Cultural-Historical Study*, Aarhus, Denmark: Aarhus University Press.

Hedegaard, M. and Chaiklin, S. (2005) *Radical–Local Teaching and Learning*, Aarhus, Denmark: Aarhus University Press.

Holliday, A. (1994) *Appropriate Methodology and Social Context*, Cambridge: Cambridge University Press.

Leont'ev, A. A. (1981) *Psychology and the Language Learning Process*, New York: Pergamon.

—— (1977) 'Activity and Consciousness', in *Philosophy in the USSR: Problems of Dialectical Materialism*, Moscow: Progress Publishers.

—— (1981) 'The Problem of Activity in Psychology', in J. V. Wertsch (ed.), *The Concept of Activity in Soviet Psychology*, Armonk, NY: M. E. Sharpe.

Leont'ev, D. A. (1992) 'Joint Activity, Communication and Interaction (toward Well-grounded "Pedagogy of Cooperation")', *Journal of Russian and East European Psychology*, 3(2): 43–58.

Luria, A. R. (1987) *The Mind of a Mnemonist*, Cambridge, MA: Harvard University Press.

Veel, R. (1999) 'Language Knowledge and Authority in School Mathematics', in F. Christie (ed.), *Pedagogy and the Shaping of Consciousness*, London: Continuum.

Vygotsky, L. S. (1978) 'Mind in Society: The Development of Higher Psychological Processes', in M. Cole, V. John-Steiner, S. Scribner and E. Souberman (eds.), (original work published in 1930, 1933 and 1935), Cambridge, MA: Harvard University Press.

—— (1987) 'Thinking and Speech', in R. W. Rieber and A. S. Carton (eds.), *The Collected Works of L. S. Vygotsky*, vol. 1, *Problems of General Psychology*, New York: Plenum.

Wertsch, J. (1998) *Mind as Action*, Oxford: Oxford University Press.

Index